Lecture Notes in Computer Science

Edited by G. Goos and J. Hartmanis

371

D. Hammer (Ed.)

Compiler Compilers and High Speed Compilation

2nd CCHSC Workshop
Berlin, GDR, October 1988
Proceedings

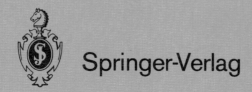

Springer-Verlag

Lecture Notes in Computer Science

Lecture Notes in Computer Science

Edited by G. Goos and J. Hartmanis

371

D. Hammer (Ed.)

Compiler Compilers and High Speed Compilation

2nd CCHSC Workshop
Berlin, GDR, October 10–14, 1988
Proceedings

Springer-Verlag

Berlin Heidelberg New York London Paris Tokyo Hong Kong

CR Subject Classification (1987): D.2.6, D.3.1, D.3.4, F.4.2, I.2.2

ISBN 3-540-51364-7 Springer-Verlag Berlin Heidelberg New York
ISBN 0-387-51364-7 Springer-Verlag New York Berlin Heidelberg

Printing and binding: Druckhaus Beltz, Hemsbach/Bergstr.
2145/3140-543210 – Printed on acid-free paper

PREFACE

vances and problems in the field of compiler generation are considered for the series of the 2-years workshop on Compiler Compilers. The first workshop especially dealt with Compiler Compilers and Incremental Compilation in 1986. The second workshop on Compiler Compilers and High Speed Compilation was held in Berlin, October 10-14, 1988.

Four invited talks were given by P. Deransart (Orleans): Current Trends in Attribute Grammars (see Lecture Notes 323), W. Aßmann (Berlin): A Short Review of High Speed Compilation, P. Fritzson (Linköping): Incremental Symbol Processing, K. Koskimies (Helsinki): Software Engineering Aspects in Language Implementation. Also, 15 other communications were chosen among 41 submissions by the program committee together with the chairmen of the single sessions. The referees were: P. Deransart (Orleans), P. Fritzson (Linköping), D. Hammer (Berlin), K. Koskimies (Helsinki), H. Oeper (Dresden), O. Mayer (Kaiserslautern), J. Penjam (Tallinn), K. J. Räihä (Tampere), G. Riedewald (Rostock), V. A. Serebriakov (Moscov), R. Wilhelm (Saarbrücken).

The workshop submissions presented a wide scale of aspects concerning improvings in the construction of compilers and higher efficiency in software development by means of new results in research and experiences from implemented complex design tools.

The interesting panel discussion "High Speed Compilation - a research task?" considered different points of view: Compiler design and (partly) improvings, user process of software development - efficient compilation, incremental compilation with error messages and error corrections for saving time during software development, intelligent compilation and automatic program construction, high speed compilation and high quality compiler components, and other. There were some pros and cons in answering the question. Summarizing, high speed compilation was pointed out research task (algorithm, compiler generation) as well as an engineering task (tuning, smart implementation).

Berlin, May 1989   Dieter Hammer

Contents

A Short Review of High Speed Compilation

Werner Aßmann

Academy of Sciences of the G.D.R.
Institute of Informatics and Computing Techniques

Abstract :

Starting with some considerations about the need for a higher speed of program development the term "High Speed Compilation" will be introduced. High speed compilers should have a speed of more than 30,000 lines per minute. High speed programming systems must be able to run through the edit/compile/link/load/run/debug phases with a waiting time less than 10 seconds. Starting with this definitions some demands on the components of compilers and programming systems are derived. Current known and applicable methods to reach this goal are discussed. This methods are divided in "Tuning" and "Better Algorithms". The effect of incremental compilation as a newer compilation technique is shown by the INDIA programming system.

1. The Need for High Speed Compilation

The latest (and sometimes longest) stage of program development takes place in the life cycle phases

> edit – compile – link – load – run – debug.

A big portion of the time needed for one cycle is only waiting time. The following example will demonstrate this situation.

> To run through the above phases we needed in case of the INDIA editor (2330 lines MODULA-2) as a part of the INDIA programming system (consisting of 65 modules, code size 270K) in a production environment (many and big directories, commercial MODULA-2 compiler) on a AT-Compatible the following times:

Editor (without any actions):	15 sec.
Compiler:	156 sec.
Linker:	221 sec.
Start (without any actions):	22 sec.
Debugger (without any actions):	139 sec.
Total:	553 sec.

That means that in the above example the waiting time amounts to more than 9 minutes - lost time! It's worth mentioning that this situation didn't occur in the past with its batch processing environments.

Reason 1: Because of working in interactive environments the waiting times must be reduced to a minimum: Waiting time is lost time!

We have two other reasons to want high speed compilation. The permanently encreasing complexity of tasks solved by computers leads to much bigger programs and program systems. On the other hand the technological evolution rate demands a higher evolution rate of some kinds of programs too. Clearly we must force up the efficiency of programming.

Reason 2: The tendency to bigger programs and a higher evolution rate.

Last not least we must have a look on the used programming languages. The newer programming languages such as MODULA-2 cause a much higher effort in the compiler (and in the other components of the programming systems). Using the traditional techniques would lead to compilation times not acceptable by the users. This development will continue in the next time. The change-over to descriptive programming techniques will complicate the compiling task another one. To solve this problem new compilation techniques must be developped. Compare under this aspect the symbol table handling in FORTRAN and MODULA-2!

Reason 3: The application of higher developped programming languages.

2. WHAT MEANS "HIGH SPEED COMPILATION"?

Clearly no exact definition of the terminus "High Speed Compilation" can be given. The ideas of the users about high speed will be very different too. Therefore a very pragmatic definition is only possible The starting point is to make some assertion about the maximal waiting time for the result of a compilation.

Our rather arbitrary definition of high speed compilation prescribes that the compilation time for a medium sized module of 2,500 lines should not exceed a period of 5 seconds. This is equivalent to:

Compilation speed >= 30,000 lines per minute.

But the above example shows that high speed compilation is only a part to reach short cycle times in the program development process. By including all the other components of a programming system such as editor, linker, loader, and debugger we can give an extended definition:

The waiting time in a "High Speed Programming System" for a full cycle must be <= 10 seconds.

The conclusion is the need not only for high speed compilers but also for

- **High Speed Loader,**
- **High Speed Linker,**
- **High Speed Debugger,** and last not least
- **High Speed File System**

as the bottleneck of all the system components.

Because the power of the used computer has a big influence of the needed time another slight different version of this definition will be given. The use of this definition lies in better possibilities comparing different products or to analyse the effort of different algorithms. The idea is the reduction to machine cycles. Using a computer with a clock rate of 25 MHz and a average number of 5 machine cycles per operation we get a maximal number of operations per line for the compiler:

Compilation effort <= 10,000 operations per line.

3. DEMANDS ON COMPILER COMPONENTS

If we suppose the traditional (logical) subdivision of a compiler into the components

- Lexical analysis (25%),
- Syntactical analysis (15%),
- Symbol table handling (25%),
- Context checking (10%), and
- Code generator (25%)

we can find out the necessary speed of all the components considering their share on the total effort:

- Lecical analysis: >= 120,000 lines per minute
- Syntactical analysis: >= 200,000 lines per minute
- Symbol table handling: >= 120,000 lines per minute
- Context checking: >= 300,000 lines per minute
- Code generator: >= 120,000 lines per minute

or according to the second definition:

- Lexical analysis: <= 2,500 operations per line
- Syntactical analysis: <= 1,500 operations per line
- Symbol table handling: <= 2,500 operations per line
- Context checking: <= 1,000 operations per line
- Code generator: <= 2,500 operations per line.

The percentual effort of the compiler components is estimated for programming languages like MODULA-2. For other languages and other compiler architectures other figures are possible so that more or less different results will be obtained. But essential is only the order of magnitude which can be used for statements about the quality of components.

To go a little more into details we look to the lexical analysis. If we suppose a number of 40 characters per line we have to perform the work of lexical analysis with <= 62 operations per character.

The lexical analysis of the INDIA system needs for a module of 892 lines respectively 26521 characters 3.300 seconds on a computer with 6 MHz. This means a effort of 149 operations per character. This is surprisingly not so far away from the goal figure especially because no special tuning was used till now.

4. REVIEW OF METHODS IN GENERAL

Three nearly orthogonal methods to increase the speed of compilers (and other programs too) exist:

- Faster hardware,
- Tuning, and
- Intelligent algorithms and data structures.

No further comment to the first method - faster hardware - wil be made. Not to mention technological and economical bounds it seems unsatisfactoryly to software developpers to spent computer time without any need.

4.1. TUNING

This term will be used for methods to optimise components of a programming system such as a compiler without general changes In principle this method can be accomplished by persons without any knowledge about the function of the program for instance by code inspection.

One simple method of this class is **Optimisation** of the program. In principle all methods known under this term from compilers can be used. The problem often lies in the contradiction to principles of structured programming. But sometimes a optimisation in space, time, and structure can be reached because some programs tends to disorder after a certain life time. Such optimisations can be:

- **Loop optimisation**
  The elimination of unaffected statements from the loop is well known. The same holds for the computation of as much as possible before entering the loop. Sometimes additional variables solve some problem. All kinds of interpreter loops must be optimised in this way.

- **Procedure call optimisation**
  The call of procedures causes in languages with recursive procedures a lot of additional actions. Another critical point is the tranfer of parameters. Therefore often called procedures should be changed to inline code or work on the base of global variables.

- **Location of variables**
  Unseen mostly by the programmer the use of imported variables and of variables declared in nested procedures is much more expensive as the use of local or global declared variables.

- **Array optimisation**
  Multidimensional arrays cause a lot of. work to compute the target address. The better way is reduction to one-dimensional arrays or substituation by pointers. The last way is the most effective one but sometimes a little dangerous.

- **Reduction of run-time checks**
  Good compilers insert a lot of run-time checks into the
  code. This arrangement increases the security of the programs considerable. But in many cases these checks can be
  eliminated after a certain stage of program correctness
  on the base of semantic information about the domain of
  variables and so on.

The effect of program optimisation in this way can be estimated
by analysis of the machine code of the compiler component. Some
interesting insights into the properties of the used compiler
(to compile the components of the programming system) are possible. The result is **Assembler-like programming**:

- **Use of efficiently compilable constructions only.**
  In dependence on the properties of compiler and machine
  code only such constructions of the implementation language will be used which will be translated to very effi-
  cent code. A good example is the problem of using a CASE-
  statement or a IF-ELSIF-ELSIF-...-statement.

- **Adaption to the used hardware.**
  The underlying components such as file system and screen
  handler must use very efficient access methods to reach a
  sufficient speed. Portability is in a direct opposition
  to this point.

Other methods must be used in case of interpreter techniques.
By **Optimisation of abstract machines and abstract machine code**
(as another word for the pairs of interpreter and associated
control table) very surprising results can be reached:

- **Optimisation of control tables.**
  Interpreter techniques are in general use for the syntactical analysis by the LR(1) or LALR(1) method but also
  for some other components. By optimisation and/or compac-
  tion of these control tables the same effects as in a
  "normal" optimisation (of code for a real machine) can be
  reached.

- **Translation into direct executable machine code.**
  By this method the abstract machine code (the control table) will be transformed into direct executable machine
  code. The interpretation of the table by the abstract machine is omitted. The big size of the generated programs
  is a little problematic but together with optimisation
  very good results are reachable (see [7], [10], [16]).

4.2. INTELLIGENT ALGORITHMS AND DATA STRUCTURES

Computer science is a relatively young field. Big efforts are
made in development of effective algorithms. Clearly the end of
this development is not reached already. Sometimes the skilful
combination of known principles has a multiple effect, sometimes a lot of research is necessary to find out a good solution for a given problem. In the field of programming systems a
lot of work was done in the last years to increase the comfort
(integrated programming systems, multi-window techniques and so

on). Only a few methods are characteristic of high speed efforts:

- **Use of fast search methods.**
  Hash search seems to be the fastest search method. The final result on this field is minimal perfect hash search using such a hash function that only one attempt for the search is necessary ("perfect") and there are no gaps in the hash table ("minimal"). Using this technique in the lexical analysis for the decision whether keyword or identifier should be the optimum. Sometimes the use of hash search is not possible without special precautions (sym- bol table handling in incremental compilers!).

- **Use of straightforward algorithms.**
  Algorithms without the need of decisions which branch to choose or without the need to transform data from one structure to another one are clearly better because the minor overhead. The use of minimal perfect hash functions is a good example for such algorithms.

- **Use of better system architectures.**
  Integrated programming systems working on a common data base can reach a much higher speed as systems divided traditionally into a lot of independent components. Some systems use syntax-oriented editors with a data structure which makes the task of lexical analysis superfluous.

- **Use of incremental techniques.**
  This method is the newest and most interesting one. The principle is not to throw away the results after doing some computation but to save all reusable data. These data will be used if the same computation task (with slightly different input data) arises a second time. The work of such systems is clearly more complicated but the effects are substantial. Compilers are very good candidates for this technique because of the frequent recompilation of programs with only a few changes.

The effects of incremental compilation techniques can be shown by the first results of the INDIA programming system (see [1] for further information):

The front-end compiler of INDIA works already incremental, the back-end compiler generates code for the whole program only. For the compilation of a small MODULA-2 module of 60 lines the following figures were measured (on a 6 MHz computer):

Normal (full) compilation:
10.160 sec. resp. 354 lines per minute.

Incremental deletion of one line (assign statement):
1.590 sec. resp. 2226 lines per minute
(0.220 sec. resp. 16091 lines per minute for front-end).

Incremental changing of one line (assign statement: deletion and following compilation of this line):
2.250 sec. resp. 1653 lines per minute
(0.880 sec. resp. 4091 lines per minute for front-end).

From this example we can learn that by incremental compilation

echniques compilation times proportional to the amount of the
program changes and not proportional to the program size can be
reached. That also means that in a good integrated programming
system the compiling process can be done during the editing
process (during the waiting time for the next input). From the
user's point of view the compilation time is exactly null in
such a system - a good contribution to a high speed programming
system!

5. REVIEW OF SPECIAL METHODS FOR SOME COMPONENTS

The most methods referenced above can be used in all the components of a compiler or a whole programming system. But for some
components very special methods are usable. In the following
the attempt will be made to gather some of such methods without
any pretensions to completeness.

The **Programming System Architecture** has nearly the biggest influence. The best way should be an

- Integrated programming system with a
- Commonly used internal program representation.

The **Compiler Architecture** should take into consideration the
following points:

- Very few passes (but sometimes dependent on the language)
- No overlays (problem of available memory).
- Incremental work.

The **Lexical Analysis** should use

- Clever input medium (if every possible the editor data
  base, situated in the memory).
- Few touches of the input characters (the best solution is
  only once!).
- Keyword decision by MPHF (minimal perfect hash function).
- Transfer of the whole lexical analysis (or of parts) to
  the editor or to the syntactical analysis.

In the **Syntactical Analysis** two basic methods are available:

- LALR(1)/LR(1) or recursive descendent procedures. Newer
  results show that LALR(1) should enable high speed together with the other advantages.
- Elimination of chain productions (if LALR(1) method).
- Clever expression handling.

As always there are scarcely general methods for the **Semantic
Analysis**:

- Limited number of "action points" during the syntactical
  analysis.
- Handling of imported objects (if there is a intermodule
  context checking) as "direct loadable" data structures
  (no additional data transformation!).

In the **Symbol Table Administration** search methods are the most
important point:

- Use of hash search methods.

- No division into name and symbol table (double search!).

The **Code Generator** should work on the base of

- Direct code generation

because template techniques are mostly to slowly. Another solution could be the use of very fast pattern techniques.

A few statements about the other components of a programming system can be made. The **Editor** should use:

- Syntax-oriented techniques to reduce the input time and to increase the reliability.
- Data structures which reduce the work of lexical analysis.

The only possibility for the **Linker** seems to be

- Incremental linking.

To reduce the effort of the **Debugger** to gather all the necessary information about the program to test only one possibility exist:

- Use of "direct loadable data structures"

At last a remark to the underlying **File System**. If the cleverness of the file system is not high enough to handle big systems some effort is necessary such as

- Own directory handling on the base of hash search techniques.
- Own buffer administration (transfer directly into the compiler data areas).
- Use of basic access functions to the file store.

6. RESULTS AND CONCLUSION

Currently some results about high speed components are available. In [8] a fast lexical analyser is described with a speed 6 times faster than LEX. The scanner generator Rex described in [7] generates scanners with a speed of 180,000 to 195,000 lines per minute running on a MC 68020 processor. Much faster parsers are available: the LALR(1) parser generated by the Lalr tool of [7] has a speed of 400,000 lines per minute, another LL(1) parser generated bei Ell [7] on the base of recursive descendent procedures even 900,000 lines per minute. The LR(1) parser of [10] reaches a speed of 500,000 lines per minute on a VAX 11/780 resp. 240,000 lines per minute on an Intel 80286. In [16] a LR(1) parser with a speed of 450,000 lines per minute running on a SUN workstation is described.

These results show clearly that the available methods enable the implementation of truly high speed components. On the other hand the results mentioned above about the possibilities of incremental compilation techniques show that integrated high speed programming systems will be available in the next time.

Literature:

[1]   W. Aßmann
      The INDIA System for Incremental Dialog Programming
      Proceedings of Workshop on Compiler Compilers and
      Incremental Compilation, Berlin, 1986
      IIR-Informationen 2(1986)12,12-34

[2]   C.C. Chang
      An Ordered Minimal Perfect Hashing Scheme Based upon
      Euler's Theorem
      Information Sciences 32(1984),165-172

[3]   N. Cercone, M. Krause, J. Boates
      Minimal and Almost Minimal Perfect Hash Function Search
      with Application to Natural Language Lexicon Design
      Comp.& Math. with Appl. 9(1983)1,215-231

[4]   G.V. Cormack, R.N.S. Horspool, M. Kaiserswerth
      Practical Perfect Hashing
      The Computer Journal 28(1985)1,54-58

[5]   P. Fritzson
      Incremental Symbol Processing
      Proceedings of Workshop on Compiler Compiler and High
      Speed Compilation, Berlin, 1988 (to appear in this issue)

[6]   R. Gerardy
      Experimental Comparison of Some Parsing Methods
      SIGPLAN Notices 22(1987)8,79-88

[7]   J. Grosch
      Generators for High-Speed Front-Ends
      Proceedings of Workshop on Compiler Compiler and High
      Speed Compilation, Berlin, 1988 (to appear in this issue)

[8]   V.P. Heuring
      The Automatic Generation of Fast Lexical Analysers
      Software-Practice and Experience 16(1986)9,801-808

[9]   R.N. Horspool
      Hashing as a Compaction Technique for LR Parser Tables
      Software-Practice and Experience 17(1987)6,413-416

[10] T.J. Pennello
      Very Fast LR Parsing
      1986 ACM 0-89791-197-0/86/0600-0145 75c

[11] D.J. Rosenkrantz, H.B. Hunt
      Efficient Algorithms for Automatic Construction and
      Compactification of Parsing Grammars
      ACM Transactions on Programming Languages and Systems
      9(1987)4,543-566

[12]   T.J. Sager
       A Polynomial Time Generator for Minimal Perfect Hash
       Functions
       Communications of the ACM 28(1985)5,523-532

[13]   T.J. Sager
       A Technique for Creating Small Fast Compiler Frontends
       SIGPLAN Notices 20(1985)10,87-94

[14]   L. Schmitz
       On the Correct Elimination of Chain Productions from LR
       Parsers
       Intern. J. Computer Math. 15(1984),99-116

[15]   W.M. Waite
       The Cost of Lexical Analysis
       Software-Practice and Experience 16(1986)5,473-488

[16]   M. Whitney, R.N. Horspool
       Extremely Rapid LR Parsing
       Proceedings of Workshop on Compiler Compiler and High
       Speed Compilation, Berlin, 1988 (to appear in this issue)

[17]   D.A. Wolverton
       A Perfect Hash Function for Ada Reserved Words
       Ada Letters IV(1984)1,40-44

INCREMENTAL SYMBOL PROCESSING

by

Peter Fritzson

Department of Computer and Information Science
Linköping University
S-581 83 Linköping, Sweden
EMAIL: paf@ida.liu.se

Abstract:

This paper introduces a novel entity-relational model for incremental symbol processing. This model forms the basis for the generation of efficient symbol processing mechanisms from high-level declarative specifications and query expressions, using program transformation techniques such as data type refinement.

The model is conceptually simple, but powerful enough to model languages of the complexity of Ada. The new model is compared to earlier, more restricted, incremental hierarchical symbol table models. The differences between symbol processing in conventional compilers and incremental symbol processing are also discussed.

1. INTRODUCTION

Symbol processing and scope analysis is one of the tasks usually performed by the syntax and semantics analysis phases of compilers. As programs grow larger, containing more interfaces and declarative information, symbol processing operations such as definition and lookup tend to consume a large fraction of the total compilation time. Also, scope analysis and lookup of definitions can be quite complex for several languages in the ALGOL family, where ADA is one example.

It is well known that interactive and incremental programming environments can enhance the programming process by preventing or quickly detecting errors, and by helping the programmer maintain and understand large programs. Thus it is essential that the programming environments use incremental methods for symbol processing.

This paper introduces a high-level declarative entity-relational data model for incremental symbol processing and scope analysis. The new model, which also can be regarded as

----
This research was supported by the National Swedish Board for Technical Development

object-oriented, gives several advantages:

Language-independence
> The model contains a few simple, yet powerful, language-independent modelling primitives. Thus it serves well as the basis for generation of language-oriented incremental symbol processing mechanisms from compact specifications.

Integration
> Since the model is entity-relational, it can be interfaced to existing relational database technology. Thus the symbol table can be viewed as a part of an integrated relational program database, which can hold both programmatic and documentation information.

Query language
> The relational formalism provides a general query language.

Efficient compilation of Queries
> The current model has been embedded into a very high level language which includes program transformation facilities [Refine-87]. Using such transformations the current model can be compiled to lower level procedural code for in-core data bases, ultimately matching the efficiency of handwritten symbol table packages.

The current model is aimed at languages such as Pascal, Modula-2, C, Ada, etc., but may well have wider applicability. An earlier incremental hierarchical symbol table model for Pascal is presented in this paper as a comparison. As mentioned, the model can be viewed either as entity-relational or object-oriented, it is largely a matter of choice. Entities are objects. A disadvantage of a pure object-oriented view is the absence of a general query language. A disadvantage of a pure relational implementation is that the performance of current relational databases is not satisfactory for compiler symbol processing applications, see e.g. [Linton-84]. Therefore, the methods presented here more or less assume an in-core database, or a database with a high degree of clustering and in-core caching of relevant data.

There are at least two alternatives of integrating this model into a compiler or editing environment. Through the fundamental operations Define and Lookup represented as procedures, the model can be interfaced to an incremental compiler [Fritzson-83] or to an editing environment based on action routines [Medina-Mora,Feiler-81]. Alternatively, Define and Lookup can be regarded as implicit relations, and the model interfaced to an editing environment based on relationally attributed grammars [Horwitz,Teitelbaum-86].

Attribute grammars are currently a popular means of specifying semantics for programming languages. Their strength is a declarative equational style notation, which enhances correctness and readability. Another advantage is the existence of general incremental attribute propagation methods for editing applications [Reps-83]. However, there are also disadvantages. The attribute grammar style of specification is somewhat low-level - each equation specifies a too small fraction of the total computation. This fragmentation can make the attribute grammar formulation of certain problems to be hard to understand. For example, the specification of syntax and semantics of Ada requires a 20000 line attribute grammar [Uhl,et.al-82]. Also, although advances have been made, efficiency still seems to be a problem. Difficulty in optimization is often due to information loss and constraints introduced when a problem is expressed in a too low-level formalism. For example, optimizers of intermediate code often need to reconstruct control-flow and data-flow which may have been explicit in higher level formalisms. Another example is the copy bypass optimization [Hoover-86], which eliminates unnecessary copy operations introduced by the constraints of attribute grammar formalisms.

We propose an alternative paradigm, based on program transformations, in the search for suitable specification languages. In this paradigm, the freedom in choosing transformations should create a greater chance of combining clarity of specification languages and efficient execution of target code. On the one hand, specialized high level notations can be devised for certain application areas. Certain notations are powerful precisely because they have a narrow applicability - more can be expressed with less. On the other hand, there are also general formalisms with powerful constructs. Examples are relational and set-theoretic operators, pattern-matching and logic. Such very high level notations can be compiled into lower level efficiently executable code by program transformation techniques such as automatic data structure refinement and control structure refinement, see [Goldberg,Kotik-83]. A special case of data structure refinement can be found in [Horwitz,Teitelbaum-86] where queries on implicit relations are transformed into queries on tree structures. The very high level specification-style notation implies greater freedom in applying various optimizations. Our symbol processing model is aimed at being a step in this direction, oriented towards the task of generating incremental programming environments from specifications.

Since the transformations from specification to executable code are automatic, correctness of executable programs follows automatically if the transformations have been proved correct, and if the specification is correct with respect to intuitions. Correctness criteria for transformations are briefly described later in this paper.

2. BACKGROUND

Programs define and use programming objects such as variables, types, and procedures. These objects are referred to in programs by means of symbols. The symbol processing component of a programming system supports all activities that define and use symbols referring to programming objects. These activities include the use of symbols by tools such as the compiler, linker, debugger, and librarian, and the browsing of symbols by users in cross reference queries.

By a *symbol table* or *symbol database* we mean the totality of the state needed to manage the definition and use of the symbols required for producing a software object, e.g., an executable module, from source program units. This state can be described as a set of relations between a set of entities. For example, there may be a relation *define* that describes all definitions within a set of source modules. It would relate entities such as the symbols being defined, the modules in which they are defined, and the declaration objects the symbols represent. A symbol processing system provides a programmatic interface to the state described in the symbol table.

A symbol processing system is *integrated* if the same symbol table is used for all programmatic and user activities, e.g., compiling, linking, debugging, cross referencing, and browsing. An integrated symbol processing system has the advantage that information is not duplicated in several places with possibly inconsistent format. A change in a source program can be incorporated once into the symbol table, and used by all applications. The system provides a uniform interface to the symbol table information, so that applications using this information are easier to write and maintain. A symbol processing system is *incremental* if the symbol table is persistent, and if a change in the source code dynamically causes corresponding updates in the symbol table. An incremental symbol table is one important prerequisite to make it possible for small changes to source code to be incorporated at minimal cost into corresponding executable program, object code modules, and symbol table database.

Before we continue our discussion on the role of incremental symbol processing in incremental compilation, let us briefly discuss the difference between separate compilation and incremental compilation. In both cases the goal is to decrease the turn-around time by re-using results from previous compilations. However, there is an order of magnitude time difference between these two technologies. In program development environments based on incremental compilation the time lag until execution can be resumed after a small program modification is usually a few seconds or less - even for big programs. By contrast, the recompilation and relink time in traditional separate compilation environments is usually measured in minutes or more, even though advanced change analysis [Tichy-86] has improved the situation. In addition the program need to be restarted from scratch after a rebuild.

The better performance of incremental compilation technology depends on several factors. The unit of recompilation is smaller for incremental compilation - a procedure or statement - than for separate compilation where it is usually a file or module. Also, maintenance of dependencies between declaration objects is at a finer granularity in an incremental environment. Incremental system components such as compiler, debugger and linker are better integrated - sometimes they even do not exist as separate entities! For example, in traditional environments, the compiler, debugger and linker usually build their own symbol tables, whereas a true incremental environment uses the same symbol table for all these purposes. In addition, an incremental environment usually preserves the current execution state, which makes debugging more convenient by providing continued execution after most small program changes.

3. INCREMENTAL SYMBOL PROCESSING IN INCREMENTAL COMPILATION

Incremental symbol processing is one important part of the total incremental compilation transformation, which translates source code and old executable code to updated executable code. Symbol processing becomes increasingly important when compiling really big programs [Rational-85], [Conradi,Wanvik-85], since there is an increased amount of declarative context in the form of include files and module specifications.

The sub-transformations which comprise incremental compilation are shown very schematically below. Note that all input arguments are not explicitly shown. For example, incremental code generation takes both an old version of the object code and an abstract syntax tree as input, and produces a new version of the object code. This means that the arrow ---> is not just a mapping, it is an update transformation.

Note also that incremental parsing is not needed if the program is stored in tree-form, and that incremental optimization is optional. In some systems incremental semantic analysis also includes incremental symbol processing.

```
Incremental Compilation:       Source code          --->  Executable code
```

The total incremental compilation transformation above can be decomposed into:

```
Incremental Code Generation:   Abstract syntax tree --->  Object code
Incremental Symbol Processing: Declarations         --->  Symbol table
Incremental Linking:           Object code          --->  Executable code
Incremental Execution:         Execution state      --->  Execution state

Incremental Parsing:           Source text          --->  Syntax tree
Incremental Semantic Analysis  Attributed tree      --->  Attributed tree
Incremental Optimization:      Intermediate code    --->  Intermediate code
```

In the rest of this paper will concentrate on incremental symbol processing, and not be concerned with other parts of incremental compilation.

4. BASIC SYMBOL PROCESSING OPERATIONS

There are two basic operations in symbol processing, *definition* and *lookup*.

The *definition* operation adds a new definition of a symbol to the symbol table. This involves adding the symbol together with a description of the declaration object it will henceforth represent. Thus a mapping is established from a symbol in some context to a declaration object. Note that a declaration object is analogous to a symbol table entry in conventional compilers.

The *lookup* operation. Given a symbol that is being used in a context somewhere in a program, find the declaration object which this symbol refers to.

In addition to the two basic operations common to all symbol processing mechanisms, an incremental symbol processing mechanism must support *insertion*, *deletion* and *update* of declaration objects. It must also incrementally maintain *dependencies* between declarations, and support navigation operations which change the current context.

5. INCREMENTAL SYMBOL PROCESSING
VERSUS CONVENTIONAL SYMBOL PROCESSING

5.1 Dependency maintenance and update of declarations

An incremental symbol processing system needs to support efficient access and updating of dependencies between declaration objects. This is especially important in order to incrementally support updating of global declarations.

The definition of a declaration object can be incrementally inserted, changed or deleted from a program. For example, after a change to an existing declaration object, e.g. a global type declaration, the system has to re-elaborate all objects which are dependent on this declaration. Thus, the system needs efficient access to global dependencies in order to quickly find the dependent objects. If a new declaration object is inserted, the system also has to determine how this affects the visibility of existing objects, e.g. if it will hide declarations in enclosing blocks.

5.2 Sequential versus Random Access

The symbol processing unit of a conventional compiler usually makes a sequential pass over a source program unit, e.g. a file, and performs actions of defining or looking up symbols as they are encountered during this sequential pass. This means that at any given point, the current state represented in the symbol table only reflects definitions which have so far been encountered before the current symbol. A conventional compiler also has schemes for remembering and updating the current block and the visibility of symbols as it progresses sequentially through a source program.

An incremental symbol processing system, on the other hand, has to be able to make "random access" to just those parts of a source program unit that have been changed. It cannot rely on assumptions based on the sequential processing of source programs. Any such assumptions that affect scope and visibility have to be explicitly represented in the symbol table. The incremental symbol table needs a way of keeping track of the relative positions of symbols in a source program unit. Many programming languages are compiled by single-pass compilers and thus require that a definition occur before its use. For such languages this positional information is of critical importance for determining the meaning of a program.

6. SYMBOL PROCESSING MODELS

In the following sections we will present three incremental symbol processing models - a *hierarchical model*, an *attributed abstract syntax tree model*, and an *entity-relational* symbol processing model. The first two are just discussed briefly. The emphasis is on the entity-relational model, which is higher-level and and declarative.

7. A HIERARCHICAL SYMBOL PROCESSING MODEL

We briefly present a simple hierarchical symbol processing mechanism for Pascal. The symbol table consists of a tree of local symbol tables, which allows both insertions and deletions of declarations. This incremental symbol table model has been implemented in the DICE system [Fritzson-83], [Fritzson-85], which is a programming environment based on incremental compilation. Note that the symbol processing mechanism presented here does not represent declaration position within a sequence of declarations. Thus, it allows forward referencing of declarations which is consistent with Modula-2, but without enforcing the Pascal define before use semantics.

A simple program example about drawing boxes will illustrate symbol processing operations in several different models, and also the structure of these models. The concept of region, defined in the next section, is also exemplified.

```
PROGRAM BoxProg;

TYPE   BoxType = RECORD
                    X1, Y1 : Integer;   X2, Y2 : Integer;
                    END;
       Color   = (Red, Green, Blue);

VAR
       BoxVar : BoxType;

PROCEDURE DrawBox(X1,Y1,X2,Y2 : Integer);
  VAR
    Dx, Dy : Integer;

  PROCEDURE DrawLine(DeltaX, DeltaY : Integer);
    BEGIN (* DrawLine *)
    .....
    END; (* of DrawLine *)

  BEGIN (* DrawBox *)
    GotoXY(X1, Y1);
    Dx := X2-X1;
    Dy := Y2-Y1;
    Drawline(0, Dy);
    Drawline(Dx, 0);
    Drawline(0, -Dy);
    Drawline(-Dx, 0);
  END; (* of DrawBox *)

BEGIN (* BoxProg)
  ClrScreen;
  .....
  WITH Boxvar DO BEGIN
    DrawBox(X1, Y1, X2, Y2);
  END;
END. (* of Main program BoxProg *)
```

Figure 1. A program example BoxProg.

```
            Systemblock
                 !
                 !
            Program BoxProg  . . . .  .  .  .  .  .  .  .
                 !            !                !                  .
                 !            !                !                  .
    Procedure DrawBox    Type BoxType    Type Color    Boxvar WITH-statement
            !
            !
    Procedure DrawLine
```

Figure 2. Slightly simplified Region hierarchy.

```
    Level 0:
                Localsymtab [GotoXY, ClrScreen, BoxProg]
                Dependencies [(GotoXY -> BoxProg), (GotoXY -> DrawBox)
                             (ClrScreen -> BoxProg)];

    Level 1:  Program BoxProg:
                LocalSymtab [Boxtype, Boxvar, DrawBox, Color, Red, Blue, Green]
                Dependencies [(Boxtype -> Boxvar), (Boxvar,DrawBox -> BoxProg)]

    Level 2:  Type Boxtype:
                LocalSymtab [X1,Y1, X2, Y2]
                Dependencies [(X1 -> BoxProg), (Y1 -> BoxProg),
                             (X2 -> BoxProg), (Y2 -> BoxProg)]
    Level 2:  Type Color:
                LocalSymtab [Red, Blue, Green]
                Dependencies [ ]

    Level 2:  Procedure DrawBox
                LocalSymtab  [X1, Y1, X2, Y2, Dx, Dy, Drawline]
                Dependencies [(Drawline -> DrawBox),
                             (X1,Y1,X2,Y2,Dx,Dy -> DrawBox)]

    Level 3:  Procedure Drawline
                LocalSymtab  [DeltaX, DeltaY]
                Dependencies [ ]
```

Figure 3. Contents of a hierarchical symbol table which includes dependencies.

The hierarchy of local symbol tables and dependencies for the small BoxProg program is shown in Figure 3. Note that only dependencies between declarations and between declarations and procedures/functions are shown. For example, (GotoXY -> DrawBox) means that DrawBox depends on and uses GotoXY. Dependencies between a set of local declarations and the procedure/program body at the same level are represented using a special form, e.g. (X1,Y1,X2,Y2,Dx,Dy -> Drawline).

Note also that the WITH-statement in the body of program BoxProg is shown connected to the block/region hierarchy with a dotted line. This means that the local symbol table of field names associated with the record type Boxtype is temporarily associated with the block hierarchy when the current position is within the WITH- statement in the BoxProg program.

8. THE NOTIONS OF REGION AND SCOPE

The term *region*, or more precisely *declarative region* [ADA-83] , is sometimes used interchangeably with the term *block*. However, the notion of region is more general - it denotes any syntactically defined portion of a program, such as e.g. a record declaration.

The notion of block is usually connected with objects which instantiate some kind of activation records, e.g. procedure blocks or program blocks. Each pair of regions are either disjoint portions of a program, or one region is completely enclosed within the other.

The *scope* of a declaration object consists of the parts of a program where it is legal to reference the declaration [ADA-83]. Scope need not conform to the nice nesting structure of certain programming languages. For example, in the C language [Harbison,Steele-84], the scope of an identifier extends from its first occurrence - see example in Appendix A. Similar rules apply for Ada and Pascal. Scope can be complicated, since it depends on both position, region structure and the nesting rules of the languge.

9. OPERATIONS ON THE HIERARCHICAL INCREMENTAL SYMBOL TABLE

In addition to manipulating the contents of the symbol table, certain symbol processing operations support navigation operations, i.e. setting the current focus in the tree-structured symbol table. This focus can be represented by a cursor, which we call the *symcursor* in the context of symbol processing. In [Fritzson-85] two similar kinds of cursors are defined: the *editcursor* which denotes the context of editing and incremental compilation operations; the *execursor* which denotes the current context during debugging and execution.

Navigational operations

To *enter a block or region*, set the symcursor to the block which is to be entered. This has the effect that subsequent definition operations will as a default be performed on the local symbol table of this block. Lookup operations will start searching in the current local symbol table. The block to be entered has to exist - it must have been previously created during some define operation. The *leave block* operation is a special case of *enter block*. It means that the symcursor should be reset from denoting the current block to instead denote the parent block, if such a block exists.

Define symbol

This operation associates a symbol in the current context with a new declaration object. First, create a declaration object and elaborate type information specified by the declaration which defines the symbol. For certain declaration objects such as procedures or records, a block with a local symbol table is also created. Then do a partial lookup to check if the symbol is already defined in the current block, in which case the new definition is illegal. Finally, enter the symbol and its declaration object in the local symbol table.

Lookup symbol

Given a symbol used to reference an object, this operation finds the corresponding object. The lookup operation can be a complex function of scope and visibility rules together with current context, position and type information. However, in the special case of our hierarchical symbol table for Pascal it is simple: first perform a lookup in the local symbol table of the current block; while not found continue the lookup in subsequent parent blocks until the outermost system block has been searched.

Declaration Update

The *insert* operation is essentially a define operation. However in an incremental symbol table more tasks need to be done. For example, it must be checked if the new definition partially hides an existing declaration which is referenced in the current context. In such a case, all objects in the current context which are dependent on the previous declaration have to be re-elaborated and recompiled.

The *delete* declaration operation removes the symbol and its associated declaration object from the symbol table. Also mark all dependent objects for incremental recompilation. If the deleted symbol represents a variable, also free its associated target memory.

Dependency Maintenance

For each use of a declaration object, update the dependency structure to reflect this use. When a use of an object is deleted, then update the dependency structure to possibly remove a dependency.

Dependency Query

This query answers the question: *Who depends on me?* It returns the set of all declaration objects which are dependent on a certain object.

10. AN ATTRIBUTED ABSTRACT SYNTAX TREE MODEL

This symbol processing model is really a special case of the hierarchical incremental symbol table model described above. We note that the region hierarchy of the symbol table corresponds to the block hierarchy of the abstract syntax tree itself, so why not use the abstract syntax tree? We need not create a special local symbol table at each block level. Instead, it is possible to do lookup operations by searching declaration nodes in the current block in the tree. Elaborated declaration objects and dependencies can be attached to the tree as attributes. Insertions and deletions are performed on the attributed tree itself. This model is used e.g. by the Rational incremental Ada environment [Rational-85].

However, there are also disadvantages in representing the symbol table as an abstract syntax tree. It is less efficient to perform a lookup as a linear search through the tree instead of a single access to a hash table. Therefore the Rational incremental ADA environment has been augmented with hashed lookup at the global level [Rational-86]. Also, the implementation of symbol processing operations may become language dependent to a greater degree, since the tree structure of declarations is peculiar for each language. This model is of course not suitable for programming environments which do not use a tree structure as the primary program representation.

11. THE ENTITY-RELATIONAL DATA MODEL

The entity-relational data model was first introduced in [Chen-76]. It can be regarded as a thin layer on top of the relational database model [Codd-70]. It is convenient to think of a relation as a table, or as a set of tuples $<v_1, v_2, .. v_n>$, where each data value v_i belongs to a data domain D_i. The columns of the table are often called attributes. In the entity-relational model, there are two kinds of attributes: associations (between entities), and properties, see Figure 4.

Concept	Informal definition	Examples
ENTITY	A distinguishable object (of some particular type)	Declaration object, (= symbol table entry in conventional systems), a node in an abstract syntax tree
PROPERTY	A piece of information that describes an entity	The name of a declared object such as variable. The memory size occupied by a variable.
ASSOCIATION (ATTRIBUTE)	A many-to-many or many-to-one relationship among entities.	CONTAINED-WITHIN: A variable X is declared within the declarative region of procedure FOO.
SUBTYPE (SUBCLASS)	Entity type Y is a subtype of entity type X if and only if every Y is necessarily an X.	The subtype EXPRESSION is a subtype of TREENODE. Subtype DECLOBJECT is a subtype of PROGRAMOBJECT.

Figure 4. The Entity-Relational data model

A query is an expression in the relational algebra in which relational operators are applied to argument relations to produce a relation as a result. The three special relational operators are JOIN, SELECT and PROJECT. PROJECT is a unary operator that forms a new relation consisting of a subset of the attributes of a relation (or of the columns of a table). JOIN is a binary operator: it merges tuples from two argument relations together into bigger tuples, but selecting only those merged tuples that fulfil a given condition. SELECT is a unary operator that selects the subset of tuples in its operand relations that satisfy a given condition.

A *view relation* is a relation which is computed from other relations when needed, using an expression consisting of relational operators.

An *implicit relation* is never constructed. Instead it is implicitly represented by some other data structure. An example is the ANCESTOR relation which can be implicitly defined by a tree, but need not be constructed explicitly. Instead, the relational query operators are transformed into different query operators that operate on this other data structure. Such an example can be found in [Horwitz,Teitelbaum-86] where it is described how certain queries of implicit relations can be transformed into a equivalent queries on tree structures. This is a special case of data structure refinement [Goldberg,Kotik-83]. The DEFINE and LOOKUP operations mentioned previously can be represented as implicit relations in our model.

12. AN ENTITY-RELATIONAL SYMBOL PROCESSING MODEL

We have chosen to express our symbol processing model as an entity-relational data model [Chen-76]. This combines most advantages of the relational approach and the object oriented approach [Zdonik,Wegner-85], [Birtwistle,et.al-73]. The relational approach provides the powerful relational operators and a query language. The object-oriented approach provides subclassing with inheritance, in addition to association of attributes and operations with objects.

There exist certain limitations of the relational model. The relational operators cannot handle (1) queries that require transitive closure, (2) queries that require order-dependent processing, and (3) arithmetic processing. Therefore our symbol processing model is augmented to allow such queries. Our model has been embedded in the Refine language [Refine-87]. This is a wide-spectrum very high level language, which provides arithmetic, set-theoretic operations, logic with universal and existential quantification, program transformation constructs, and object-oriented programming with single inheritance. Note however, that all explicit relations in our model are pure entity-relational. This added query power is convenient when defining the implicit LOOKUP relation.

Our entity-relational symbol processing model is currently implemented as a set of mappings (associations) between objects. Since mappings can be defined between an object and a set of objects, or between a set of objects and another set of objects, many-to-many or one-to-many relations can readily be represented as mappings.

ENTITIES

```
Declobject:    subtype-of  Programobject

Region:        subtype-of  Programobject

Declaration:   subtype-of  Programobject

Statement:     subtype-of  Programobject
```

Figure 5. Entities in the entity-relational model.

BINARY RELATIONS/ASSOCIATIONS

Each binary relation is represented as a mapping together with its converse mapping. Since many-to-one mappings are not invertible, we can instead form a converse mapping, where the range consists of sets of entities. The REGION_OBJECT relation is sparse - not all declobjects have regions, and vice versa.

```
Relation  DEPENDENCY:
   USED_BY  : map  Declobject    -> set(Programobject)
   USES     : map  Programobject -> set(Declobject)
Comments
   USED_BY  The set of program objects which depend on a declobject.
   USES     The set of declobjects a program object is dependent on.
```

```
Relation  REGION_NESTING:
  PARENT_REGION  : map  Region  ->  Region
  CHILD_REGIONS  : map  Region  ->  set(Region)
Comments
  PARENT_REGION  The innermost surrounding region.
  CHILD_REGIONS  The set of child regions of a region.

Relation  DEFINED_WITHIN:
  DECLS_IN_REGION    :  map  Region      ->  seq(Declobject)
  REGION_AROUND_DECL :  map  Declobject  ->  Region;
Comments
  DECLS_IN_REGION     The sequence of declobjects defined in a region.
  REGION_AROUND_DECL  The region within which a declobject is defined.

Relation  INHERIT:
  INHERITS     : map  Region  ->  Region
  INHERITED_BY : map  Region  ->  set(Region)
Comments
  INHERITS      The region which exports declobjects into this region.
  INHERITED_BY  The set of regions by whom this region is inherited.

Relation  PRINT_NAME
  PRNAME       : map  Declobject  ->  Symbol
  PRNAME_OF    : map  Symbol      ->  set(Declobject)
Comments
  PRNAME       The printname of an object.
  PRNAME_OF    The declobject of which this is a printname.

Relation  REGION_OBJECT
  OBJ_REGION    : map  Declobject  ->  Region
  OBJ_REGION_OF : map  Region  ->  Declobject
Comments
  OBJ_REGION     A region which may be associated with a declobject.
  OBJ_REGION_OF  The programobject which is associated with a region.
```

Figure 6. Relations/associations in the entity-relational model.

BOOLEAN PROPERTIES OF REGIONS

TRANSPARENT
  Declobjects from within a transparent region are directly visible outside.
QUALIFIED
  Declobjects from within a qualified region are visible by qualification.
PARTIALLY_QUALIFIED
  Declobjects which are explicitly named as exported from within a region.
ORDINAL_QUALIFIED
  Declobject are visible by their ordinal position - procedure parameters.
PARTIALLY_NESTED

A partially nested region inside an outer region may introduce new
declobjects, but their names may not collide.

Figure 7. Boolean properties of regions.

PROPERTIES OF DECLOBJECTS

POSITION   : ProgramPoint
  Position of a declaration or program object. It can be represented as
  line number, character position, or tree node address.
TYPE_OF   : Typespec
  Type of a declaration object.

Figure 8. Properties of declobjects and certain programobjects.

We currently identify five boolean properties of regions: transparent, qualified,
partially_qualified, ordinal_qualified and partially_nested regions. An example of a
transparent region is the definition of the enumeration type Color, where all components are
externally visible. A record declaration is a typical example of a qualified region -
components defined within the region are externally visible by qualified access. A procedure
declaration which introduces a block of local declarations is an example of a partially_nested
region. Finally, a region which inherits another region, can extend the visibility of
declarations from this other region to itself. The Pascal WITH-statement is an example of a
region which inherits other regions. Thus, it makes the fields from some record declaration
visible within itself.

For Pascal or Modula-2, type analysis is not needed for lookup or definition of symbols.
However, for the Ada language, type information is necessary in order to resolve overloaded
symbols.

The DEPENDENCY Relation:

```
Dependenton:   Used-by:
  <GotoXY,      {BoxProg,DrawBox}>
  <ClrScreen,   {BoxProg}>

  <BoxVar,      {BoxProg}>
  <DrawBox,     {BoxProg}>
  <BoxType,     {BoxVar}>

  <X1,          {BoxProg}>
  <Y1,          {BoxProg}>
  <X2,          {BoxProg}>
  <Y2,          {BoxProg}>

  <Drawline,    {DrawBox}>
  <X1,          {DrawBox}>
  <Y1,          {DrawBox}>
  <X2,          {DrawBox}>
  <Y2,          {DrawBox}>
  <Dx,          {DrawBox}>
  <Dy,          {DrawBox}>
```

The REGION_NESTING Relation:

```
parent_region:   child_regions:

  <R-Systemblock, {R-BoxProg}>
  <R-BoxProg,     {R-BoxType, R-Color, R-DrawBox, R-Boxvar_WITH}>
  <R-DrawBox,     {R-Drawline}>
```

The DEFINED_WITHIN Relation:
  parent_region: decl_objects:

```
  <R-Systemblock  {GotoXY, ClrScreen}>
  <R-BoxProg,     {Boxtype, Boxvar, DrawBox}>
  <R-BoxType,     {X1, Y1, X2, Y2}>
  <R-Color,       {Red, Green, Blue}>
  <R-DrawBox,     {X1-2, Y1-2, X2-2, Y2-2, Dx, Dy, Drawline}>
  <R-Drawline,    {DeltaX, DeltaY}>
```

The PRINT_NAME Relation:

  Namestring: Object:

```
  <"BoxProg",    BoxProg>
  <"BoxType",    BoxType>
  <"DrawBox",    DrawBox>
  <"X1",         X1>
  <"X1",         X1-2>
  <"Y1",         Y1>
  .....          .....
```

The INHERIT relation:
  Donor: Inheritor:

```
  <Boxtype,      Boxvar-WITH>;
```

Figure 9. An example of relations. The simplified version of the entity-relational model has been applied to the BoxProg program example. Note that when two objects have the same name, e.g. the record field X1 and the formal parameter X1, these objects are denoted X1 and X1-2 respectively.

13. INFORMAL DESCRIPTION OF OPERATIONS

This section provides an informal description of the incremental symbol processing operations with emphasis on the lookup operation, which later in this paper is expressed formally.

A printname and a current region are input to most variants of the lookup operations. In addition, the current position need to be supplied for certain languages, and a typespec for overload resolution. The lookup will return a matching declaration object, or a special *Undefined* value.

Qualified lookup

A typical example of qualified lookup is the lookup of record field names which are qualified by a record variable using dot-notation, e.g. Recordvariable.Fieldname, or the lookup of procedures defined in some Modula-2 module, e.g. Modulename.Procname. It is conceptually simple: perform the lookup among declaration objects defined within the record region or the module region. This region is here denoted by the current region.

In relational terminology this can be expressed using our relations PRINT_NAME and DEFINED_WITHIN. Find all declaration objects obj, such that DEFINED_WITHIN(obj, current_region) and PRINT_NAME(printname, obj). This can be conceptually performed by first joining the relations PRINT_NAME and DEFINED_WITHIN, and then performing a selection using printname and current_region as a combined key. The search can be made more efficient by performing most of the selection operations before the join, or maintaining a precomputed joined relation.

Visibility lookup

This is a lookup operation where the given name directly implies some declaration object which is visible in the current context. The visibility of declaration objects is the primary criterium in this lookup. Typical examples are the lookup of a variable name, a procedure name, or a type name.

However, several factors complicate the lookup operation. Declarative regions are usually nested, and declarations in inner regions may redefine symbols with the same name in outer regions. Certain regions inherit declarations from other regions. For example, the Pascal WITH-statement inherits field declarations from some record type region. Certain regions are transparent, e.g. Pascal enumeration type declarations, which makes their components visible in the parent region.

A simple, but perhaps inefficient, way of performing the lookup is as follows. Use the current printname to index the PRINT_NAME relation in order to select all objects with that printname. Then use the DEFINED_WITHIN relation to find within which region each such object is defined. Now the second phase of the lookup starts. We must find the set of regions which have declarations that can be visible from the current region. This includes the parent region, the parent of the parent region etc., following the REGION_NESTING relation to the uppermost region. It also includes transparent child regions, and regions which are inherited by such regions.

First example:

Here the current printname is "X1" and the current region is DrawBox. Selections using "X1" as an index into PRINT_NAME, yield two objects: X1 and X1-2. The DEFINED_WITHIN relation further yields X1-2 which is defined within the DrawBox region and X1 which is defined within the Boxtype region. Then we look for the set of possibly relevant regions in addition to DrawBox. Using REGION_NESTING, we obtain the parent region BoxProg and Systemblock. The child region Color is transparent and should also be included. Thus, the set of possible regions becomes {DrawBox, BoxProg, Systemblock, Color}. Finally we intersect with the regions of our two possible objects, eliminating X1 since it is defined within Boxtype. Thus the final result of our lookup is X1-2.

Second example:

The current printname is again "X1", but we now perform the lookup from a position in the WITH-Boxvar statement region, which thus is the current region. As in the previous example, "X1" first matches the two objects X1 and X1-2. Using the nesting hierarchy we then obtain {WITH-Boxvar, BoxProg, SystemBlock} as possible defining regions. The Boxtype region is added since it is inherited by the WITH-Boxvar region - see the INHERIT relation. The Color region is also added since it is transparent and is a child of BoxProg. This yields the set {WITH-Boxvar, BoxProg, SystemBlock, Boxtype, Color}. Since X1 is defined within Boxtype, but X1-2 is defined within Drawline, the final result is X1.

So far we have ignored the possibility that declarations in inner blocks redefine symbols which are declared in outer blocks. Such ambiguities can be resolved by introducing an auxiliary relation REDEFINED between declaration objects [Reiss-83]. However, the random access nature of incremental symbol processing makes REDEFINED somewhat unsuitable, since the contents of this relation is dependent of the current focus of processing. In the worst case REDEFINED would have to be rebuilt at each lookup. A more efficient solution is used in the precise formulation of the lookup algorihm further on in this paper.

Define symbol

This operation associates a symbol in the current context with a new declaration object. First, create a declaration object and elaborate type information specified by the declaration which defines the symbol. This means updating the PRINT_NAME relation with a tuple <printname, object> and some other object attributes. Then do a partial lookup of the symbol in the current region, and in regions which are transparent to or inherited into the current region. If the lookup succeeds, then there are multiple definitions of the symbol, in which case the new definition is illegal.

Otherwise, enter the symbol and its declaration object into the current region in the symbol table. This means inserting a tuple <object, current_region> in the relation DEFINED_WITHIN. If the new declaration introduces a region, e.g. procedure, function, record- declarations, the object also belongs to the class of region objects. Then the relations REGION_NESTING and REGION_OBJECT should be updated. The INHERIT relation should be updated if the new region inherits declarations from some other region. If the new region object contains component declaration, then we first have to introduce this new region. For example, the symcursor denoting the current region should be set to this new region before the components are defined.

Navigation operations

Enter region will set the current region to be the region which is to be entered. Subsequent definition operations will insert definitions within the current region. Lookup operations start searching for object definitions within the current region. *Leave region* is really a special case of Enter region, since it means that we should enter the parent region of the current region. The parent region is found by indexing the REGION_NESTING relation using the current region object as a key.

Declaration update

As mentioned before, the insert operation is essentially a define operation. However, in an incremental symbol table we have to check if the inserted declaration will hide some existing declaration which is already used in the current context. This is done by performing a full lookup on the symbol at the definition point - not a partial lookup as in an ordinary define operation. Suppose the new definition partially hides an existing declaration which is referenced in the current context. In such a case, all objects in the current context which are dependent on the previous declaration have to be re-elaborated and recompiled. The checking is performed by doing a lookup.

To delete a declaration, remove the symbol and its associated declaration object from the symbol table, i.e. update the relations PRINT_NAME and DEFINED_WITHIN. If the removed object has a region, then also update REGION_NESTING and INHERIT. Use the removed object as a key to the DEPENDENCY relation to find all dependent objects, and mark those for incremental recompilation. Also mark transitively dependent objects in the same way.

Dependency update

For each new use of a declaration object, update the dependency structure to reflect this use by inserting a tuple <current_region, object> into the DEPENDENCY relation. If a use of a declaration object is removed, and there are no more uses of that object within the current region, then delete the tuple <current_region, object> from the DEPENDENCY relation.

Dependency Query

This query answers the question: *Who depends on me?* Return the set of all declaration objects which are dependent on a certain object by making a selection from the DEPENDENCY relation, using this object as a key. Many other query variants can be expressed using the relational algebra.

14. AN EXTENDED ENTITY-RELATIONAL MODEL

Our simple incremental relational symbol processing model cannot exactly represent languages with single pass symbol processing semantics, where a symbol cannot be referenced before it has been defined. This problem can be solved by introducing the notion of *Position* for declaration objects.

Another problem is that formal parameters can be accessed outside their defining procedures by qualification on their ordinal positions in parameter lists. In addition to ordinal qualification, languages such as Ada also support named qualification on parameter names. Thus, we need to extend our previous model, which for each procedure has a single declarative region for both parameters and local variables. In the extended model we introduce at least two declarative regions for each procedure: one qualified region enclosing the whole procedure including the formal parameters, and one or more additional regions nested within, for blocks with local declarations.

This model suits Ada and C, where declarations in nested local blocks are allowed to hide parameter declarations. In Pascal however, local declarations are not allowed to hide parameter declarations - they are conceptually part of the same block. Our solution to this problem is to introduce another class of regions called *partially nested regions*. This kind of region is similar to nested regions except that declarations within partially nested regions are not allowed to hide declarations from outer regions.

Remember that the *scope* of a declaration object consists of the parts of a program where it is legal to reference the declaration. It can be expressed as a function of simpler notions such as position, nesting of regions, visibility rules etc. This is expressible within our extended model. Scope need not conform to the nice nesting structure of programming languages. For example, in the C program example in Appendix A, the scope XX1 of the global variable XX covers the initial part of the body of the function foofunc, whereas the scope XX2 of the local variable XX covers the rest of foofunc.

15. PRECISE FORMULATION OF THE LOOKUP ALGORITHM

There are two basic variants of the lookup operation, which define the implicit LOOKUP relation. Those two are lookup by direct visibility and lookup by qualification. Visibility lookup is the most common case, where an occurrence of a name in the current context should be associated with some declared program entity. This can be a complex function of nesting structure, local context, positions of declarations, import and export of declarations, and types when there is a possibility of overloading. Simple overload resolution with type comparison is included in the present lookup algorithm. A complete overload resolution algorithm for Ada is presented by [Baker-82].

The function Visibility_Lookup starts searching within the innermost region that includes the current program point. If there is no match, continue at the next outer level in the region nesting hierarchy. According to the nesting rules only the first match should be returned. Thus positional and type-checking predicates, when relevant, must be applied during the search. The Undefined value is returned when there is no match. Note that at each nesting level we consider both declarations from the current region, declarations from regions which are inherited into the current region (e.g. Pascal WITH), and declarations from transparent child-regions (e.g. Pascal Enumeration). PRNAME_OF(Name) returns the set of declaration objects with a certain print name. For single-pass compiled languages such as Pascal and C, which require that a definition occurs before its use, the Check_position predicate is relevant.

Lookup by qualification is far simpler. Just lookup the qualified name within the region where it is defined. For example, in the common case of a record field reference, search for it within the declarative region of the record type. A special case is ordinal qualification, where instead of a name, an integer index denotes the declaration object. For certain languages [Refine-87] it is possible to denote a fieldname in this way, e.g. xrec.2 would reference the second field in xrec. However, ordinal lookup is most commonly used for accessing procedure parameters to make type checking possible at call sites.

```
FUNCTION  Visibility_Lookup(Name          : Symbol;
                           Currentregion  : Region;
                           Currentposition: ProgramPoint;
                           Currenttype    : Typespec): Declobject
(* Lookup of Name in the current context, which is denoted by Currentregion.
   Start Looking in the current region, and all regions (transparent or
   inherited) which are visible at the current nesting level.
   Continue searching outwards at each level in the nesting hierarchy,
   until a matching declaration object is found, or
```

```
     the root, which has no parent, is encountered.
*)
BEGIN
     r   :=  Currentregion;
   REPEAT
       rset  :=  {r} union {INHERITS(r)} union
                          {x | x in CHILD_REGIONS(r) and TRANSPARENT(x) }
       FOR  d:Declobject  IN  PRNAME_OF(Name)  DO
          IF  REGION_AROUND_DECL(d) in  rset
               and  Check_Type(d, Currenttype)
               and  Check_Position(d, Currentposition)
          THEN
               RETURN  d;
       END FOR;

       r   :=  PARENT_REGION(r);
   UNTIL  Undefined(r);

   RETURN   Undefined;
END;


FUNCTION  Check_Position(d: Declobject; p: Position): Boolean;
(* Predicate to check if d is accessible before or at position p.
   For languages which require define before use *)
BEGIN
  RETURN  BEFORE(POSITION(d), p);
END;


FUNCTION  Check_Type(d: Declobject; t: Typespec): Boolean;
(* Predicate to check if d is compatible with typespec t.
   For languages which allow overloading with respect to type/signature *)
BEGIN
  RETURN  TypeCompatible(TYPEOF(d), t);
END;



FUNCTION  Qualified_Lookup(Name            : Symbol;
                           Currentregion    : Region;
                           Currenttype      : Typespec): Declobject;
(* Qualified lookup of Name, example:  Qualifyname.Name
   Currentregion can be obtained by OBJ_REGION(Qualifyobject), where
   Qualifyobject is the declaration object associated with Qualifyname.
   Currenttype is useful when overloading is a possibility.
 *)
BEGIN
   FOR  d:Declobject  in  DECLS_IN_REGION(Qualifyregion)  DO
       IF  PRNAME(d) = Name;
           and  Check_Type(d, Currenttype)
       THEN
           RETURN  d;
   END FOR;
   RETURN Undefined;
END;



FUNCTION   Ordinal_Lookup(Ordernumber   : Integer;
                          Qualifyregion : Region): Declobject;
(* Lookup by ordinal qualification. Example:  lookup of a procedure
   parameter for type checking at some call site.  In this case
   Qualifyregion can be obtained by REGION-OF(Procedureobject).
 *)
BEGIN
   RETURN   the element extracted by
            indexing the Ordernumber:th element in the sequence
            DECLS_IN_REGION(Qualifyregion);
END;
```

Figure 10.

The lookup procedures for our incremental symbol processing model are shown in pseudo code in Figure 10. Note that the procedures are fairly short in this model, despite the apparent complexity of lookup. The Refine implementation of this pseudo code has approximately the same length.

16. WHY IS THIS ENTITY-RELATIONAL MODEL INCREMENTAL?

Incremental means that the work needed to introduce a change is more or less proportional to the size of the change. Thus it is essential that the datastructures of the model, in our case relations, *permit efficient updating* - both insertions and deletions. Also, the *dependency* relation permits the effects of changes to be propagated only to affected program entities, without affecting others. *Direct access* and order-independent processing: changes can be processed in any order anywhere in the program. The symbol table is *independent of the current focus of processing*. For example, if we introduced a relation REDEFINED - that represents which declarations have been redefined in the current nesting context - it would violate this rule, since it would need to change if the current focus changed.

17. REPRESENTATION OF CERTAIN LANGUAGE CONSTRUCTS

In this section we show how some special language constructs can be represented in the entity-relational symbol processing model. The current list of examples are from Pascal, Modula-2 and Ada. Regions are marked in these examples.

Pascal declaration of enumeration scalars
> This construct introduces a set of named entities within a small region of the program. This is easily modelled by a TRANSPARENT region, which causes entities from inside it to be directly visible in the surrounding region.
>
> Example: TYPE Color = (Red, Blue, Green);
>   ----------------

Pascal record type declaration
> A record type declaration introduces a number of field entities. If the body of the declaration is modelled by a QUALIFIED REGION, then the fields will be visible by qualification in the surrounding region.
>
> Example: TYPE Personrec = RECORD Age:Integer; Weight:Integer END;
>   ---

Pascal WITH statement
> A Pascal WITH statement causes the fields of a record variable to be directly visible within its body. This is modelled by a region around its body. This regions INHERITS the region around the record type where the fields are declared. Thus the fields become directly visible.

Two nested regions are associated with this example WITH-statement. The xrec record type region is imported/inherited by the outer WITH-region, and the yrec region by the inner region.

```
Example:    WITH xrec,yrec DO .... ;
                 --------------  Outer region
                 ---------  Inner region
```

Modula-2 IMPORT declaration, Ada WITH-declaration

Even though it sounds strange, we introduce a small QUALIFIED REGION for each module identifier. Each such region covers only the identifier itself, and INHERITS the region around the module/package specification part. Thus all declaration objects from within the module/package are available within this small region. Since it is a QUALIFIED REGION, declarations are also visible outside it by qualified access.

In this example there are two small qualified regions, where each only covers the relevant module/package identifier. Xmodule is inherited by the first region, and ymodule by the second.

```
Examples:
   Modula-2:    IMPORT xmodule,ymodule;
   Ada     :    WITH   xmodule,ymodule;
                       -------  -------
                     region 1  region 2
```

Modula-2: Selective import statement

Here, a PARTIALLY TRANSPARENT region is introduced around the list of identifiers. The xmodule region is inherited by this underlined partially transparent region. Thus only these explicitly mentioned identifiers are made directly visible outside this region.

```
Example:
   Modula-2:    FROM xmodule IMPORT  foo1,foo2,foo3;
                                    --------------
```

Ada USE declaration

This case is similar to the Ada WITH-declaration, but here a TRANSPARENT region is introduced around each identifier. Thus declarations from inherited regions are made directly visible.

In our example we introduce a sequence of two transparent regions, where the first inherits xmodule and the second inherits ymodule. All definitions from these modules are made directly visible outside the transparent regions.

```
Example:
   Ada  :       USE xmodule, ymodule;
                    -------  -------
```

18. CORRECTNESS

In this section we discuss correctness of queries and very high level specifications, where queries on our symbol processing model is one special case. Since the transformations from specification to executable code are automatic, correctness of executable programs follows automatically if the transformations have been proved correct, and if the specification is correct with respect to intuitions. In the following, we will use the normal definition of correctness which only requires that the implementation has the same semantics as the specification, without taking intuitions into account.

Data type refinement is an especially important program transformation from our point of view, since it allows transformation of relational queries to query operations on other data structures which may be more efficient in certain respects. A special case of such data structure refinement is described in [Horwitz,Teitelbaum-86] where queries on implicit relations are transformed into queries on tree structures. In the rest of this section we will focus on how to define correctness of data type refinements, which follows the treatment in [Goldberg,Kotik-83].

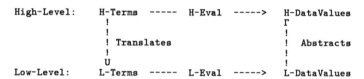

```
High-Level:    H-Terms  ----- H-Eval  ----->  H-DataValues
                  !                            Г
                  !                            !
                  ! Translates                 !  Abstracts
                  !                            !
                  U                            !
Low-Level:     L-Terms  ----- L-Eval  ----->  L-DataValues
```

Figure 11. Correctness of a data-type refinement, expressed through
            a commutating diagram.
            A refinement is a pair I = <Translates, Abstracts>. It is correct
       iff: forall t1 in H-Terms, forall t2 in L-Terms
            [(t1 --> t2) => (H-Eval(t1) = Abstracts(L-Eval(t2)))]

Informally, we can define a data type D as a pair $<Operations_D, DataValues_D>$. We also assume the existence of a function *Eval*, which maps terms into terms, where a term is an expression involving only the operations of some data type. A *refinement* I of a type $H = <Operations_H, DataValues_H>$ to a type $L = <Operations_L, DataValues_L>$, is a pair <Translates, Abstracts>. *Translates* is a relation between H-Terms and L-Terms. It specifies the possible translations from expressions in H-Terms to expressions in L-Terms. *Abstracts* is an abstraction map, that maps each value in $DataValues_L$ to the unique value in $DataValues_H$, which it represents in the refinement, and is the identity function for all other values. Remember that there are usually several lower level concrete representations for each higher level abstract data type.

It is then natural to define a data type refinement as correct, if translated expressions always preserve the semantics of the original expressions. This is the same as requiring that the diagram in Figure 11 commutes. More formally, a refinement I = <Translates, Abstracts> is correct if

```
        forall t1 in H-Terms, forall t2 in L-Terms
        [(t1 --> t2) => (H-Eval(t1) = Abstracts(L-Eval(t2))) ]
```

Refinements can be composed under certain conditions. By the above definition it is easy to realize that the composition of two correct refinements is itself correct.

19. COMPARISON WITH PREVIOUS WORK

The DICE hierarchical incremental symbol processing model [Fritzson-85], is too specialized, and lacks a general declarative query language. A more general incremental model is clearly needed.

The [Reiss-83] paper presents a general model for the generation of non-incremental symbol processing mechanisms from ad-hoc declarative specifications. In addition, that paper contains a separate formal relational symbol processing model. However, that relational model is not suitable as a basis for generation of efficient symbol processing mechanisms. Also, that relational model is not incremental, and it does not correctly model the fact that for many languages the scope of a declaration extends forward from the actual point of declaration. However, its non-relational implementation still works correctly because of the sequential processing nature of non-incremental symbol processing.

The present entity-relational model is an improvement in several respects. It is incremental and it can be used to generate efficient symbol processing mechanisms from high-level declarative specifications through transformations. It is also conceptually simplified, e.g. the complex notion of scope group [Reiss-83] is eliminated. Our model uses the more precise notion of declarative region as a basis for expressing scope. We also include the notion of position, which is needed in an incremental context.

The PSG system [Bahlke,Snelting-86], has the possibility of generating simple scope analysis. However, PSG context relations are primarily designed for use on type analysis, which includes the reconstruction of types from unification on incomplete program fragments.

Attributed-relational grammars [Horwitz,Teitelbaum-86] appears useful as a possible means of communication between a language-based editor and our entity-relational model. However, only very simple scope analysis for a Pascal subset is mentioned in that paper. It could clearly be extended by integrating the entity-relational model presented in this paper.

20. FUTURE WORK

We are currently planning to use similar transformational techniques to generate other parts of compilers than the symbol processing module.

Finite differencing techniques [Paige,Koenig-82] have so far been used to transform powerful set-theoretic operations to cheap incremental counterparts. We are considering the investigation of finite differencing techniques in order to compile code that will cheaply and incrementally update relational expressions and maintain invariants, after small updates to basic input relations.

Another interesting area concerns the extension of our current incremental model to support programming-in-the-large: version handling and configuration control. A design for a distributed network version of our relational program database is desirable. Solve the efficiency problems of current relational databases, for example by relaxing the consistency requirement at the single tuple level, and use invisible caching techniques. There is the question if clustering, caching, query-optimization and relaxed consistency requirements are enough to achieve good performance?

APPENDIX A - C LANGUAGE EXAMPLE OF SCOPE, REGION, POSITION

The scope of a declaration object consists of the parts of a program where it is legal to reference the declaration. Scope need not conform to the nice nesting structure of programming languages. For example, in the C program example below the scope XX1 of the global variable XX covers the initial part of the body of the function foofunc, whereas the scope XX2 of the local variable XX covers the rest of foofunc.

The example below contains six declarative regions: R-File for the whole file, R-foofunc for the function foofunc, and R-block for the body of foofunc. R-foofunc is a qualified region to provide positional access to parameters from the rest of the program; R-block is a nested region for the body of the function.

```
R-File region
 !
 !
 !                   int   XX = 3;            -!
 !                                             ! Scope XX1 for XX (int)
 !   R-foofunc  void foofunc(ch)               !
 !   !               char ch;                  !
 !   ! R-block {                               !
 !   !  !              int     ZZ = XX;       -!                  <-- Position P1
 !   !  !                                      !
 !   !  !              double  XX;            -!                  <-- Position P2
 !   !  !                                      ! Scope XX2 for XX (double)
 !   !  !              ....                    !
 !   !  !      }                              -!
 !
 !
 !
 !   R-X1:         define   X  3             -!
 !   !                ....                    ! Scope X1 for X
 !   !                ....                   -!
 !
 !   R-X2:         undef    X               -!
 !   !                ....                    ! Scope X2 for X
 !   !                ....                   -!
 !
 !   R-X3:         define   X  10           -!
 !   !                ....                    ! Scope X3 for X
 !   !
```

Figure 12: C language program example

The DEPENDENCY Relation:

```
  Dependenton:   Used-by:
  <XX,           {foofunc}>
```

The REGION_NESTING Relation:

```
  parent_region:  child_regions:

  <R-Systemblock,  {R-File}>
  <R-File,         {R-foofunc}>
  <R-foofunc,      {R-block}>
  <R-file,         {R-X1, R-X2, R-X3}>
```

The DEFINED_WITHIN Relation:
```
  parent_region:  decl_objects:
```

```
<R-File,              {XX, foofunc}>
<R-foofunc,           {ch}>
<R-block,             {ZZ, XX-2}>          ;  the second XX declaration
<R-File,              {X, X-2, X-3}>       ;  the second X = undef
                                           ;  the third  X = 10
```

The PRINT_NAME Relation:

```
   printname:     object:

   <"XX"          XX>
   <"XX"          XX-2>
   <"ch"          ch>
   <"ZZ"          ZZ>
   <"foofunc"     foofunc>
   <"X"           X>
   <"X"           X-2>
   <"X"           X-3>
```

The INHERIT relation:
  Donor: Inheritor:

     ....empty....

Figure 13. Relational symbol table for the C language program of figure 12.

REFERENCES

[ADA-83] United States Department of Defense, "Reference Manual for the Ada Programming Language", ANSI/MIL-STD-1815A/1983, February 17, 1983.

[Bahlke,Snelting-86] Rolf Bahlke, Gregor Snelting: "The PSG System: From Formal Language Definitions to Interactive Programming Environments", TOPLAS Vol 8, No 4, October 1986.

[Baker-82] T. P. Baker: "A One-Pass Algorithm for Overload Resolution in Ada", ACM TRansactions on Programming Languages and Systems, Vol. 4, No 4, Oct. 1982, pp 601-614.

[Birtwistle,et.al-73] G M Birtwistle, O-J Dahl, B Myhrhaug, K Nygaard: "SIMULA BEGIN", 391 pp, AUERBACH Publishers Inc, Philadelpia, Pa., 1973.

[Chen-76] Peter Pin-Shan Chen· "The Entity-Relationship Model - Towards a Unified View of Data", ACM Transactions on Database Systems, Vol. 1, No. 1, March 1976.

[Conradi,Wanvik-85] Reidar Conradi and Dag Wanvik, "Mechanisms and Tools for Separate Compilation", Technical Report No 25/85, Nov 1985, The University of Trondheim, Division of Computer Science, N-7034 Trondheim-NTH.

[Fritzson-83] Peter Fritzson, "Symbolic Debugging Through Incremental Compilation in an Integrated Environment", The Journal of Systems and Software 3, 285-294 (1983).

[Fritzson-85] "The Architecture of an Incremental Programming Environment and some Notions of Consistency" Workshop on Software Engineering Environments for Programming-in-the-Large, Harwichport, Massachusetts, June 9-12, 1985.

[Goldberg,Kotik-83] Allen Goldberg and Gordon Kotik: "Knowledge-Based Programming: An Overview of Data Structure Selection and Control Structure Refinement", KES.U.83.7, November 1983, Kestrel Institute, 1801 Page Mill Road, Palo Alto, CA 94304. Also in: Software Validation, H.L. Hausen, Ed., North-Holland, 1984.

[Harbison,Steele-84] Samuel P. Harbison and Guy L. Steele Jr., "C - A Reference Manual", Prentice-Hall, 1984.

[Hoover-86] Roger Hoover: "Dynamically Bypassing Copy Rule Chains in Attribute Grammars", 13:th Annual ACM Symposium on the Principles of Programming Languages, St. Petersburg, Florida, Jan 1986.

[Horwitz,Teitelbaum] Susan Horwitz, Tim Teitelbaum: "Generating Editing Environments Based on Relations and Attributes", ACM Transactions on Programming Languages and Systems, Vol. 8, No. 4, October 1986.

[Linton-84] M. A. Linton: "Implementing Relational Views of Programs" In Proceedings of the ACM SIGSOFT/SIGPLAN Software Engineering Symposium on Practical Software Development Environments (Pittsburgh, Pa., April 1984), ACM New York, 132-140.

[Paige,Koenig-82] Robert Paige, Shaye Koenig: "Finite Differencing of Computable Expressions", TOPLAS 4.3, July 1982, pp 402-454.

[Rational-86] "Private communication on the Rational Incremental Ada Compiler" Rational, 1501 Salado Drive, Mountain View, California 94043.

[Rational-85] James E. Archer, Michael T. Devlin: "Rationals Experience Using Ada for Very Large Systems", Proc of the First International Conference on Ada Programming Language Applications for the NASA Space Station, Houston, Texas, June 2-5, 1986.

[Refine-87] Reasoning Systems: "Refine^{TM} User's Guide", Version 2.0, September 1987. Reasoning Systems Inc., 1801 Page Mill Rd., Palo Alto, CA 94304.

[Reiss-83] Steven P. Reiss, "Generation of Compiler Symbol Processing Mechanisms from Specifications", ACM TOPLAS 5.2 April 1983.

[Reps-83] Thomas W. Reps: "Generating Language-Based Environments", The MIT Press, Massachusetts Institute of Technology, Cambridge, Massachusets 02142

[Smith,et.al] Douglas Smith, Gordon Kotik, Stephen Westfold: "Research on Knowledge-Based Software Environments at Kestrel Institute", IEEE Trans. on Software Engineering, Vol SE-11, No 11, Nov 1985.

[Uhl,et.al-82] J. Uhl, S. Drossopoulou, G. Persch, G. Goos, M. Dausmann, G. Winterstein, W. Kirchgässner: "An Attribute Grammar for the Semantic Analysis of Ada", IX, 511 pages, Lecture Notes in Computer Science, Springer Verlag, 1982.

[Zdonik,Wegner-85] Stanley B. Zdonik and Peter Wegner, "A Database Approach to Languages, Libraries and Environments", Workshop on Software Engineering Environments for Programming-in-the-Large, Harwichport, Massachusetts, June 9-12, 1985.

SOFTWARE ENGINEERING ASPECTS IN LANGUAGE IMPLEMENTATION

Kai Koskimies*
GMD Forschungstelle an der Universität Karlsruhe
Haid-und-Neu Strasse 7, 7500 Karlsruhe, BRD

Abstract

Current implementations of programming languages are modularized according to implementation techniques rather than to the natural units of the language to be implemented. It is argued that such implementations have poor software engineering qualities like reusability and maintainability. A syntax–directed, modular language implementation technique is sketched, based on an object–oriented view of the source language. The technique makes use of the extended types offered by the language Oberon.

1. INTRODUCTION

Typical language implementation software consists of large, complex programs. One could think that traditional software engineering issues like reusability, maintainability, and modularity would play a particularly important role in the developing of such software. Hence it is somewhat surprising to note that practical language implementations are usually bulky, monolithic programs that have relatively weak software engineering qualities. A typical one–pass compiler (see e.g. [WMK80]) consists of a single module taking care of the entire analysis of the source text and synthesis of the target program, assisted by some smaller service modules for scanning, symbol table, etc. The main module may be structured, but it basically follows the programming style of the 60's. This kind of module division is virtually the same for all languages, independently of the size of the language. Hence for sizable languages the main module becomes very large (say, over 10000 lines), exceeding the reasonable limit of a software unit.

The reason for this unsatisfactory situation is probably the fact that programming languages are regarded as complex, indivisable objects. Hence, from the software engineering point of view the language to be implemented is a black box: the implementor tends to think in terms of services needed by the translation process, and does not try to divide the language itself into logical pieces that would be represented by separate modules.

In this paper we try to demonstrate that the implementation of programming languages can be cut into pieces in a sensible and natural way. In particular, we will study how two popular software engineering paradigms could be applied in language implementation, namely *object–oriented programming* and *modular programming.* Both of these techniques contribute to the division of the language implementation into software units that closely correspond to the concepts and structures of the source language as they are presented e.g. in the reference manual. We expect that this will improve especially the maintainability and reuse of language implementation software. Naturally, this topic is not new in the sense that modular and/or

---

* On leave from University of Helsinki, Finland. This work is in part supported by Deutsche Forschungsgemeinschaft and by the Academy of Finland.

object–oriented languages have been used in language implementation for a long time. The (perhaps) new aspect of this study is the systematic syntax–directed method of modularization. The ideas presented here originate to some extent from the object–oriented language implementation system TOOLS ([KoP87], [KELP88]), and from the experiences in using it [KoM88].

The syntactic structure of a programming language is the most obvious basis for modularizing the implementation. Although many computer philosophers regard the syntax as something irrelevant and superficial, it is nevertheless the only concrete form of manifestation of the language. An older programming paradigm, *structured programming,* has been applied to language implementation in a syntax–directed way, and the result has been one of the most successful language implementation strategies, recursive descent. However, instead of mapping the various parts of a language into procedures we will map them into separately compiled modules. These modules will usually be interpreted as representatives of classes in the sense of object–oriented programming.

We will proceed as follows. Chapter 2 studies our syntax–directed view of the objects constituting a program in detail, with respect to structures found in Pascal–like languages. In Chapter 3 we will present the basic method for modularizing language implementation, and Chapter 4 provides an example of the application of this method. Finally, in Chapter 5 we will discuss the advantages of the method. We assume that the reader is familiar with the concepts of object–oriented programming (e.g. [Weg87]).

2. SYNTAX–DIRECTED OBJECTS

Notion objects

Let us consider a nonterminal symbol of a context–free grammar as the name of a class. An instance of such a class represents a realization of a particular language notion; we call these instances *notion objects.*

How well do the notion objects cover the natural objects that constitute a program? First, we note that many of the notion objects may be needed only for syntactic analysis (possibly required by a particular parsing method), or for some trivial information passing. The other, more essential notion objects constitute something which is near to an abstract representation of the source text. However, here we will not make any distinction between "essential" and "non–essential" notion objects (or nonterminal classes).

Second, sometimes there is no clear one–to–one correspondence between syntactic notion objects and logical language objects. First, there may be "syntactic discontinuity" so that a logical language object is represented by disconnected pieces of text. In such a situation it may be difficult to assign naturally a particular nonterminal for the class of the objects, although the objects have clearly a syntactic representation. A typical example is the grouping of variable declarations that have the same type:

```
VariableDeclaration ::= 'VAR' IdList ':' TypeId
IdList ::= IdList ',' Identifier | Identifier
```

A single variable declaration (representing a variable object) consists of an identifier and of the type denotation following the list of identifiers; between these pieces of text there may be an unbounded number of other identifiers. Note that in this case a piece of text (the type denotation) is shared by several objects.

In some languages (e.g. Ada) the above form of variable declarations is viewed as a short-hand notation for a sequence of declarations of single variables. The expanded form would of course eliminate the problem. In general, short-hand notations may cause problems in finding the syntactic counterparts for the classes of the language definition.

Third, in some cases a nonterminal instance actually represents a set of objects. This situation arises when the nonterminal acts either in the role of a *metaclass* or in the role of a *collective class*.

An instance of a metaclass nonterminal corresponds to a class definition so that an unlimited number of objects may be generated during run-time as instances of the nonterminal instance. A trivial case of a metaclass is a nonterminal which produces something that corresponds to a class in the source language, e.g. class definitions in Simula. In general, if a language concept has the property that it can be instantiated, the corresponding nonterminal belongs to the category of metaclasses. Such concepts include e.g. type and procedure definitions in Pascal-like languages.

Metaclass nonterminals are usually associated with other nonterminals that produce the instantiation structure. For example, in Pascal variable declarations and calls of the standard procedure "new" are used to create instances of types, and procedure calls are used to instantiate procedures. The notion objects created in response to these nonterminals are "generative" in the sense that the activation of some of their methods will give rise to an instance of a class defined by an instance of a "metaclass nonterminal".

An instance of a collective nonterminal class represents invariably a fixed group of objects. The most frequent example is a list structure (declaration list, statement list etc.); in this case the objects belonging to the group (i.e. the list elements) are represented by other notion objects. However, in some cases the objects belonging to the group are not syntactically represented. Such a situation may arise e.g. in the declaration of a structured variable, in which the components are not represented by distinct pieces of text.

Note the difference between collective classes and metaclasses: an instance of a collective class is a set of objects, possibly of different classes, while an instance of a metaclass is a class that may or may not be later used for creating instances of this class.

Finally, in some cases a natural object is not at all represented by a notion object, not even via a metaclass nonterminal. A trivial example is the standard environment in Pascal (i.e. standard constants, types, etc.). However, in this case the additional syntactic structures can be easily introduced, generating an empty string at the beginning of the program. If a class has no association with syntax, we call it a *semantic class*. In Pascal-like languages the existence of such classes is not quite obvious, although a particular implementation technique may require them.

Class hierarchies

Although the hierarchic relations implied by the syntactic production rules provide a seemingly obvious basis for establishing a class hierarchy for nonterminal classes, this idea makes sense only in certain special cases. The fact alone that production rules are usually recursive makes it impossible to build a general class hierarchy on this basis. However, sometimes a production rule exhibits a classification of nonterminals that can be understood as an introduction of a superclass. We will call these *superclass productions.* In standard Pascal (BSI[82]), such productions are e.g.:

```
new–type::= simple–type | structured–type | pointer–type
simple–type::= ordinal–type | real–type
ordinal–type::= enumerated–type | subrange–type | ...
structured–type::= ["packed"] unpacked–structured–type |
structured–type–identifier
unpacked–structured–type::= array–type | record–type | ...
```

These productions actually define the hierarchic type system in Pascal: "simple–type", "structured–type", and "pointer–type" are subclasses of "(new–)type"; "ordinal–type" and "real–type" are subclasses of "simple–type" etc.

In general, a superclass production is of the form

```
S ::= C1 | C2 | ... | Cn
```

where S is the *superclass nonterminal* and C1, C2, ... , and Cn are *subclass nonterminals.* Typical superclass productions can be found easily in Pascal:

```
simple–statement::= empty–statement | assignment–statement | ...
structured–statement::= compound–statement |
conditional–statement | ...
conditional–statement::= if–statement | case–statement
```

Except for types and statements, superclass productions can be found e.g. for operators and elementary value accessing:

```
multiplying–operator::= "*" | "/" | "div" | "mod" | "and"
factor::= variable–access | unsigned–constant | ...
```

In the first case subclasses are represented directly by terminal symbols. In the second case the subclasses are intuitively not so clear, partly because the naming conventions of various factors do not emphasize the common aspect.

In Pascal declarations must be given in a fixed order, implying that there is no superclass production for declarations. However, if such a restriction were not imposed by the syntax, a superclass production would appear in the form:

```
declaration::= constant–declaration | type–declaration | ...
```

Note that superclass nonterminals should not give rise to separate notion objects: the logical language concept is represented by the most accurate nonterminal. Hence, a chain of superclass nonterminal instances in the syntax tree should be regarded as a single instance of the lowest–level class; the instances of the superclass nonterminals then represent only different levels of the object.

Attributes and methods

The attributes (local data) and methods of notion objects vary considerably depending on the nature of the language concept represented by the nonterminal. First we note that the attributes are usually divided into two categories: those contributing to the structural relations of the objects (structural attributes), and those describing some non–structural properties of the objects. The first category essentially establishes an abstract tree structure of the source text. Note that the attributes do not merely provide local connections, but also non–local. For example, a nonterminal instance denoting a variable reference in an expression probably has an attribute referring to the variable object, which might be represented by a nonterminal instance far from the expression. However, we consider such attributes non–structural: structural attributes are related only to the substructures.

Maybe the most notable special feature of notion objects (when compared to the conventional objects) is the creation operation: instead of an explicit operation these objects are assumed to be created implicitly on the basis of some pattern matching process applied to an input text. Normally this is done through parsing. In the top–down approach discussed in the following section the creation operation can be directly implemented as the parsing procedure of the nonterminal in question.

A typical method possessed by many notion objects is a check on the values of the non–structural attributes (or sometimes on the non–structural attributes at the objects referenced by other attributes). Such a check is usually required by the "static semantics" of the language, and can be carried out immediately after the creation of the object. These checks concern e.g. various conditions imposed by the type system, like type compatibility rules. Since the static checks can be carried out at creation time, it is natural to consider them as part of the creation operation. Some checks cannot be done until at run–time because they depend on dynamic information; these checks can be usually regarded as part of the method describing the dynamic behaviour of the object in question. For example, a range check may be necessary in connection with the execution of an assignment statement in Pascal.

Besides the creation operation and the possible associated checking operation, notion objects very seldom seem to have more than one method. Normally each language concept has a single role or activity throughout the interpretation of the source text; indeed, this should probably be a basic language design principle. Typical methods are e.g. the evaluation of an expression or some part of it, or the execution of a statement. In a compiling implementation the corresponding methods would produce the code for executing these actions.

3. MODULAR LANGUAGE IMPLEMENTATION METHOD

In a conventional recursive descent compiler the main module consists of a set of procedures, one for each nonterminal of the source language. The main module is assisted by several "implemetation service" modules for scanning, symbol tables etc. Our basic idea is to reverse this scheme: we want to have a separate module for each nonterminal, and to provide all the implementation services in one module (see Fig. 1 and 2). The latter module is assumed to be the same for all implemeted languages; hence it can be viewed as a kind of a language implementation system, although in a slightly different sense than the conventional metacompilers.

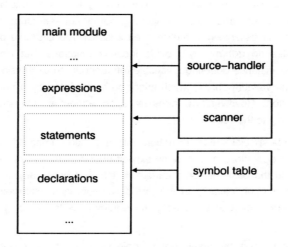

Fig. 1. Conventional module division

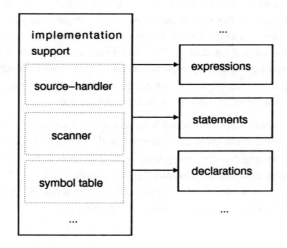

Fig. 2. Source language oriented module division.

The nonterminal modules are viewed as the specifications of the corresponding nonterminal classes. Each such module will therefore define in its visible part the class type, which will always be a pointer to a record consisting of the attributes of the notion objects, and the methods of the class. One of these methods must be the creation operation, but otherwise they can be freely chosen.

Implementation language

We will present the method using Wirth's new language Oberon [Wir88a]. It turned out that the type extension mechanism provided by this language [Wir88b] fits very nicely with the requirements of our task. Two problems arise when a conventional modular language (like Modula–2 or Ada) is used. First, structural attributes cannot be handled naturally because of the rigidity of the type system. If we want that the class type is defined by each module, then the class type definition of module A needs the class type of module B, if A–objects need to refer to the B–objects. Since the class type must be given in the definition part, this means that the definition part of A must import B. However, since nonterminals may be recursive, it may be that B also needs to refer to A–objects (possibly indirectly through a chain), and therefore the definition part of B must also import A. This leads to forbidden circular importing. In Ada the problem is particularly difficult because even the opaque types must be completely defined in the definition part (in the private section). In Modula–2 the problem can be solved by making the class type an opaque type, and by defining the attributes in the implementation part. However, this would mean that *all* attributes are invisible for the outsiders, which in turn leads to the introduction of additional methods only for reading the values of some attributes.

In Oberon a visible record type, defined in the definition part of a module, can be extended with a non–visible part in the implementation module. This is exactly what we want: the structural attributes can be conveniently represented in the non–visible extension. Note that the structural attributes should indeed be invisible; they are needed only for implementing some of the methods of the class, and should not be touched by the outsiders.

The other problem concerns the construction of class hierarchies. In Ada or Modula–2 such hiearchies must be presented using variant records in a rather clumsy way. This can be done e.g. by defining all the subclasses in the uppermost level (that is, in the root class) as a variant record, and by importing this type to all the subclasses. Such a solution is however very unnatural, and it in fact breaks the modularization by introducing implicit dependencies between the modules.

In Oberon, the superclass module must also be imported by the subclass module, but the subclass can be defined simply as an extension of the superclass. Hence the attributes of each class level can be naturally defined in the right place. There are no hidden dependencies between modules: the superclass module need not know anything about the subclasses.

We will assume the existence of a module which provides all the necessary language–independent implementation services; this module is called "Support". These services include at least support for scanning, for deterministic modular recursive descent parsing (as proposed in [Kos88]), a general object retrieval mechanism, and a collection of useful data types (e.g. lists). In fact, some of the facilities of this module can be viewed as "system" classes, so that certain nonterminals will be their subclasses. For example, a declaration can be viewed as a subclass of "the class of objects to be found on the basis of an identifier"; the latter class is provided as a type of "Support". Similarly, a statement list structure can be presented as a subclass of a general list.

Again, the presenting of such system classes becomes very natural in Oberon. For example, the class record of a declaration can be defined as an extension of an element type (exported from "Support"), allowing these declarations to be inserted into a general–purpose object–base with a fast search mechanism.

Construction of modules

For each nonterminal, the definition module is constructed as follows:

1) Import list:

    If the nonterminal is a subclass nonterminal, import the module of the superclass nonterminal. If the nonterminal is a subclass for a system class, import "Support".

2) Data part:

    Define the following type:

    > **type** Attr = **record** (S)
    > A_1: T_1;
    >   ...
    > A_n: T_n;
    > **end**;

    where S is either the attribute record type of the form X.Attr of the superclass nonterminal X, or some system class of the form Support.C, and A_1...A_n are the visible attributes of the instances of the class. This type describes all the data contained by the objects. The actual class type is defined as:

    > **type** Class = **pointer to** Attr;

    so that objects will always be represented by dynamic variables.

3) Methods:

    Define the heading of the creation operation as

    > **procedure** Create(): Class;

    Define the headings of other methods, possibly with parameters of type "Class".

For each nonterminal, the implementation module is constructed as follows:

1) Import list:

    Import all the modules of the syntactic substructures of the nonterminal. If the syntactic structure contains terminal symbols, or if the methods otherwise make use of "Support", import it.

2) Data part:

    If the notion objects have structural attributes, define an extension of Attr:

```
type Attr = record (S)
    A₁: T₁;
    ...
    Aₙ: Tₙ;
    X₁: U₁;
    ...
    Xₖ: Uₖ;
end;
```

where $X_1,...,X_k$ are the structural attributes of the notion objects. Types $U_1,...,U_k$ are of the form W.Class, where W is an imported module.

3) Methods

Implement the creation method in the style of a parser routine of a recursive descent parser, by calling the creation methods of the constituent structures in appropriate places. In the case of a superclass nonterminal, return the value returned by the creation method of one of the substructures (subclasses) as such. Otherwise create a dynamic variable representing the object, and initialize the attributes. Implement other methods as required.

Comments

The above rules are the basic guidelines that should be followed in the design of the modules. Sometimes additional importing is necessary, for example when an object has a non–structural attribute that refers to another object. Then the class type of some other module has to be imported into the definition module. Additional types required for defining the "Attr" type may also be necessary in the definition module.

A particular problem arises in parsing, because in principle a module should not know anything about the other modules, except what is available through the interface. Hence a nonterminal module should not make use of any information concerning the syntactic structure of other nonterminals, either. This requirement rules out conventional recursive descent parsing, where the starter and follower tokens are assumed to be known globally for the entire grammar. The problem can be solved by collecting necessary parsing information dynamically, during parsing [Kos88]. We will not discuss this method here, but we merely assume that deterministic parsing is in some way possible.

We have not paid any attention to metaclass nonterminals. The simplest way to present them is to let the generating notion object have an attribute that refers to an instance of the metaclass nonterminal. A method of the generating notion object (e.g. variable declaration) can then make use of this reference, and create an instance according to the referenced object (type definition).

4. AN EXAMPLE

As an example of the application of the modular language implementation method, we will examine the developing of an interpreter for the following toy language:

```
Prog ::= DeclList StatList
DeclList ::= (Decl ';')*
Decl ::= TypeDecl | ConstDecl | VarDecl
TypeDecl ::= 'TYPE' id '=' number '..' number
ConstDecl ::= 'CONST' id '=' number
VarDecl ::= 'VAR' id ':' id
StatList ::= Stat (';' Stat)*
Stat ::= AssStat | LoopStat | IfStat
AssStat ::= id ':=' Expr
LoopStat ::= WhileStat | RepeatStat
WhileStat ::= 'WHILE' Expr 'DO' StatList 'END'
RepeatStat ::= 'REPEAT' StatList 'UNTIL' Expr
IfStat ::= 'IF' Expr 'THEN' StatList ElsePart 'END'
Expr ::= Term (Oper Term)*
Term ::= number | id | SubExp
SubExp ::= '(' Expr ')'
Oper ::= '+' | '−'
```

For simplicity, only integers and their subranges are allowed types; logical values are assumed to be represented by integers (0: false, <>0: true). Hence type checking consists only of run–time range checks. Standard identifier "INTEGER" denotes the type of integers provided by the underlying system.

In the sequel we will examine some of the modules required for this implementation; a complete listing of the modules can be found in Appendix.

Let us first study the modules for declarations. A declaration can be viewed as a subclass of "identifiable" objects provided by the support module. Hence we write the definition part as follows:

```
definition Decl;
    import Support;
    type Attr = record (Support.EntryType)
                    name: String;
               end;
        Class = pointer to Attr;
    -- methods:
    procedure Create(): Class;
    procedure Find(Key: String): Class;
end Decl.
```

We assumed here a general string type "String". This specification implies that the common properties of declarations are 1) that they are identifiable objects, 2) that they have a string–valued name for identification, and 3) that function "Find" can be used to access an object through its name.

A type declaration is a subtype of a declaration:

```
definition TypeDecl;
    import Decl;
    type Attr = record (Decl.Attr)
                        lo: Integer;
                        hi: Integer;
                   end;
        Class = pointer to Attr;
```

```
    --methods:
      procedure Create(): Class;
    end TypeDecl.
```

This states only that each type has two visible attributes, the lower and the upper bound of the range. Type declarations (or types) have further a subtype, namely (the declaration of) the standard type:

```
    definition StandTypeDecl;
      import TypeDecl;
      type Attr = record (TypeDecl.Attr) end;
           Class = pointer to Attr;
      --methods:
      procedure Create(): Class;
    end StandTypeDecl.
```

The attributes of the standard type will be the same as for other types; hence the definition module is practically identical to type declaration. The essential difference appears only in the implementation part, because the creation method of standard types is implemented differently (i.e., without parsing).

Let us examine another class chain. A statement has the property that it belongs to a list of sequentially executable statements. Hence a statement is a subclass of list elements provided by the support module. A common method to all the statements is the execution of the statement:

```
    definition Stat;
      import Support;
      type Attr = record (Support.ListElemType) end;
           Class = pointer to Attr;
      -- methods:
      procedure Create(): Class;
      procedure Execute(S: Class);
    end Stat.
```

An assignment statement is further a subclass of a statement. An assignment statement has no visible attributes, but two structural hidden attributes referring to the left–hand side and to the right–hand side of the assignment.

```
    definition AssStat;
      import Stat;
      type Attr = record (Stat.Attr) end;
           Class = pointer to Attr;
      -- method:
      procedure Create(): Class;
      procedure Execute(AS: Class);
    end AssStat.
```

Note that in the "Stat" module the execution method only selects the appropriate lower class method on the basis of the actual class of the parameter object. This arrangement is necessary in the absence of virtual methods. Let us look at the implementation part:

```
module AssStat;
    import Support, VarDecl, Decl, Expr;
    type Attr = record
            lhs: VarDecl.Class;
            rhs: Expr.Class;
            end;
    procedure Create(): Class;
            var AS: Class;
                D: Decl.Class;
    begin   -- AssStat ::= id ':=' Expr
            New(AS);
            D:= Decl.Find(Support.ScanTC(Support.identifier));
            Support.ScanSymbol(":=");
            if (D is VarDecl.Class) and (D<>nil)
                    then AS.lhs:= D(VarDecl.Class);
                    else Support.Error("Declaration error");
            end;
            AS.rhs:= Expr.Create();
            return AS;
    end Create;
    procedure Execute(AS: Class);
    begin
            Expr.Evaluate(AS.rhs);
            VarDecl.Assign(AS.lhs, AS.rhs.val);
    end Execute;
end AssStat.
```

In this case we have a taken short–cut: "lhs" is not really a structural attribute but a direct reference to the left–hand side variable; in this way we avoid the introduction of an additional nonterminal on the left–hand side. For this reason we have to import "VarDecl". Note also that we have to import "Decl" because we apply the searching mechanism defined for declarations. "Expr" has to be imported because the creation of an assignment requires the creation of an expression.

Note that this kind of modularization turns the language structures into replaceable, separately compiled units. For example, if we wish to add a new statement into the language, we only need to modify the implementation part of "Stat", and recompile it together with the new module for the additional statement. If we want to change the form of a while statement, or its implementation, it is enough to modify and recompile the implementation part of "WhileStat". The definition parts of modules are affected only if there are some changes in the abstract, visible properties of the language structures, and even then the recompilation is reduced to a minimum.

5. DISCUSSION

One of the most crucial part of software engineering is our ability to make use of the existing software for developing new systems. This ability is known to be very low, e.g. a study [Jon84] indicates that only about 15% of written code is original, the rest being some kind of adaptation or copying of existing software. We feel that in language implementation software the situation is at least as bad. For example, in each new language implementation the concept of an arithmetic expression is re–implemented, although this part of the software is practically identical to numerous other implementations. One could imagine that in many cases some general form of an expression would be quite sufficient. Similar examples can be found easily.

Our study suggests that programming languages are perhaps not so indivisable beasts as people tend to think. Rather, it seems that the possible non–modular features of present programming languages are a consequence of the monolithic implementation paradigm. If programming languages had evolved with the support of truly modular implementation paradigms, they might look very different from what they are today. It could be even possible that the concept of a programming "language" would gradually vanish in such development, in favour of a programming "system" consisting of relatively loosely coupled, replaceable parts. In the author's view, this kind of development would be profitable to software engineering in general: various kinds of differently oriented programming systems could be rapidly developed, and the programmers would be easily adapted to using these systems because they consist of familiar, generally known components.

REFERENCES

[BSI82] British Standards Institution: Specification for Computer Programnming Language Pascal. BSI6192, BSI 1982.

[Jon84] Jones C.: Reusability in Programming: A Survey of the State of the Art. IEEE Transactions on Software Engineering, SE–10,5 (Sept 1984), 488–493.

[Kos88] Koskimies K.: Modular Recursive Descent Parsing. Unpublished manuscript, September 1988.

[KELP88] Koskimies K., Elomaa T., Lehtonen T., Paakki J.: TOOLS/HLP84 Report and User Manual. Report A–1988–2, Department of Computer Science, University of Helsinki, 1988.

[KoM88] Koskimies K., Meriste M.: Experiences with Class–Based Implementation of Program– ming Languages. Technical Report, Department of Computer Science, University of Helsinki, 1988.

[KoP87] Koskimies K., Paakki J.: TOOLS – A Unifying Approach to Object–Oriented Language Interpretation. In: Proc. of ACM Sigplan '87 Symposium on Interpreters and Interpretive Techniques, Sigplan Notices 22,7 (June 1987), 153–164.

[Weg87] Wegner P.: Dimensions of Object–Oriented Languages. In: OOPSLA '87, Sigplan Notices 22,12 (Dec 1987), 168–182.

[WMK80] Welsh J., McKeag M.: Structured System Programming. Prentice–Hall International, 1980.

[Wir88a] Wirth N.: The Programming Language Oberon. Software Practice and Experience 18,7 (July 1988), 671–690.

[Wir88b] Wirth N.: Type Extensions. ACM TOPLAS 10,2 (April 1988), 204–214.

OPTRAN - A Language/System for the Specification of Program Transformations: System Overview and Experiences*

Peter Lipps, Ulrich Möncke, Reinhard Wilhelm

FB 10 - Informatik
Universität des Saarlandes
D-6600 Saarbrücken
Federal Republic of Germany

ABSTRACT

OPTRAN is a batch-oriented system for the generation of compilers that support program transformations. Programs are represented by attributed abstract syntax trees (AAST). The transformation of AAST's is a powerful method to describe problems in compiler writing such as machine-independent optimisations, language-based editors, and source-to-source translations.

The specification language OPTRAN allows for a static and declarative description of tree transformations. Given such a specification, the system will automatically generate the transformation system, mainly consisting of an attribute evaluator and reevaluator, as well as a tree analyzer and transformer.

The paper presents an introduction to the description mechanisms together with an overview of the system, showing the interaction of several generators. The main goal of the system design is the usage of precomputation methods wherever possible. This generative approach is explained. The static view of transformations makes it possible to generate highly efficient transformers but also has its limitations, which we mention.

The system is written in Pascal and generates Pascal programs. Pascal also serves as host language, i.e. semantic rules are specified as Pascal procedures. This complicates the error diagnosis of the runtime system as the semantics of these procedures is not obvious to the generator system. Furthermore it inhibits the recognition of certain properties of the specification like invariance of attribute assignments under non-trivial transformations.

We report practical experiences for some applications, e.g. a compiler for MiniPascal producing M68000 code and a frontend for Ada producing DIANA intermediate descriptions. [Li88] contains an annotated bibliography on OPTRAN.

---

*partially supported by the Deutsche Forschungsgemeinschaft under Project "Manipulation of Attributed Trees" and the Commission of the European Community under Esprit Project Ref. No. 390 (PROSPECTRA)

1. Introduction

Attributed abstract syntax trees (AASTs) have become a standard representation for programs in software development and compiling environments. Many tasks such as standardization, code optimization, source-to-source translation, and transformational program development can be specified by attributed tree transformations. The **OPTRAN specification language** allows the definition of sets of such tree transformation rules. The **OPTRAN system** consists of a set of generators producing efficient tree transformers from an OPTRAN specification.

We will now abstract from the applications listed above and discuss different views of the concept "tree transformation".

The Term rewriting view

Transformations of attributed trees can be seen as being derived from term rewriting: There, transformations are specified by a set of simple transformation rules (term rewriting rules, oriented equations). The rules are specified independently and not linked together by any superimposed control structure. Rules may be applied ("fired") wherever their left sides match inside the object tree. Rule application causes local changes in an object tree, which represents the state of the transformation system. OPTRAN is based on this batch oriented pure term rewriting scheme with the following extensions:

- rule application may depend on attribute values
- rule application may modify attribute values
- rule application conflicts are solved by user defined strategies mainly concerning the orientation in the object tree (bottom-up, top-down, left-to-right, right-to-left).

The enrichment of term rewriting by attributes leads to the problem of attribute updating and ensuring attribute consistency, which is solved by reevaluation techniques. The advantage of this approach is the locality both of rule and attribute specification, the latter locally to a (operator resp.) production. On the other hand, this scheme lacks powerful constructs for describing strategies, linking rules together, building rule packages, coupling application of different rules, conditional and (locally) iterative rule application, and specifying tree walking. This deficit of describing control was recognized early. Proposals for a PASCAL like control structure have been made, see for example [GMW80] . In addition, proposals for language extensions like list constructs [Ba86] and their attribution [Ra86, BMR85] as well as more powerful patterns [BMR86] exist. [Th88] investigates coupling of transformation units and the maintenance of transformation rule packages.

The Functional view

Transformations are not specified as a set of unrelated rules, but as functions to be applied to the subject tree. The style of describing control is very different from the term rewriting or the OPTRAN style. Functional composition may be used to form bigger transformations from smaller ones. The simple patterns and rules mentioned above do not vanish, but are embedded as parts of the functional expression describing the whole transformation. Higher order functions may be used to formulate transformation strategies. Nevertheless, the experience from the construction of pattern matching automata etc. may be amortised in the implementation of such a functional language. The reader is referred to [He88] for more details.

System overview

OPTRAN is a very-high-level language for the specification of attributed abstract syntax trees and tree transformations. The structure of an abstract syntax tree is described by a regular tree grammar. A set of attributes is associated with each node of a tree. Context information may be collected in attributes and passed over the tree. There is a set of semantic rules for each production of the tree grammar describing the functional dependencies between attributes. Transformation rules specify the possible modifications of trees. Each rule consists of an application condition (left hand side) and an output description (right hand side). The syntactic part of an application condition is described by an input pattern. An additional context condition can be formulated by means of a predicate over attributes of the input pattern. A transformation rule is said to be applicable at a node of a tree if there is a match for the input pattern at that node and the predicate is satisfied. If a rule is a applicable the part of the tree that is matched by the input pattern is replaced by the output pattern. Hereby, the bindings of the variables of the input template resulting from the successful match are used to construct the new tree. In general, the transformation of a tree changes the functional dependencies of attributes. Therefore, the values of inconsistent attributes, i.e. attributes for which the dependencies have been changed by a transformation, have to be recomputed.

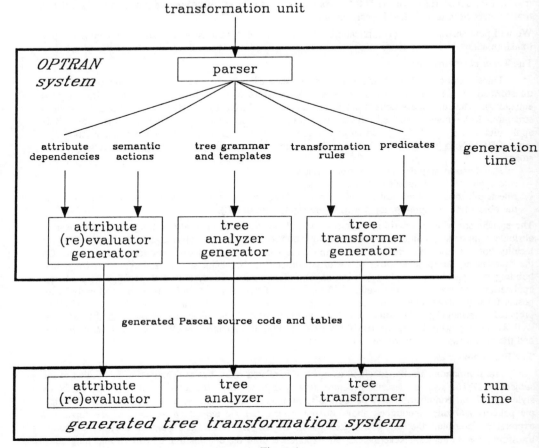

Figure 1

An OPTRAN specification of a tree transformation system is called a *transformation unit (t-unit)*. A t-unit mainly consists of three parts, i.e.

- a tree grammar, describing the structure of abstract syntax trees,
- attributes associated with nodes of the tree and semantic rules associated with productions denoting the functional dependencies between attributes,
- a set of tree transformation rules.

The OPTRAN system generates a *transformation system (t-system)* for a given t-unit. At run time, the t-system takes an abstract syntax tree and basically performs the following actions:

- initially, the *attribute evaluator* computes the value of all attributes according to the functional dependencies specified in the t-unit
- the *tree analyzer* searches the attributed abstract syntax tree for a node where a tree template matches and the corresponding predicate is satisfied;

- the *tree transformer* applies the selected transformation rule to,the tree;
- the *attribute reevaluator* recomputes the value of inconsistent attributes of the transformed tree.

Extensive analysis of the static properties of a t-unit at generation time makes it possible to perform these tasks in a very efficient way.

- the *attribute (re)evaluator generator* analyses the attribute dependencies
- the *tree analyzer generator* analyzes the set of input patterns of the transformation rules and produces an efficient tree pattern matcher from it [We83] ;
- the *tree transformer generator* generates efficient tree transforming programs for the transformation rules [Wi81] ;

Figure 1 shows the basic components of the OPTRAN system and how they are connected.

2. Specification language

Abstract syntax trees are described by a regular tree grammar in OPTRAN. The grammar corresponds to the tree part of a string-to-tree grammar and makes linking to a compiler frontend possible. At this time, such a frontend can be generated with the POCO LALR(1)-Parser-Generator [Eu88] or the ELL(2)-Parser-Generator [He86a, He86b] both developed at the Universität des Saarlandes.

A *tree grammar* is a quadrupel $TG = (N, OP, P, S)$, where N is a finite set of *nonterminals*, OP is a finite set of *operators* with fixed arity, $S \in N$ is the *axiom*, and P is a set of *productions* of the form $X_0 ::= X_1$ or $X_0 ::= <op, X_1,..., X_n>$, where $n \in N_0$ is the *arity* of the operator op, $X_0, \cdots, X_n$ are nonterminals, and $<op, X_1,..., X_n>$ is the linear representation of a tree with depth 1. An operator op must not appear in more than one production.

An *abstract syntax tree* t of TG is a finite ordered tree. The nodes of t are labeled with operators.

Example:

STATLIST	::=	<sepop, STATLIST, STAT>
STATLIST	::=	STAT
STAT	::=	ASSIGNSTAT
STAT	::=	WHILESTAT
STAT	::=	IFSTAT
ASSIGNSTAT	::=	<assop, VARIABLE, EXPR>
WHILESTAT	::=	<whileop, EXPR, STATLIST>
IFSTAT	::=	<ifop, EXPR, STATLIST, STATLIST\2>
EXPR	::=	<addop, EXPR\1, EXPR\2>
EXPR	::=	<relop, EXPR\1, EXPR\2>
EXPR	::=	<intconst>
EXPR	::=	<boolconst>
EXPR	::=	VARIABLE
VARIABLE	::=	<varid>

Figure 2

Attributes are used to collect context information and to spread this information over the tree. Each attribute has a type. Two disjoint sets of attributes, i.e. the set of *inherited* attributes $Inh(op)$ and the set of *synthesized* attributes $Syn(op)$, are associated with each operator op. The set of all attributes of op is denoted by $Attr(op) = Inh(op) \cup Syn(op)$. *Instances* of these attributes are attached to each node of a syntax tree labeled with op.

A (possibly empty) set of *semantic rules* is specified for each production $X_0 ::= <op, X_1, \cdots, X_n>$, describing the functional dependencies between attribute occurrences of this production. We call the occurrences of the inherited attributes at op and the synthesized attributes at X_i *used attribute occurences* and the occurrences of the synthesized attributes at op and the inherited attributes at X_i *defined attribute occurences*, where $i \in \{1, ... , n\}$. There is exactly one *implicit* semantic rule r for each defined attribute occurrence of a production, that is not imported. Each used attribute occurrence can be an argument of r. Some defined attribute occurrences do not have an associated defining rule. The corresponding instances will initially receive their value by importing it from a preceding frontend. These attribute occurrences are called *imported*.

The set of transformation rules specifies how to manipulate a given tree. A *transformation rule tr* consists of an *application condition* and an *output description*. The application condition has a syntactic and a semantic part. An input pattern specifies the *syntactic application condition*. A leaf of a pattern may be labeled with a *parameter*. A parameter matches every tree. Input patterns have to be linear, that is no parameter appears twice in the pattern. The semantic application condition is given by a *predicate* over the attributes of the input pattern. A rule *tr* is **applicable** at a node *n* of a tree *t* if the input pattern matches at *n* and the predicate over attribute instances of the subtree at *n* is satisfied. *n* is called *transformation node*. The predicate can be omitted.

Application of a transformation rule *tr* restructures the tree: the instance of the matching input pattern is replaced by the corresponding output pattern and each parameter of the output pattern is replaced by the matched subtree. The value of an imported attribute is specified by a so called *explicit* semantic rule, which may take any attributes of the input pattern as argument. The value of the non-imported attributes is defined by the implicit semantic rules specified for each production of the tree grammar.

Example:

```
transform
        <ifop, <boolconst>, THENPART, ELSEPART>
if istrue(svalue of boolconst) into
        THENPART
else into
        ELSEPART
fi;


transform
        <varid>
if (sconst of varid) and (stype of varid = inttype) into
        <intconst>
elsif (sconst of varid) and (stype of varid = booltype) into
        <boolconst>
fi;
```

Figure 3

In general, there may be more than one transformation rule applicable in a tree at the same time. A user defined *strategy* [We83] resolves the conflict: the user can specify if a given tree is searched for rule application *bottom-up* or *top-down*, *left-to-right* or *right-to-left*. In addition, a *(strictly) monotonic* strategy guarentees that only (proper) ancestors/descendants of a transformation node are tested for rule application. The rule with the most specific input pattern is chosen if there is more than one transformation rule applicable at the same node. If two patterns are incomparable the textually preceding rule is chosen.

An attributed tree grammar, a set of transformation rules and the specification of a strategy for conflict resolution together constitute a *transformation unit*.

3. Attribute (re)evaluation

3.1. Generation time analysis

The analysis of static properties of a given transformation unit at generation time renders it possible to generate very efficient transformation systems. The generative approach to tree pattern matching is explained in [MWW86], where it is compared to an interpretative approach. In this paper, we only give a short overview of the generative aspects of attribute (re)evaluation. A detailed description of attribute (re)evaluation in OPTRAN can be found in [LMOW87].

Using a pure interpretaive approach an attribute (re)evaluator would at run time follow the attribute dependencies in a given tree. The generated attribute (re)evaluator uses precomputed information about attribute dependencies. The precomputation is based on the analysis of the tree grammar at generation time. In the OPTRAN system it is performed using *grammar flow analysis (GFA)* [MW83, Mö85, Mö86a]. GFA simulates the transformation time behaviour at generation time by computing fixed points in a graph structure, called *grammar graph* [MW83], that represents the tree grammar. Depending on the actual *grammar flow problem*, the precomputed information can be exact or approximative. At run time, this information is associated with the nodes of the actual abstract syntax tree.

The computation of characteristic graphs, ordered partitions of attributes, attribute evaluation plans [Ol86] and identity classes [Ti86] can be formulated as grammar flow problems. In addition, grammar flow analysis can be used to generate tree pattern matching automata [Mö86a] and code generators [Mö87].

The generative support for attribute (re)evaluation is motivated in several ways. Utilization of characteristic graphs makes reevaluation in time O(lnumber of changed attribute instancesl) feasible [Re82]. The set of characteristic graphs resp. the IO-graph [KW76] can be precomputed for each nonterminal. At run time, there is no need to propagate graphs in the actual tree or to build transitive closures. Instead, only encodings of graphs are propagated and an automaton selects the right graph from the set of graphs at a nonterminal, depending on the encodings of graphs at the children. In addition, the partition of attribute instances into classes of simultaneously evaluable instances together with a total order on these classes can be preplanned. Furthermore, the automata that perform the selection process at run time can be compressed at generation time [BMW87].

OPTRAN can handle absolutely noncircular attribute grammars, if the IO-graphs, i.e. approximative subordinate characteristic graphs, are precomputed. A pass evaluation scheme can be incorporated [LMOW87].

3.2. Language features

A detailed survey of the following language features and a description of their implementation can be found in [GPSW86, LMOW87].

Demand and data driven reevaluation

The OPTRAN system offers a *data driven* and a *demand driven* attribute (re)evaluator. Both evaluation mechanisms can be freely mixed. Using the data driven scheme, all attributes that may have changed their value are recomputed, i.e. a new consistent attribute value for an attribute instance is computed if at least one argument of the semantic rule defining the value of this instance has received a new value. The demand driven scheme allows to delay the reevaluation of attributes until their values are needed.

Complex attributes and footholds

When using the demand driven scheme attributes can be declared *complex*. Utilization of complex attributes instead of so-called simple attributes leads to smaller memory requirements since the value of a complex attribute instance is not stored. To speed up the reevaluation process some complex attributes can be made *footholds* (actually denoted *based* attributes): the value of a foothold is stored permanently in the tree.

Local attributes

Local attributes associated with a production rather than a nonterminal [Mö86b] can be used to store some temporary result of a computation that is used by more than one semantic rule.

Identity classes

Attribute instances identically depending on each other constitute an *identity class* and share the same memory allocation. An application of a transformation rule can modify identity classes.

4. Host and implementation language

Pascal is used as *implementation language* and as *host language*, i.e. the OPTRAN system itself is written in Pascal, semantic rules have to be coded as Pascal procedures/functions and attribute types are Pascal data types. In the following we will comment on both design decisions. When judging these descisions, one has to keep in mind that the developement of OPTRAN started in the late 70's. A first system including all parts described in section 1 except an attribute reevaluator was available in 1982 [SSW82, MWW84] .

Implementation language

The source of all generators makes up more than 39.000 lines of code and the static part of a run time transformation system has nearly 14.000 lines. The following deficiencies of Pascal made the implementation and maintenance of the OPTRAN system particularly hard, as will be the case for any system of comparable size:

- lack of modularity
  During the development of OPTRAN, there were more than 13 programmers involved in the implementation of the system. Even though the system itself consists of several modules, some modules had to be maintained by more than one programmer at the same time. Here, we suffered from the absence of an accepted module concept in Pascal.
- under-developed operating system interface
  The system's resource management (file system, memory manager) could have been optimized if there was better access to OS services than those offered by standard Pascal (e.g. no random file access). Using non-standard features of some Pascal dialects is no solution since it makes the OPTRAN system non-portable.
- strong type checking
  The strong type checking of Pascal has to be circumvented using Pascal variant records leading to somewhat unnatural formulation of otherwise (e.g. in C) fairly obvious parts. In addition, some (generic) operations had to be recoded for several data types, leading to a great amount of code duplication. A less rigid type system, generic procedures or polymorphic functions would have solved this problem;
- no separate compilation
  The fact that a lot of the system's modules are fixed or won't be changed after their generation can not be exploited by the system, i.e. changing a single semantic rule forces one to recompile the whole run time transformation system. Berkeley Pascal offers seperate compilation, but again this is a non-standard feature.

Making a UNIX host (SUN 3/160 running SUN-OS 3.4) our development machine the situation has been improved. The usage of the source code control system (SCCS) and the make utility facilitated the maintenance of the system and made it possible to reflect the modularity of the system in a reasonable way. However, the modularity of the generated transformation system is only exploited with Berkeley Pascal's seperate compilation feature.

The run time system still suffers from a few specific Pascal limitations. Generated static tables can not be included in the Pascal source but have to be read from a file during the initialisation phase of the transformation system. Interfacing a frontend, i.e. reading an abstract syntax tree, is done via file i/o, too, since Pascal does not support input/output of dynamic data structures. Practical experiences reveal that the system's run time is dominated by the time spent for i/o.

The run time library of some Pascal compilers is another cause for unsatisfying run times. Automatic translation of some system components from Pascal to C cut down the generator run time significantly.

We have successfully ported the system to a Siemens 7.5xx running BS2000. Unfortunately, we encountered several Pascal compiler errors and limitations (e.g. incorrect code generation, static internal symbol tables) during this port and an attempt to bring it to another UNIX system. Especially, the unusual size (> 64 KBytes) of data structures used in some part of the OPTRAN system lead to several problems.

Host language

Attribute types are specified as Pascal data types (e.g. integer, record) and semantic rules are written as Pascal procedures/functions. In addition, one has to specify special compare and copy/dispose operations for each attribute type which is used internally by the system at run time. The behaviour of the system can be manipulated by changing these operations. Such a modification can be intended, e.g. to artificially restrict the region of reevaluation in the transformed tree or to make access to context information more efficient. On the other hand, these modifications are the source of errors that are hard to find since it is not easy to distinguish them from possible bugs of the system itself.

Furthermore, users of the system misuse side effects of Pascal routines to manipulate global data structures. This again may lead to hard-to-locate errors, especially because the user's expectation of system behaviour often differs from what is really going on inside the system.

Besides, the possibility of side effects seriously interferes with the analysis of a transformation's semantics at generation time. In general, the generating system has no knowledge of the effect of a given semantic rule. Actually, there is one exception to this statement: identity functions (called copy rules in [Ho86]) are treated in a special way by the system.

Using a functional language as host language would - at least in some cases - make it possible to reason about safeness and invariance of attribute values with regard to application of transformations [GMW81] . There is a trade-off between an improvement of generation time analysis that can be achieved by the usage of a functional language and the exploitation of side effects in an imperative language, e.g. manipulation of a global state. However, taking into account the inherent functional nature of attribute grammars we plead for a functional host language.

5. Practical experience

Code optimisation and data flow analysis

OPTRAN has proven its usefulness in classical fields of compiler construction, i.e. machine-independent code optimisation and data flow analysis [LMOW87] . [Li86] contains a transformation unit for a toy language called BLAN. A fraction of this t-unit is shown in the appendix. The generated t-system performs static semantic checking, global data flow analysis and constant propagation. The attribution for global data flow analysis and the transformation rules for constant propagation are based on algorithms presented in [Wi79a] . For this application the power of OPTRAN tree patterns is sufficient. The mixture of demand and data driven attributes accelerates the (re)evaluation process. Automatic reevaluation is fully utilized since most of the transformation rules affect the set of constant variables, which is represented by a special demand attribute. In addition, this attribute is an argument of some predicates. As stated in [Wi79a] , non-circular attribute grammars compute good approximations to the exact data flow information. The class of absolutely noncircular attribute grammars which can be handled by OPTRAN is sufficient for BLAN. Currently, [Ti88] investigates the effect of circular grammars into the specification language and the generation mechanism. A simple way of simulating circular attribute grammars by transformations and attribute reevaluation is described inTh88 .

Ada→DIANA frontend

The Ada DIANA frontend produces an intermediate description in DIANA for a given Ada program. The specification of this frontend consists of two t-units.

The transformation system that is generated for the first t-unit [Ke88] produces a normalized OPTRAN tree, where general operators are replaced by specific operators after name class analysis, e.g. the tree for an Ada construct like $f(a)$ is replaced by a subtree that represents either a function call or an array access. The actual choice is dependent on the context, which is accumulated in attributes. These attributes serve as arguments for predicates, thereby driving the transformation process. The replacement of subtrees itself is described by the syntactic part of the transformation rules. The specification for this t-unit (14300 lines) contains 116 transformation rules, 569 productions and 4211 semantic rules.

The second t-unit (15000 lines) [Ma88] mainly specifies overload resolution. It contains no transformation rules. The generated run time system is merely used as an attribute evaluator. The specification contains 550 productions and 4950 semantic rules.

The frontend itself will be described in [KM88] . Both t-units do not make use of the full power of the OPTRAN system. As said before, the second one even does not contain any transformations. Therefore, there is no need for a sophisticated reevaluation process. On the other hand, the evaluator is designed with transformations in mind: special memory management techniques that are only useful in "pure" attribute evaluators [FY86] are not exploited. In the first t-unit context information is collected in symbol table attributes during initial attribute evaluation. The transformations are guaranteed to leave this information unchanged. Unfortunately, there is no explicit way to specify invariance of attributes with regard to a transformation. However, there is an implicit way, i.e. modifying the corresponding compare function, as described in section 4. Using a kind of global attribute is another dangerous possibility. [Li86] exhibits the special risks of using global attributes in transformation systems.

Code generator for Pascal

An early version of the OPTRAN system without reevaluation (the reevaluation process was replaced by several runs of the initial attribute evaluator) was used to generate Motorola 68000 machine code for a subset of Pascal [Ra86] . Code emission is done by explicit rules when replacing Pascal tree fragments with special register nodes. Semantic rules describe register allocation and assignment. The assignment is computed during initial evaluation and is protected against reevaluation. The emphasis lays more on efficient tree transformation than on clever reevaluation. The generated t-system was modified by hand to make attribute values dependent on the transformation history. However, the OPTRAN philosophy does not support this view: in OPTRAN, the value of an attribute instance is solely defined by the functional attribute dependencies.

At the time of writing the specification is adapted to the current system.

Other applications

A source-to-source translator, that translates SPL4 (Siemens system programming language) programs into C programs is part of [Ho88] .

These partly nontrivial examples show, that OPTRAN can be successfully used for complex translation and transformation tasks. It, however, requires a disciplined specifier, which withstands the temptation to gain efficiency by using all the possibilities Pascal as a specification language offers him.

6. Acknowledgements

Over the years, the following persons were involved in the design and/or implementation of the OPTRAN system and/or wrote specifications in OPTRAN: Peter Badt, Jürgen Börstler, Michael Greim, Bernd Edelmann, Stefan Edelmann, Thomas Geiger, Günther Horsch, Paul Keller, Peter Lipps, Thomas Maas, Ulrich Möncke, Matthias Olk, Stefan Pistorius, Peter Raber, Thomas Rauber, Peter Schley, Michael Schmigalla, Alois Schütte, Monika Solsbacher, Winfried Thome, Elisabeth Tieser, Heiner Tittelbach, Beatrix Weisgerber, and Reinhard Wilhelm.

Appendix A¡

```
{  1}  t-unit B_LAN;
{  2}  (* Authors:    Peter Lipps, Matthias Olk    *)
        ...
{ 17}  (* constant declaration part      *)
{ 18}  const
        ...
{ 22}     maxvector    =   127;
{ 23}     maxnesting   =   4;
        ...
{160}  (* attribute type declaration part*)
{161}  simpletype mputype
{162}       (* user defined type for mod, pre, use *)
{163}     veclen  = 1..maxvector;
{164}     bitvector    = set of veclen;
{165}     bvindex = 0..maxnesting;
{166}     bvarray = array [bvindex] of bitvector;
{167}     mputype      = bvarray;
```

```
{ 168}    operations
{ 169}      compare
{ 170}        function mputypecomp (mpu1, mpu2 : mputype) : boolean;
{ 171}      copy
{ 172}        procedure mputypecopy (mpu1 : mputype; var mpu2 : mputype);
{ 173} endtype
        ...
{ 295}  (*  attribute declaration part    *)
{ 296}  (*        synthesized attributes   *)
{ 297}  synthesized

{ 324}      spre    : mputype attached to
{ 325}        (* preserved variables *)
{ 326}        parid, nopar, parlistop, procop, whileop, ifop, assop, sepop;
        ...
{ 348}  (*         inherited attributes     *)
{ 349}  inherited
        ...
{ 365}      ipool    : symtabtype attached to
{ 366}        (* constant pool *)
{ 367}        sepop, assop, ifop, whileop, procop, relop, addop, intconst, boolconst, varid;

{ 384}  (*  declaration of semantic rules  *)

{ 515}  procedure unionmpu (bvarr1, bvarr2 : mputype; var bvarr3 : mputype);
{ 516}  procedure intersectmpu (bvarr1, bvarr2 : mputype; var bvarr3 : mputype);
        ...
{ 591}  procedure searchinpool (pool : symtabtype; scan : scanattrtyp; var ausscan : scanattrtyp);
        ...
{ 622}  (*  productions of attributed grammar  *)
{ 623}  grammar is
{ 624}
{ 626}  prog ::=  <op_prog, block>;
        ...
{ 697}  block ::= <op_block, blockhead, declpart, applpart>;
        ...
{ 740}  applpart ::=    <applpartop, stats>;
        ...
{ 744}    (* constant pool *)
{ 745}      create(solstruct, true, ipool of stats);
        ...
{ 747}  applpart ::=    <noapplpart>;
        ...
{ 751}  stats ::= <sepop, stats\1, stats\2>;
{ 752}    local luse : mputype;
{ 753}    based spre of stats\1;
        ...
{ 757}    (* mod, pre, use *)
{ 758}      intersectmpu (suse of stats\2, spre of stats\1, luse);
{ 759}      unionmpu    (suse of stats\1, luse, suse of sepop);
{ 760}      intersectmpu (spre of stats\1, spre of stats\2, spre of sepop);
{ 761}      unionmpu    (smod of stats\1, smod of stats\2, smod of sepop);
{ 762}    (* constant pool *)
{ 763}      ipool of stats\1 := id(ipool of sepop);
{ 764}      ipool of stats\2 := id(spool of stats\1);
{ 765}      spool of sepop   := id(spool of stats\2);
{ 767}  stats ::= stat;
{ 768}
{ 770}  stat ::=    callstat;
```

```
{ 772}  stat ::=   assstat;
{ 774}  stat ::=   whilestat;
{ 776}  stat ::=   ifstat;
        ...
{ 780}  assstat ::=      <assop, assvariable, expr>;
        ...
{ 788}     (* mod, pre, use *)
{ 789}     suse of assop := id(suse of expr);
{ 790}     inittoO     (selement of assvariable, spre of assop);
{ 791}     inittol (selement of assvariable, smod of assop);
{ 792}     (* constant pool *)
{ 793}     ipool of expr := id(ipool of assop);
{ 794}     spool of assop := insertinpool (sconst of expr, scvalue of expr,
{ 795}                        sscanattr of assvariable, selement of assvariable, ipool of assop);
        ...
{ 801}  ifstat ::=   <ifop, expr, stats\1, stats\2>;
{ 802}     local luse : mputype;
        ...
{ 810}     (* mod, pre, use *)
{ 811}     unionmpu (suse of stats\1, suse of stats\2, luse);
{ 812}     unionmpu (suse of expr, luse, suse of ifop);
{ 813}     unionmpu (spre of stats\1, spre of stats\2, spre of ifop);
{ 814}     unionmpu (smod of stats\1, smod of stats\2, smod of ifop);
{ 815}     (* constant pool *)
{ 816}     ipool of expr := id(ipool of ifop);
{ 817}     ipool of stats\1 := id(ipool of ifop);
{ 818}     ipool of stats\2 := id(ipool of ifop);
{ 819}     spool of ifop := intersect(equalpoolkey, lesskey, getobjkey,
{ 820}                        spool of stats\1, spool of stats\2);
        ...
{ 824}  whilestat ::=   <whileop, expr, stats>;
        ...
{ 831}     (* mod, pre, use *)
{ 832}     unionmpu (suse of expr, suse of stats, suse of whileop);
{ 833}     allmpu   (spre of whileop);
{ 834}     smod of whileop := id(smod of stats);
{ 835}     (* constant pool *)
{ 836}     ipool of expr := intersect (equalpoolkey, lesskey, getobjkey,
{ 837}                        ipool of whileop, spool of stats);
{ 838}     ipool of stats := minuspool (equalkey, lesskey, getobjkey,
{ 839}                        ipool of whileop, smod of stats);
{ 840}     spool of whileop := intersect (equalpoolkey, lesskey, getobjkey,
{ 841}                        ipool of whileop, spool of stats);
        ...
{ 916}  expr ::= simpleexpr;
        ...
{ 939}  simpleexpr ::= <addop, simpleexpr, simpleopd>;
        ...
{ 947}     (* mod, pre, use *)
{ 948}     unionmpu (suse of simpleexpr, suse of simpleopd, suse of addop);
{ 949}     (* constant propagation *)
{ 950}     sconst of addop := sconst of simpleexpr and sconst of simpleopd;
{ 951}     addcvalue(sconst of simpleexpr, sconst of simpleopd,
{ 952}                scvalue of simpleexpr, scvalue of simpleopd, scvalue of addcp);
{ 953}     (* constant pool *)
{ 954}     ipool of simpleexpr := id(ipool of addop);
{ 955}     ipool of simpleopd := id(ipool of addop);
{ 957}  simpleexpr ::= simpleopd;
        ...
```

```
{ 961}  simpleopd ::=   variable;
{ 963}  simpleopd ::=   <intconst>;
{ 964}     local scanattr : scanattrtyp;
{ 965}     imported scanattr (*of intconst*);
{ 966}       stype of intconst := inttype;
{ 967}       sscanattr of intconst  := id( scanattr (*of intconst*));
{ 968}    (* mod, pre, use *)
{ 969}       creatempu (suse of intconst);
{ 970}    (* constant propagation *)
{ 971}       sconst of intconst := true;
{ 972}       makecvalue(scanattr (*of intconst*), scvalue of intconst);
        ...
{ 987}  variable ::=      <varid>;
        ...
{ 995}    (* mod, pre, use *)
{ 996}       inittol (extractelemcode(info), suse of varid);
{ 997}    (* constant propagation *)
{ 998}       sconst of varid := isinpool2 (ipool of varid, scanattr);
{ 999}       makecvalue(scanattr (*of varid*), scvalue of varid);
        ...
{1022}   (* declaration of transformation rules *)
{1023}   transformation is
{1024}   strategy bulr sm;
{1025}
{1026}   (tr1) transform
{1027}           <varid>
{1028}        if sconst of varid and (stype of varid = inttype)
{1029}        into
{1030}             <intconst>
{1031}        apply
{1032}             searchinpool(ipool of varid, scanattr of varid, scanattr of intconst);
{1033}        elsif sconst of varid and (stype of varid = booltype)
{1034}        into
{1035}             <boolconst>
{1036}        apply
{1037}             searchinpool(ipool of varid, scanattr of varid, scanattr of boolconst)
{1038}        fi;
        ...
{1056}   (tr4) transform
{1057}           <addop, <intconst\1>, <intconst\2>>
{1058}        into
{1059}             <intconst>
{1060}        apply
{1061}             trafoaddop(sscanattr of intconst\1, sscanattr of intconst\2, scanattr of intconst);
        ...
{1131}   (tr11) transform
{1132}           <ifop, boolconst, thenpart, elsepart>
{1133}        if boolfalse(sscanattr of boolconst)
{1134}        into
{1135}             elsepart
{1136}        else into
{1137}             thenpart
{1138}        fi.
```

References

[BMR85]   Badt, P., P. Raber, and U. Möncke, **Attributation Schemata for List-Structured Nodes**, ESPRIT: PROSPECTRA Project Report S.1.3-R-1.0, FB 10 - Informatik, Universität des Saarlandes, 1985.

[BMR86]   Badt, P., P. Raber, and U. Möncke, **Specification of Recursive Patterns**, ESPRIT: PROSPECTRA Project Report S.1.6-SN-4.0, FB 10 - Informatik, Universität des Saarlandes, 1986.

[BMW87]   Börstler, J., U. Möncke, and R. Wilhelm, **Table Compression for Tree Automata**, Aachener Informatik Berichte No. 87-12, RWTH Aachen, Fachgruppe Informatik, Aachen, 1987.

[Ba86]   Badt, P., **OPTRAN - Ein System zur Generierung von Baumtransformatoren: Rekursive Schablonen und Listenkonstrukte**, Diploma Thesis (in german), FB 10 - Informatik, Universität des Saarlandes, Saarbrücken, 1986.

[Eu88]   Eulenstein, M., **POCO - Ein portables System zur Generierung portabler Compiler**, *Informatik Fachberichte 164*,1988.

[FY86]   Farrow, R. and D. Yellin, **A Comparison of Storage Optimizations in Automatically-Generated Attribute Evaluators**, *Acta Informatica* 23(4),Springer-Verlag, 1986.

[GMW80]   Glasner, I., U. Möncke, and R. Wilhelm, **OPTRAN - A Language for the Specification of Program Transformations**, pp. 125-142 in *Informatik Fachberichte, 7th GI Workshop on Programming Languages and Program Development*, Springer-Verlag, 1980.

[GMW81]   Giegerich, R., U. Möncke, and R. Wilhelm, **Invariance of Approximative Semantics with respect to Program Transformations**, pp. 1-10 in *11. GI Fachtagung für Programmiersprachen und Programmentwicklung,Informatik Fachberichte 50,* , Springer-Verlag, 1981.

[GPSW86]   Greim, M., St. Pistorius, M. Solsbacher, and B. Weisgerber, **POPSY and OPTRAN-Manual**, ESPRIT: PROSPECTRA-Project Report, S.1.6-R-3.0, Technical Report No. A 08/86, FB 10 - Informatik, Universität des Saarlandes, Saarbrücken, 1986.

[He86a]   Heckmann, R., **An efficient ELL(1)-Parser Generator**, *Acta Informatica* 23, pp. 127-148, 1986.

[He86b]   Heckmann, R., **Manual for the ELL(2)-Parser Generator and Tree Generator Generator**, Technical Report No. A 05/86, FB 10 - Informatik, Universität des Saarlandes, Saarbrücken, 1986.

[He88]   Heckmann, R., **A Functional Language for the Specification of Complex Tree Transformations**, *Proceedings of the 2nd European Symposium on Programming (ESOP'88)*, LNCS 300, , pp. 175-190, Springer-Verlag,

[Ho86]   Hoover, R., **Dynamically Bypassing Copy Rule Chains in Attribute Grammars**, ACM Symposium on Principles of Programming Languages, January 1986.

[Ho88]   Horsch, G., **Source-to-source-Transformationen: Eine Studie des Compiler-Generierenden Systems OPTRAN anhand eines SPL4→C-Compilers**, Diploma Thesis (in german), FB 10 - Informatik, Universität des Saarlandes, Saarbrücken, 1988.

[KM88]   Keller, P. and Th. Maas, **An OPTRAN generated Ada→DIANA frontend**, Technical Report (forthcoming), FB 10 - Informatik, Universität des Saarlandes, Saarbrücken, 1988.

[KW76]   Kennedy, K. and S.K. Warren, **Automatic Generation of Efficient Evaluators for Attribute Grammars**, *Conf. Record of 3rd Symposium on Principles of Programming Languages*, , pp. 32-49, 1976.

[Ke88]   Keller, P., **Spezifikation und Implementierung eines Compilerfrontends für Ada: Deklarations- und Nameclassanalyse** , Diploma Thesis (in german), FB 10 - Informatik, Universität des Saarlandes, Saarbrücken, 1988.

[LMOW87]   Lipps, P., M. Olk, U. Möncke, and R. Wilhelm, **Attribute (Re)evaluation in OPTRAN**, ESPRIT: PROSPECTRA Project Report S.1.3-R-5.0, FB 10 - Informatik, Universität des Saarlandes, 1987. (to be published in Acta Informatica)

[Li88]   Lipps, P., **OPTRAN: A Language/System for the Specification of Program Transformations - Annotated Bibliography**, Internal Report, FB 10 - Informatik, Universität des Saarlandes, 1988.

[Li86]	Lipps, P., **Komplexe Attribute - Mechanismen zur Verwaltung und Berechnung in einem baumtransformierenden System**, Diploma Thesis (in german), FB 10 - Informatik, Universität des Saarlandes, Saarbrücken, 1986.
[MW83]	Möncke, U. and R. Wilhelm, **Iterative algorithms on grammar graphs**, pp. 177-194 in *Proc. 8th Conference on Graphtheoretic Concepts in Computer Science*, ed. H.J. Schneider, H. Goettler, Hanser Verlag, München, 1983.
[MWW84]	Möncke, U., B. Weisgerber, and R. Wilhelm, **How to implement a system for manipulation of attributed trees**, pp. 112-127 in *Informatik Fachberichte, 8th GI Workshop on Programming Languages and Program Development*, Springer-Verlag, Zürich, March 1984.
[MWW86]	Möncke, U., B. Weisgerber, and R. Wilhelm, **Generative support for transformational programming**, pp. 511-527 in *ESPRIT: Status Report of Continuing Work*, Elsevier Sc., Brussels, 1986.
[Mö85]	Möncke, U., **Generierung von Systemen zur Transformation attributierter Operatorbäume - Komponenten des Systems und Mechanismen der Generierung**, Ph.D. Thesis (in german), FB 10 - Informatik, Universität des Saarlandes, Saarbrücken, 1985.
[Mö86a]	Möncke, U., **Grammar Flow Analysis**, ESPRIT: PROSPECTRA-Project Report S.1.3-R-2.1, FB 10 - Informatik, Universität des Saarlandes, 1986. (submitted for publication)
[Mö86b]	Möncke, U., **Production Local Attributes**, ESPRIT: PROSPECTRA-Project Study Notes, S.1.3-SN-3.0, FB 10 - Informatik, Universität des Saarlandes, Saarbrücken, 1986.
[Mö87]	Möncke, U., **Simulating Automata for Weighted Tree Reductions**, ESPRIT: PROSPECTRA-Project Report S.1.6-R-5.1 and Technical Report No. A 10/87, FB 10 - Informatik, Universität des Saarlandes, 1987.
[Ma88]	Maas, T., **Spezifikation und Implementierung eines Compilerfrontends für Ada: Auflösung der Überladung und Erzeugung von DIANA**, Diploma Thesis (in german), FB 10 - Informatik, Universität des Saarlandes, Saarbrücken, 1988.
[Ol86]	Olk, M., **Generierung eines effizienten Attributschedulers für ein baumtransformierendes System**, Diploma Thesis (in german), FB 10 - Informatik, Universität des Saarlandes, Saarbrücken, 1986.
[Ra86]	Raber, P., **Listenkonstrukte und ihre Attribuierung in einem System zur Generierung von Baumtransformatoren**, Diploma Thesis (in german), FB 10 - Informatik, Universität des Saarlandes, Saarbrücken, 1986.
[Ra86]	Rauber, Th., **Registerverteilung und Codeselektion für wechselnde Zielmaschinen**, Diploma Thesis (in german), FB 10 - Informatik, Universität des Saarlandes, Saarbrücken, 1986.
[Re82]	Reps, Th., **Generating Language-Based Environments**, Ph.D. Thesis, Cornell University, 1982.
[SSW82]	Schmigalla, M., A. Schütte, and B. Weisgerber, **OPTRAN'82-Manual**, Internal Report, FB 10 - Informatik, Universität des Saarlandes, Saarbrücken, December 1982.
[Th88]	Thome, W., **Ein Konzept zur Bibliotheksverwaltung von Transformationseinheiten und deren Hintereinanderschaltung**, Diploma Thesis (in german), FB 10 - Informatik, Universität des Saarlandes, Saarbrücken, 1988.
[Ti88]	Tieser, E., **Attributauswertung für zyklische Attribuierung**, Diploma Thesis (in german), FB 10 - Informatik, Universität des Saarlandes, Saarbrücken, 1988.
[Ti86]	Tittelbach, H., **Effiziente Attributspeicherverwaltung für ein baumtransformierendes System**, Diploma Thesis (in german), FB 10 - Informatik, Universität des Saarlandes, Saarbrücken, 1986.
[We83]	Weisgerber, B., **Attributierte Transformationsgrammatiken: Die Baumanalyse und Untersuchungen zu Transformationsstrategien**, Diploma Thesis (in german), FB 10 - Informatik, Universität des Saarlandes, Saarbrücken, 1983.
[Wi79a]	Wilhelm, R., **Computation and Use of Data Flow Information in Optimizing Compilers**, *Acta Informatica* 12, pp. 209-225, Springer-Verlag, 1979.
[Wi81]	Wilhelm, R., **A Modified Tree-To-Tree Correction Problem**, *Information Processing Letters* 12(3), pp. 127-132, North-Holland, 1981.

COMPILER CONSTRUCTION BY OBJECT-ORIENTED SYSTEM NUT

Jaan Penjam

Institute of Cybernetics of the Estonian Academy of
Sciences, Akadeemia tee 21, Tallinn 200 108, U.S.S.R.

1. Introduction

The idea of logic programming concernes computing relations
specified by logic formulas. Logic programming is often considered
as programming in PROLOG which works in a first order predicate
calculus. In this paper we describe in a way an alternative logic
programming system, conceptually based on the intuitionistic
propositional calculus. This system is named NUT and it is
developed at the Institute of Cybernetics of the Estonian Academy
of Sciences [TMPE86]. The system runs under the operating systems
CP/M and Unix.

Actually, the NUT system is the most advanced representative
of the family of the programming systems called PRIZ [TM88]. This
family includes systems PRIZ ES, Solver, MicroPRIZ, ExpertPRIZ,
NUT etc., which have been developed in last 15-20 years. All these
systems support knowledge-based programming style and they are
successfully used in the solving engineering problems and in
scientific investigations of artificial intelligence as well.
First of all the PRIZ-systems are known as AI-systems.

Knowledge-based programming can be briefly characterized by
the following four features [Tyugu87]:
- programming in terms of a problem domain;
- using the computer in the whole problem-solving process
  beginning with the discription of a problem;
- synthesizing programs automatically;
- using a knowledge base for accumulating useful concepts.

In the PRIZ systems these conditions are satisfied by combi-

ning conventional programming technique with automatic synthesis
of programs from specifications. G. Mints and E. Tyugu have proved
that the method for synthesis of programs used in the PRIZ systems
is complete whereas every partially recursive function can be
synthesized [MT82]. In this article the usage of computational
models and structural synthesis of programs for compiler specification and implementation is discussed.

2. Computational models and structural synthesis of programs

The PRIZ systems are based on the idea that a program should
explicitly state what properties the desired result is required to
exhibit but does not state how the desired result is to be
obtained. To describe requirements for results of a program, logic
formulae as a programming language can be used. Unlike the PROLOG,
structural synthesis of programs uses propositional calculus for
this purpose. (A more detailed comparison of the PRIZ and PROLOG
systems can be found in [MT88]). Here the so called computability
statements are used like Horn clauses in PROLOG. In our case, only
propositional formulae of the following two different forms are
considered:

1.Unconditional computability statement

$$|-\ A_1\ \&\ .\ .\ .\ \&\ A_n\ \xrightarrow{f}\ B$$

or in a shorter way

$$|-\ \overline{A}\ \xrightarrow{f}\ B; \tag{1}$$

2.Conditional computability statement

$$|-\ (\overline{A}_1\ \xrightarrow{g1}\ B_1)\ \&\ .\ .\ .\ \&\ (\overline{A}_n\ \xrightarrow{gn}\ B)\ \longrightarrow (\overline{C}\ \xrightarrow{F(g)}\ D),$$

or in a shorter way

$$\vdash (\overline{A} \xrightarrow{g} B) \longrightarrow (\overline{C} \xrightarrow{F(g)} D). \tag{2}$$

where f and F are function symbols and g denotes a list of function symbols $g_1, \ldots, g_m$.

Relation (1) means that computability of some objects a_1, a_2, $\ldots$, a_k implies computability of object b by function (program) f In other words, for any given values of objects a_1, a_2, $\ldots$, a_k the value of object b can be computed and $b = f(a_1, a_2, \ldots, a_k)$. Statement (2) expresses functional dependencies of higher order (function F uses functions g_1, $g_2, \ldots, g_m$ as arguments). The computability of object d depends on the computability of c_1, $c_2, \ldots, c_n$ under the condition that there exist functions g_i ($i = 1, \ldots, m$), for computing object b_i from $a_{i1}, \ldots, a_{il}$.

A computational model is a set of computability statements of form (1) or (2).

If there a correspondance between the propositional variables and the actual objects is arranged and if the proper interpretation of function symbols is given, then the computation model describes some real object or phenomenon via its inner relations between its structural components.

Usually a computational problem can be formulated as: "Knowing values of objects $x_1, \ldots, x_n$, compute the value of y, so that conditions $S_1, \ldots, S_r$ are satisfied." If these conditions are simulated by computational model S, then the problem can be solved by such a function f that the sequent

$$S \vdash X \xrightarrow{\lambda x.f} Y \ . \tag{3}$$

is valid. All PRIZ systems derive sequent (3) automatically from the computability statements of model S and from the so called logic axioms of form $A \vdash A$ by means of the inference rules called Structural Synthesis Rules (SSR) - see [MT82].

Example 2.1.

Let the computational model S contain one statement
|-(N--->F) ---> (N------>F), where G(g) is a function with the
      g   G(g)
following property

$$G(g,n) = \underline{if}\ n=0\ \underline{then}\ n*g(n-1)\ \underline{fi}\quad .$$

The synthesizer will prove the sequent S |- N------>F, where g is
                                              $\lambda n.g$
the recursive programm to compute n! :

$$g(n) = \underline{if}\ n=0\ \underline{then}\ n*g(n-1)\ \underline{fi}\quad .$$

3. Object-oriented system NUT.

The "pure logic" formulas as a programming language is
suitable for knowledge representation inside the computer and for
automatic program construction. But this is not proper form for
knowledge representation for humans. For this purpose in the PRIZ
systems different high level input languages are used. Problem
description presented in these languages is automatically
translated into computational models and after that all manipu-
lations with knowledge: analysis of the model, proof of
correctness of a problem description, synthesis of programs etc.
are made at the level of logic programming, i.e. at the level of
computability statements.

The translation from the input language of the system into
computational models is concerned in paper [MT88].

The basic concepts of the NUT language are object and class.
Values, programs, data types etc. are objects. The objects of the
same kind are joined together into some abstract object called
class, for example real numbers, arrays, geometric figures and so
on.

A problem specification in the NUT language begins with a
description of classes of objects involved in this problem. A
class is a carrier of the knowledge about commom properties of its
objects, such as the structure of objects and relations applicable
to them, initializations of components and so on.

Every class declaration begins with the name of the class followed by the class description in parentheses. The structure of a object, i.e. components of the object, their names and types are defined at the beginning (after the keyword <u>var</u>). The type of component can be the name of some class. There are also some predefined classes of objects in the NUT, these are <u>numeric,</u> <u>bool</u>, <u>text</u>, <u>program</u>, <u>array</u> and <u>any</u>. In a simple case of class specification only components are specified, for example

```
point: (var x,y: numeric);
pair:  (var P,Q: point;
            distance: numeric);
```

The component specification may be followed by some amendment which determine some parameters of the component, its relations with other components and so on. As example, let us describe the class 'scheme' of objects consisting of two pairs of points, where one point of te first pair is at the origin of coordinates and the second poit coincides with the first point of the other pair.

```
scheme: (var
        A: pair P=[0,0];
        B: pair P=A.Q);
```

In the more complicated cases the description of structure of objects is usually followed by relations (after the keyword <u>relations</u>). The relations may be represented by equations. For example:

```
bar: (var P,Q: point;
            l, alpha: numeric;
        relations
            Q.x-P.x=l*cos(alpha);
            Q.y-P.Y=l*sin(alpha));
```

In othes cases relations are represented by the implications (computability statements) followed by the program in braces. The

language for presentating these programs is similar to the conventional high level programming languages extended by some specific operators, such as creation of a new object by a given
class, call of synthesizer etc. For instance, the class of fac-
torial that corresponds to the computational model of example 2.1,
is written in the NUT as follows.

```
fact (var n,f: numeric;
    :   relations
        [n -> f], n -> f {if n=0 -> f:=1 ||
                          n>0 -> subtask 1 (n-1, f1);
                          f:=n*f1 fi}
);
```

Another basic entity of the language is an object. New
objects are generated during computations by the predefined
function new. For example, bar AB with length 7 and angle of
elevation $\pi/3$ will be formed by the operator

```
AB:= new bar l=7, alpha = 3.14/3;
```

Components a and b of the object X may be evaluated by the
operator X.compute(a,b). By this operator the NUT system attempts
to synthesize a program for computing mentioned components and if
it succeeds, the synthesized program is used for evaluating
objects X.a and X.b. Hence, to compute 17! it is enough to write

```
f17:=new fact n:=17;
f17.compute(f);
```

If there are no parameters in compute operator, the system
computes values for all components of X which are not evaluated
before. So, 17! might have been computed by operator f.compute().

The classes and objects are drawn together into packages,
which are stored in the semantic memory (archive) of the NUT
system. Usually a package contains the knowledge from a single
field, such as geometry, electrisity, etc.

4. Dynamic realization of attribute grammars

An attribute grammars (AG) provides an universally recognized formalism for the description of formal languages and compilers. Let us consider here relational AG, where semantic rules are presented by relations on the attributes of the productions [DM85]. In the following example these relations are represented by algebraic equations.

Example 4.1

Let us consider a simple language for a specification language of electrical circuits. The syntax of the language is presented by the following productions.

p1: S --> resistor (Pars)   p5: Pars --> Pars ; Par
p2: S --> par (S , S)   p6: Par --> r= <number>
p3: S --> ser (S , S)   p7: Par --> i= <number>
p4: Pars --> Par   p8: Par --> u= <number>

Production p1 defines a phrase to describe a single resistor, productions p2 and p3 determine phrases for presenting a parallel and a serial connections of less circuits, respectively. Productions p4-p8 describe how to express parameters (resistance, current and voltage) of some elements of the circuit.

The scheme shown in Fig. 1 has the folowing specification in this language.

ser(resistor(r=2),par(resistor(r=2,i=0.5),resistor(r=2)))   (8)

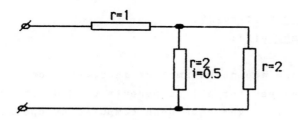

Fig. 1.

To attach the semantics to the sentences, we associate attributes r, i and u with symbols S, Parm, Parms to denote the parameters of the corresponding parts of the scheme. The semantic rules are represented by the equations as follows

$$R_{p1} = \{r_{n0} = r_{n3},\ i_{n0} = i_{n3},\ u_{n0} = u_{n3},\ i_{n0} = u_{n0}/r_{n0}\};$$

$$R_{p2} = \{1/r_{n0} = 1/r_{n3} + 1/r_{n5},\ i_{n0} = i_{n3} + i_{n5},\ u_{n0} = u_{n3},\ u_{n0} = u_{n5},$$
$$i_{n0} = u_{n0}/r_{n0}\};$$

$$R_{p3} = \{r_{n0} = r_{n3} + r_{n5},\ i_{n0} = i_{n3},\ i_{n0} = i_{n5},\ u_{n0} = u_{n3} + u_{n5},\ i_{n0} = u_{n0}/r_{n0}\};$$

$$R_{p4} = \{r_{n0} = r_{n1},\ i_{n0} = i_{n1},\ u_{n0} = u_{n1}\};$$

$$R_{p5} = R_{p4}\ \{r_{n0} = r_{n3},\ i_{n0} = i_{n3},\ u_{n0} = u_{n3}\};$$

$$R_{p6} = \{r_{n0} = <number>\};$$

$$R_{p7} = \{i_{n0} = <number>\};$$

$$R_{p8} = \{u_{n0} = <number>\};$$

The decorated abstract syntax tree t of text (8) is represented in Fig. 2. The unique possible valuation of this tree is computed from the system of algebraic equations. The nodes of the tree are denoted by their labels, the productions used in the nodes are written in parentheses.

The AG is called consistent (well-defined) if attributes of all syntax trees are uniquely determined. Well-definedness of AG can be dynamically checked (separately with respect to every syntax tree) in linear time. In this section we demonstrate the possibilities to use the system NUT for this purpose. When the SSR rules are used the proof of consistency is constructive: the program for attribute evaluation is built simultaneously.

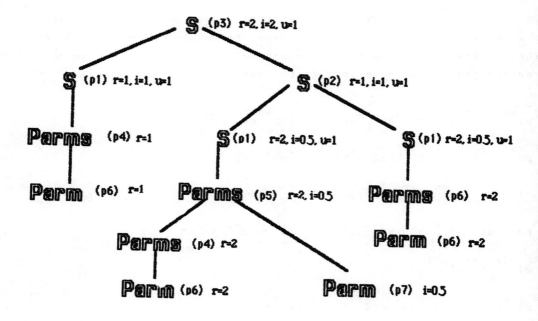

Fig. 2

Fig. 3 shows the place of the NUT system in a compiler when dynamic realization of AG is used. System NUT itself is in the role of the semantic processor, some spetsialized parser has to be used to get syntax tree in the form proper for the NUT system.

To design the attribute evaluator for consistent partial relational AG it is desirable to join the classes required for language definition into a separate package. The staying components of this package are knowledge about attributes and semantic rules of the underlying grammar (in Fig. 3 denoted by attribute models). In order to compute the semantics of the single program, the model of the parse tree of the program has to be constructed in the same package.

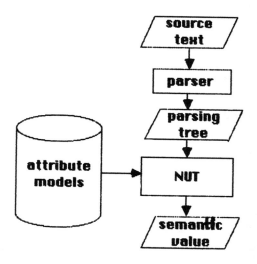

Fig.3.

The description of AG represents for every symbol of the underlying grammar the sets of attributes and their types. In the relational AG presented in example 3.1 the attributes are expressed in the NUT language in the following way.

S, P, Parm, Parms: (<u>var</u> i, u, r: <u>numeric</u>);

The class representing the semantic rule of production $p:X_0 \longrightarrow X_1, \ldots, X_n$ defines objects with components $C0, C1, \ldots, Cn$, correspondingly to symbols $X_0, X_1, \ldots, X_n$. The type of a component C_i is determined by the attributes of symbol X_i. Thus for example 3.1 the classes for productions may be written as follows.

```
P1: (var C0:S;C3:Parms;
      relations
           C0.r=C3.r;
           C0.i=C3.i;
           C0.u=C3.u;
           C0.i=C0.u/C0.m);
P2:(var C0,C3,C5:S;
      relations
           1/C0.R=1/C3.r+1/C5.r;
           ..................),
   .   .    .    .    .    .    .    .    .    .
P8:(var C0: Par; C4: numeric;
      relation
           C0.u=C4);
```

To compute the semantics of the syntax tree t the corresponding object has to be built and after that the program computing the semantics of t has to be synthesized. Syntax tree has
components (elementary trees) as instances of productions which
together with its semantic rules indicate dependencies between
attributes of t. So the class of the object associated with syntax
tree in Figure 2 may be designed as follows.

```
TREE: (N1: P6 C4=1;  /*prod p6 is used at node n1 */
                     /*nonterminal <number>=1 */
      N2:P4  C1=N1.C0:   /*prod p4 is used at node n2 */
                         /*node n2 is father for node n1*/
      N3:P1 C3=N2.C0;    /*like previous ones*/
      N4: P6 C4=2;
      N5: P4 C1=N4.C0;
      N6: P7 C4=0.5;
      N7: P5 C1=N5.C0, C3=N6.C0;
      N8: p1 C3=N7.C0;
      N9: P6 C4=2;
      N10:PU C1=N9.C0;
```

```
N11:P1 C3=N10.CO;
N12:P2 C3=N8.CO,C5=N11.CO;
N13:P3 C3=N3.CO,C5=N12.CO);
```

The semantics of the tree described above is computed by the operators.

```
t:=new TREE;
t.compute (N13.CO);
```

By the operators the system generates an object t and the corresponding computational model M(t). The last operator imposes on the system to prove the formula $|- \xrightarrow{f} t.N13.CO$ by the SSR rules.

To develop a complete translator we need a proper syntax parser. The output of the parser must be either text of class TREE or, what is more desirable, the corresponding model M(t) in the internal representation form used by the program synthesizer. In an experimental realization of RAG we used parsers generated by the yacc. The output of these parsers was the abovedescribed text in the NUT language.

5. Static realization of ANCAG.

It is well-known that the task to test well-definedness of AG has intrinsically exponential time complexity. In practice some subclasses of AG are used the well-definedness of which can be checked in polynomial time. Let us consider absolutely noncircular attribute grammars (ANCAG) [CF82]. The cosistency of ANCAG can be statically proved by the SSR rules.

In this case the NUT system is used as a constructor of semantic parts of compilers or interpretators as shown in Fig. 4.

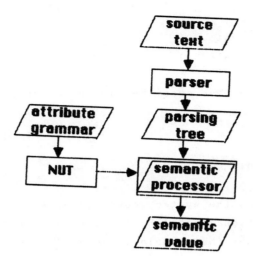

Fig.4.

In this case we also compose classes representing symbols and productions of the grammar. Differently from the last section, we suppose the given splitting of attributes as $\Pi(x)=\{<I_1,S_1>,...,<I_n,S_n>\}$ [Pen83]. It is desirable to preserve this splitting when attribute models are being written:

$$X:(\underline{var}\ inh_1:(v_1;t_1,...i_k:t_k);$$
$$syn t_1:(s_1:u_1;...;s_e:u_2);$$
$$inh_2:(i_{k+1}:t_{k+1},\ i_m:t_m);$$
$$syn_2:(s_{l+1}:u_{+1};...,u_m);$$
$$.\quad.\quad.\quad.\quad.\quad.\quad.\quad.\quad.\quad.\quad.\quad.$$
$$);$$

where $t_1,t_2,...,u_1,u_2,...$ are texts which correspondingly declare the types of attributes $i_1,i_2,...s_1,s_2,...$.

An attribute model $M(p)$ of production p: $X_0 \rightarrow X_1...X_n$ is given by the class

Mp: ($\underline{var}$ X_0: X_0,... X_n:X_n ; /*components of production*/
T: $\underline{any}$; /*pointer to syntax tree*/
$\underline{relations}$
<Semantic rules>
[Mq|-T,X_1.inh$_1$ -> X_1.synt$_1$],...,T,X_1.inh$_1$ -> X_1.synt$_1$
{$\underline{call}$ visit($\underline{subtask1}$(T,X_1.inh$_1$), $\underline{subtask2}$(T,X_2.inh$_1$),...
...,T,X_1.inh$_1$)});

. . . .

);

The function visit is preprogrammed so that visit(g^{q1},g^{q2}...,t^q,i)=g^q(i). Here t^q is subtree, where the production $q \in \{q1,q2,...\}$ is used at root and g^q is procedure implementing a visit to subtree t^q.

In this case the semantic processor will be synthesized by the operators Gr:=new MpO; Gr.compute (S_0.synt), where p_0 is the production with the start symbol of the grammar on the left-hand side.

6. Conclusion

The development of the abovesuggested methods for realization of semantics has initiated investigations with the goal to use computational models immediately as specification formalism for the definition of languages and compilers. The preliminary results in this direction are observed in [MP88]. Our experiments of specifying and implementing some aspects of languages (first of all contextual properties and semantics) in the manner described in the paper allow to expect success in a project of a language implementing system based on the presented methods.

References

1. [CF82]   B.Courcelle,P.Franchi-Zannetacci. Attribute Grammars and Recursive Program Schemes. Theor.Comput.Sci, 1982, Vol.17, pp 163-191 and 235-257.

2. [DM85]   P.Deransat, J.Maluszinski. Relating Logic Programs and Attribute Grammars. J.Logic Programming, 1985, Vol.2, pp.119-155.

3. [MP88]   M.Meriste,J.Penjam.   Computational   Models   and Attribute Grammars. In Proc. of WG-23 "Specialized Languages as Tools for Programming Technology", Tallinn, 1988 (in preparation).

4. [MT82]   G.Mints, E.Tyugu. Justification of the Structural Synthesis of Programs. Sci.Comput.Progr. 1982, Vol.2, pp.215-240.

5. [MT88]   G.Mints, E.Tyugu. The Programming System PRIZ. J.Symbolic Computation. 1988, Vol.5, pp.359-375.

6. [Pen83]   Ya.Pen'yam. Synthesis of a Semantic Processor from an Attribute Grammar. Programming and Computer Software (Programmirovanie). 1983, Vol.9, No.1, pp. 29-30.

7. [TMPE86] E. Tyugu, M. Matskin, J. Penjam, P. Eomois. NUT - an Object-Oriented Language.- Computers and AI, 1986, Vol. 5, No. 6, pp. 521-542.

8. [Tyugu87] E.Tyugu. Knowledge-Bsed Programming. Turing Institute Press, Addison-Wesely Publ.Co., Glasgow, 1987,-243pp.

Generators for High-Speed Front-Ends

Josef Grosch
GMD Forschungsstelle für Programmstrukturen an der Universität Karlsruhe
Haid-und-Neu-Str. 7, D-7500 Karlsruhe 1, West Germany

Abstract

High-speed compilers can be constructed automatically. We present some existing tools or the generation of fast front-ends.

Rex (Regular EXpression tool) is a scanner generator whose specifications are based on egular expressions and arbitrary semantic actions written in one of the target languages C or Modula-2. As scanners sometimes have to consider the context to unambiguously recognize a oken the right context can be specified by an additional regular expression and the left context can be handled by so-called start states. The generated scanners automatically compute he line and column position of the tokens and offer an efficient mechanism to normalize dentifiers and keywords to upper or lower case letters. The scanners are table-driven and run t a speed of 180,000 to 195,000 lines per minute on a MC 68020 processor.

Lalr is a LALR(1) parser generator accepting grammars written in extended BNF notaion which may be augmented by semantic actions expressed by statements of the target anguage. The generator provides a mechanism for S-attribution, that is synthesized attriutes can be computed during parsing. In case of LR-conflicts, unlike other tools, *Lalr* proides not only information about an internal state consisting of a set of items but it prints a lerivation tree which is much more useful to analyze the problem. Conflicts can be resolved y specifying precedence and associativity of operators and productions. The generated arsers include automatic error reporting, error recovery, and error repair. The parsers are able-driven and run at a speed of 400,000 lines per minute. Currently parsers can be generated in the target languages C and Modula-2.

Ell is a LL(1) parser generator accepting the same specification language as *Lalr* except hat the grammars must obey the LL(1) property. The generated parsers include automatic rror reporting, recovery, and repair like *Lalr*. The parsers are implemented following the ecursive descent method and reach a speed of 450,000 lines per minute. The possible target anguages are again C and Modula-2

A comparison of the above tools with the corresponding UNIX tools shows that ignificant improvements have been achieved thus allowing the generation of high-speed comilers.

1. The Scanner Generator Rex

The scanner generator *Rex* has been developed with the aim to combine the powerful pecification method of regular expressions with the generation of highly efficient scanners. The name *Rex* stands for *regular expression tool,* reflecting the specification method.

A scanner specification consists in principle of a set of regular expressions each assoc
ated with a semantic action. Whenever a string constructed according to a regular expressio
is recognized in the input of the scanner its semantic action which is a sequence of arbitrar
statements written in the target language is executed. To be able to recognize tokens depend
ing on their context *Rex* provides start states to handle left context and the right context ca
be specified by an additional regular expression. If several regular expressions match th
input characters, the longest match is preferred. If there are still several possibilities, the reg
ular expression given first in the specification is chosen.

Rex generated scanners automatically provide the line and column position of eac
token. For languages like Pascal and Ada where the case of letters is insignificant tokens ca
be normalized to lower or upper case. There are predefined rules to skip white space lik
blanks, tabs, or newlines.

The generated scanners are table-driven deterministic finite automatons. The tables ar
compressed using the so-called comb-vector technique [ASU86]. Whereas the generator *Rex* i
implemented in Modula-2 it can generate scanners in the languages C and Modula-2
Currently *Rex* is available for PCS Cadmus/UNIX and SUN/UNIX workstations.

The most outstanding feature of *Rex* is its speed. The generated scanners process nearl
200,000 lines per minute without hashing of identifiers and up to 150,000 lines per minute
hashing is applied. This is 4 times the speed of *Lex* [Les75] generated scanners. In typica
cases *Rex* generated scanners are 4 times smaller then *Lex* generated ones (around 15 KB
Usually *Rex* takes only 1/10 of the time of *Lex* to generate a scanner. All figures have bee
measured on a MC 68020 processor.

In the following we will demonstrate the powerful specification method provided b
Rex and present a comparison with other scanner generators.

1.1. Structure of Specification

A complete scanner specification is structured like shown in Figure 1. The regula
expressions may be preceded by six sections containing arbitrary target code, which may cor
tain declarations to be used in the semantic actions or statements for initialization and final
zation of data structures. The DEFINE and START sections serve to abbreviate regula
expressions by identifiers and to declare start states (see below). A complete definition of th

```
EXPORT { external declarations }
GLOBAL { global   declarations }
LOCAL  { local    declarations }
BEGIN  { initialization code   }
CLOSE  { finalization   code   }
EOF    { end of file    code   }
DEFINE   definition of regular expressions
START    definition of start states
RULE     regular expressions and semantic actions
```

Fig. 1: Structure of Specification

specification language can be found in the user manual [Gro87].

83

.2. Right Context

There are languages where the strategy of the longest match fails. For example in
Modula-2 the input 1.. has to be recognized as tokens "1" and "..", not as "1." and ".",
which are also two legal Modula tokens. The problem can be solved using an additional regular expression to describe this situation where the right context of a token leads to an exception in the longest match strategy. Figure 2 shows the syntax used in *Rex* for regular expressions and semantic actions to describe the 4 tokens involved in the above problem. The character '/' separating two regular expressions specifies to recognize a sequence of digits only if it is followed by two dots.

```
{0-9} +              : { return SymDecimal; }
{0-9} + / ".."       : { return SymDecimal; }
{0-9} + "." {0-9} *  : { return SymReal    ; }
".."                 : { return SymRange   ; }
"."                  : { return SymDot     ; }
```

Fig. 2: Scanner Specification Using Right Context

.3. Start States

To handle tokens whose recognition depends on the left context or to process even
tokens which cannot be specified by regular expressions the scanners can have several start
states. In every start state a different set of regular expressions is recognized. There is a special statement to change the current start state (yyStart). For example nested comments like
in Modula can be scanned as shown in Figure 3.

```
GLOBAL   {VAR NestingLevel: CARDINAL;}

BEGIN    {NestingLevel := 0;}

EOF      {IF yyStartState = Comment THEN Error ("unclosed comment"); END;}

DEFINE   CmtCh   = - {*(\t\n}.

START    Comment

RULES
             "(*" : {INC (NestingLevel); yyStart (Comment);}

#Comment# "*)" : {DEC (NestingLevel);
                  IF NestingLevel = 0 THEN yyStart (STD); END;}

#Comment# "(" | "*" | CmtCh + : {}
```

Fig. 3: Scanner Specification Using Start States

1.4. Ada Quote Problem

The Ada quote problem can also be solved using start states. The problem is to sca
for example

```
t'(',',',',',',')  as
t      '     (     ',',    ,     ',',    ,    ',',    )    and not as
t      '('         ,     ',',    ,    ',',    ,    '    )
```

which are both possible sequences of Ada tokens. The correct solution again violates the long
est match strategy. A careful study of the language definition reveals that single quotes onl
appear behind identifiers and closing parentheses. Figure 4 shows the structure of a solutio
After recognizing one of these two tokens we switch to start state QUOTE which recognize
among other tokens single quotes. After all the other tokens we switch to the predefined sta
state STD where quotes are only accepted as delimiters for character literals. More exam
ples of scanner specifications can be found in [Gro88a].

```
LOCAL    {char  Word [256]; int   L;}

DEFINE   character = {\ -~}.
         letter    = {A-Z a-z}.
         digit     = {0-9}.

START    QUOTE

RULES

#STD# ' character ' : {
      L = GetWord (Word);
      Attribute.vChar = Word [1];
      return SymCharacterLiteral;}

#QUOTE# ' : {
      yyStart (STD);
      return SymApostrophe;}

"(" : {yyStart (STD); return SymLParenthesis;}

")" : {yyStart (QUOTE); return SymRParenthesis;}

letter (_? (letter | digit)+ )* : {
      yyStart (QUOTE); L = GetLower (Word);
      Attribute.vSymbol = MakeSymbol (Word, L);
      return SymIdentifier;}
```

Fig. 4: Scanner Specification Solving the Ada Quote Problem

1.5. Comparison of Scanner Generators

Figure 5 compares *Rex* to the classical UNIX scanner generator *Lex* [Les75] and to th
new public domain remake of *Lex* called *Flex* [Pax88] (for fast *Lex*). The table compares th
specification technique and the performance of the generators as well as of the generate
scanners. The specification dependent numbers for generation time and scanner size are for

	Lex	Flex	Rex
specification language	regular expressions	regular expressions	regular expressions
semantic actions	yes	yes	yes
right context	yes	yes	yes
start states	yes	yes	yes
conflict solution	longest match first rule	longest match first rule	longest match first rule
source coordinates	line	-	line + column
case normalization	-	yes	yes
predefined rules to skip white space	-	-	yes
several solutions (REJECT)	yes	yes	-
adjustment of internal arrays	by hand	automatic	automatic
scanning method table compression	table-driven comb-vector	table-driven comb-vector	table-driven comb-vector
implementation language	C	C	Modula
target languages	C	C	C, Modula
speed [lines/min.] without hashing with hashing	36,400 34,700	139,000 118,000	182,700 141,400
table size [bytes] scanner size [bytes]	39,200 43,800	57,300 64,100	4,400 11,200
generation time [sec.]	73.7	7.2	4.9
availability	UNIX	UNIX	PCS/UNIX SUN/UNIX VAX/UNIX BSD 4.2

Fig. 5: Comparison of Scanner Generators (speed measured on MC 68020 processor)

odula-2 scanner.

The Parser Generator Lalr

The parser generator *Lalr* has been developed with the aim to combine a powerful ecification technique for context-free languages with the generation of highly efficient rsers. As it processes the class of LALR(1) grammars we chose the name *Lalr* to express e power of the specification technique.

The grammars may be written using extended BNF constructs. Each grammar ru[
may be associated with a semantic action consisting of arbitrary statements written in t[
target language. Whenever a grammar rule is recognized by the generated parser the assoc[
ated semantic action is executed. A mechanism for S-attribution (only synthesized attribute[
is provided to allow communication between the semantic actions.

In case of LR-conflicts a derivation tree is printed to ease in locating the problem. T[
conflict can be resolved by specifying precedence and associativity for terminals and rule[
Syntactic errors are handled fully automatically by the generated parsers including err[
reporting, recovery, and repair. The mentioned features are discussed in more detail in t[
following chapters.

The generated parsers are table-driven. Like in the case of *Rex* comb-vector techniqu[
is used to compress the parse tables. The generator *Lalr* is implemented in the langua[
Modula-2. Parsers can be generated in the languages C and Modula-2. The generator uses t[
algorithm described by [DeP82] to compute the look-ahead sets although the algorithm pu[
lished by [Ive86] promises to perform better. Currently *Lalr* is available f[
PCS-Cadmus/UNIX and SUN/UNIX workstations.

Parsers generated by *Lalr* are twice as fast as *Yacc* [Joh75] generated ones. They rea[
a speed of 400,000 lines per minute on a MC 68020 processor excluding the time for scannin[
The size of the parsers is only slightly increased in comparison to *Yacc* (e. g. 37 KB f[
Ada), because there is a small price to be paid for the speed.

In the following we will discuss some features of *Lalr* in detail and present a con[
parison to other parser generators. Further information about the implementation of *La[
can be found in [Gro88b].

2.1. Structure of Specification

The structure of a parser specification follows the style of a *Rex* specification as show[
in Figure 6. Again, there may be five sections to include target code. The TOKEN sectic[
defines the terminals of the grammar and their encoding. In the OPER (for operator) sectic[
precedence and associativity for terminals can be specified to resolve LR-conflicts. The RUL[
section contains the grammar rules and semantic actions. A complete definition of t[
specification- language can be found in the user manual [Vie88].

```
EXPORT { external declarations }
GLOBAL { global    declarations }
LOCAL  { local     declarations }
BEGIN  { initialization code    }
CLOSE  { finalization   code    }
TOKEN    coding of terminals
OPER     precedence of operators
RULE     grammar rules and semantic actions
```

Fig. 6: Structure of Specification

.2. S-Attribution

Figure 7 shows an example for the syntax of grammar rules and semantic actions. The :mantic actions may access and evaluate attributes associated with the nonterminals and ter-inals of the grammar rules. This attributes are currently denoted in the less readable tumeric" style of *Yacc* [Joh75].

```
expr : expr '+' expr { $0.value := $1.value + $3.value; } .
expr : expr '*' expr { $0.value := $1.value * $3.value; } .
expr : '(' expr ')'  { $0.value := $2.value; } .
expr : number        { $0.value := $1.value; } .
```

Fig. 7: Parser Specification Using S-Attribution

.3. Ambiguous Grammars

The grammar of Figure 7 as well as the example in Figure 8 are typical examples of mbiguous grammars. Like *Yacc* we allow to resolve the resulting LR-conflicts by specifying recedence and associativity for terminals in the OPER section. Figure 9 gives an example. he lines represent increasing levels of precedence. LEFT, RIGHT, and NONE denote ·ft-associativity, right-associativity, and no associativity. Rules can inherit the properties of terminal with the PREC suffix.

```
stmt : 'IF' expr 'THEN' stmt               PREC LOW
     | 'IF' expr 'THEN' stmt 'ELSE' stmt   PREC HIGH .
```

Fig. 8: Ambiguous Grammar (Dangling Else)

```
OPER  LEFT '+'
      LEFT '*'
      NONE LOW
      NONE HIGH
```

Fig. 9: Resolution of LR-Conflicts Using Precedence and Associativity

.4. LR-Conflict Message

To ease in locating the reason for LR-conflicts we adopted the method proposed by)eP82]. Besides reporting the type of the conflict and the involved items (whatever that is)r the user) like most LR parser generators a derivation tree is printed. Figure 10 shows an <ample. It shows how the items and the look-ahead tokens get into the conflict situation. In :neral there can be two trees if the derivations for the conflicting items are different. Each ·ee consists of 3 parts. An initial part begins at the start symbol of the grammar. At a cer-.in node (rule) two subtrees explain the emergence of the item and the look-ahead.

Every line contains a right-hand side of a grammar rule. Usually the right-hand side is idented to start below the nonterminal of the left-hand side. To avoid line overflow dotted lges also refer to the left-hand side nonterminal and allow to shift back to the left margin. ι Figure 10 the initial tree part consists of 5 lines (not counting the dotted lines). The

```
State 266

read reduce conflict

program End-of-Tokens
'PROGRAM' identifier params ';' block '.'
..............................:
:
labels consts types vars procs 'BEGIN' stmts 'END'
......................................:
:
stmt
'IF' expr 'THEN' stmt 'ELSE' stmt
                        :
                        'IF' expr 'THEN' stmt
                        :
reduce    stmt -> 'IF' expr 'THEN' stmt.  {'ELSE'}  ?
read      stmt -> 'IF' expr 'THEN' stmt.'ELSE' stmt   ?
```

Fig. 10: Derivation Tree for an LR-Conflict (Dangling Else)

symbols 'stmt' and 'ELSE' are the roots of the other two tree parts. This location is indicated by the "unnecessary" colon in the following line. After one intermediate line the left
subtree derives the conflicting items. The right subtree consists in this case only of the root
node (the terminal 'ELSE') indicating the look-ahead. In general this can be a tree of arbitrary size. The LR-conflict can easily be seen from this tree fragment. If conditional statements are nested like shown there is a read reduce conflict (also called shift reduce conflict).

2.5. Error Recovery

The generated parsers include information and algorithms to handle syntax errors completely automatically. We follow the complete backtrack-free method described in
[Röh76, Röh80, Röh82] and provide expressive reporting, recovery, and repair. Even
incorrect input is "virtually" transformed into a syntactically correct program with the
consequence of only executing a "correct" sequence of semantic actions. Therefore the following compiler phases like semantic analysis don't have to bother with syntax errors. Lalr
provides a prototype error module which prints messages as shown in Figure 11. Internally
the error recovery works as follows:

- The location of the syntax error is reported.
- All the tokens that would be a legal continuation of the program are computed and
  reported.
- All the tokens that can serve to continue parsing are computed. A minimal sequence of
  tokens is skipped until one of these tokens is found.

Source Program:

```
program test (output);
begin
   if (a = b] write (a);
end.
```

Error Messages:

```
3, 13: Error       syntax error
3, 13: Information expected symbols: ')' '*' '+' '-' '/' '<' '<='
                   '=' '<>' '>' '>=' 'AND' 'DIV' 'IN' 'MOD' 'OR'
3, 15: Information restart point
3, 15: Repair      symbol inserted : ')'
3, 15: Repair      symbol inserted : 'THEN'
```

Fig. 11: Example of Automatic Error Messages

The recovery location is reported.

Parsing continues in the so-called repair mode. In this mode the parser behaves as usual except that no tokens are read from the input. Instead a minimal sequence of tokens is synthesized to repair the error. The parser stays in this mode until the input token can be accepted. The synthesized tokens are reported. The program can be regarded as repaired, if the skipped tokens are replaced by the synthesized ones. With leaving the repair mode parsing continues as usual.

.6. Comparison of Parser Generators

Figure 12 compares *Lalr* with:

Yacc well known from UNIX [Joh75]

Bison public domain remake of *Yacc* [GNU88]

PGS Parser Generating System also developed at Karlsruhe [GrK86, KlM88]

Ell recursive descent parser generator described in chapter 3.

The language dependent numbers exclude time and size for scanning and refer to experiments with a Modula-2 parser.

The measurements of the parser speed turned out to be a hairy business. The results can be influenced in many ways from:

The hardware: We used a PCS Cadmus 9900 with a MC68020 processors running at a clock rate of 20 MHz.

The compiler: We used the C compiler of PCS.

The language: We used Modula-2.

The size of the language: In the case of *Lalr* the size of the language or the size of the grammar does not influence the speed of the parser because the same table-driven algorithm and the same data structure is used in every case. This can be different for other

	Bison	Yacc	PGS	Lalr	Ell
spec. language	BNF	BNF	EBNF	EBNF	EBNF
grammar class	LALR(1)	LALR(1)	LALR(1) LR(1) SLR(1)	LALR(1)	LL(1)
semantic actions	yes	yes	yes	yes	yes
S-attribution	numeric	numeric	symbolic	numeric	-
L-attribution	-	-	-	-	planned
conflict message	state, items	state, items	state, items	derivation-tree	-
conflict solution	precedence associativity	precedence associativity	modification	precedence associativity	
chain rule elim.	-	-	yes	-	-
error recovery	by hand	by hand	automatic	automatic	automatic
error repair	-	-	yes	yes	yes
parsing method	table-driven	table-driven	table-driven	table-driven	recursive descent
table compression	comb-vector	comb-vector	comb-vector	comb-vector	-
impl. language	C	C	Pascal	Modula	Modula
target languages	C	C	C Modula Pascal Ada	C Modula	C Modula
speed [lines/min.]	105,000	184,000	200,000	385,000	437,000
table size [bytes]	8,004	10,364	11,268	11,795	-
parser size [bytes]	11,136	12,548	17,616	17,416	14,344
gen. time [sec.]	5.0	19.6	69.5	29.6	6.4
availability	UNIX	UNIX	PCS/UNIX VAX/UNIX BSD 4.2 SIEMENS/ BS2000	PCS/UNIX SUN/UNIX	PCS/UNIX SUN/UNIX

Fig. 12: Comparison of Parser Generators (speed measured on a MC 68020 processor)

parsers. For example the speed of directly coded parsers decreases with an increasi
grammar size. PGS stores states in one byte if there are less than 256 states and in tw
bytes otherwise. This increases the speed for small grammars, too, at least
byte-addressable machines.

- The grammar style, the number of rules, especially chain rules and the like: We used t
  same grammar for most experiments which had as few chain rules as possible and whi
  caused as few reduce actions as possible. This means e. g. we specified expressions in

ambiguous style like shown in Figure 7. Exceptions are *Ell* which needs an LL(1) grammar and PGS, because modifications are inelegant to resolve many ambiguities.

The test input: We used the same large Modula program as test data in every case, of course. Nevertheless the programming style or the code "density" influence the resulting speed. This effect could be eliminated by selecting tokens per minute as measure. In spite of this we chose lines per minute as measure because we find this to be more expressive. (In the average there are 4 tokens in a line).

The timing: We measured CPU-time and subtracted the total time and the scanner time to get the parser time.

The semantic actions: We specified empty semantic actions for all rules in order to simulate the conditions in a realistic application. This has more consequences as one might think. It disables a short cut of *Yacc* and the chain rule elimination [WaG84] of PGS, decreasing the speed in both cases. A further experiment with PGS revealed even more problems. To allow chain rule elimination we deleted the empty semantic actions for chain rules. Surprisingly, instead of getting faster the parser was slower. The reason is that chain rule elimination increases the number of states. Accidentally we exceeded the number of 256. Now states have to be stored in two bytes instead of one. The additional memory accesses are more expensive than the win from the chain rule elimination.

The Parser Generator Ell

The parser generator *Ell* processes LL(1) grammars which may contain extended BNF nstructs and semantic actions and generates a recursive descent parser. A mechanism for attribution (inherited and synthesized attributes evaluable during one preorder traversal) is be added. Like *Lalr* syntax errors are handled fully automatic including error reporting om a prototype error module, error recovery, and error repair. The generator *Ell* is impleented in Modula-2 and can generate parsers in C and Modula-2. Those satisfied with the stricted power of LL(1) grammars may profit from the high speed of the generated parsers ich lies around 450,000 lines per minute. For a detailed comparison see Figure 12.

Conclusion

We presented the tools *Rex*, *Lalr*, and *Ell* that allow the generation of efficient comer front-ends. The combination of generated scanners and parsers reach speeds of more an 100,000 lines per minute or almost 2,000 lines per second. As scanning itself is one of e dominating tasks in a compiler we belief that compilers with a total performance of 1,000 es per second can be generated automatically. Our current work concentrates on tools for mantic analysis based on attribute grammars and code generation based on pattern match-
.

cknowledgement

The author implemented *Rex* and contributed the parser skeletons in C and Modula-2
 Lalr. The generator program *Lalr* was written and debugged by Bertram Vielsack who
o provided the experimental results for the parser generators. The parser generator *Ell*
s programmed by Doris Kuske.

References

[ASU86]   A. V. Aho, R. Sethi and J. D. Ullman, *Compilers: Principles, Techniques, a* *Tools*, Addison Wesley, Reading, MA, 1986.

[DeP82]   F. DeRemer and T. Pennello, Efficient Computation of LALR(1) Look-Ahe Sets, *ACM Trans. Prog. Lang. and Systems 4*, 4 (Oct. 1982), 615-649.

[GNU88]   GNU Project, *Bison - Manual Page*, Public Domain Software, 1988.

[GrK86]   J. Grosch and E. Klein, *User Manual for the PGS-System*, GM Forschungsstelle an der Universität Karlsruhe, Aug. 1986.

[Gro87]   J. Grosch, Rex - A Scanner Generator, Compiler Generation Report No. GMD Forschungsstelle an der Universität Karlsruhe, Dec. 1987.

[Gro88a]   J. Grosch, Selected Examples of Scanner Specifications, Compiler Generati Report No. 7, GMD Forschungsstelle an der Universität Karlsruhe, Mar. 1988.

[Gro88b]   J. Grosch, LALR - Generates Efficient Table-Driven Parsers, Compi Generation Report No. 10, GMD Forschungsstelle an der Universität Karlsru Sep. 1988.

[Ive86]   F. Ives, Unifying View of Recent LALR(1) Lookahead Set Algorithms, *SIGPL. Notices 21*, 7 (1986), 131-135.

[Joh75]   S. C. Johnson, Yacc — Yet Another Compiler-Compiler, Computer Scier Technical Report 32, Bell Telephone Laboratories, Murray Hill, NJ, July 1975.

[KlM88]   E. Klein and M. Martin, The Parser Generating System PGS, *to appear Software—Practice & Experience*, , 1988.

[Les75]   M. E. Lesk, LEX — A Lexical Analyzer Generator, Computing Scier Technical Report 39, Bell Telephone Laboratories, Murray Hill, NJ, 1975.

[Pax88]   V. Paxson, *Flex - Manual Pages*, Public Domain Software, 1988.

[Röh76]   J. Röhrich, Syntax-Error Recovery in LR-Parsers, in *Informatik-Fachberich* vol. 1, H.-J. Schneider and M. Nagl (ed.), Springer, Berlin, 1976, 175-184.

[Röh80]   J. Röhrich, Methods for the Automatic Construction of Error Correcti Parsers, *Acta Inf. 13*, 2 (1980), 115-139.

[Röh82]   J. Röhrich, Behandlung syntaktischer Fehler, *Informatik Spektrum 5*, 3 (198 171-184.

[Vie88]   B. Vielsack, The Parser Generators Lalr and Ell, Compiler Generation Rep No. 8, GMD Forschungsstelle an der Universität Karlsruhe, Apr. 1988.

[WaG84]   W. M. Waite and G. Goos, *Compiler Construction*, Springer Verlag, New Yo NY, 1984.

INCREMENTAL ALGORITHMS IN PROF-LP

T. Gyimóthy, T. Horváth, F. Kocsis and J. Toczki
Research Group on Theory of Automata
Hungarian Academy of Sciences
Somogyi u. 7. SZEGED
H-6720 HUNGARY

ABSTRACT

PROF-LP is a programgenerator system for IBM XT/AT compatible computers. On the basis of an attribute grammar description the system generates a Pascal program which can be considered as the processor of the given specification. PROF-LP can be used for generating one-pass and multi-pass language processors. The generated one-pass processors use LL(1) method for syntactic analysis and L-attribute evaluation strategy. The multi-pass processors use LALR(1) type syntactic parser and OAG attribute evaluation strategy.

The attribute grammar definition can be created in an incremental way as well. In this paper an incremental method for generating LL(1) parsing table is presented. The main advantage of the incremental system is the very fast generation of language processors.

Keywords: attribute grammars, incremental parsing,
          software generation

1. INTRODUCTION

PROF-LP (Professional Language Processor) is a program-generator for IBM XT/AT compatible computers. The system has been developed on the basis of HLP/PAS [3], [8].

The input of the PROF-LP is an attribute grammar
description from which a Pascal program is generated. The
system is able to generate MS-Pascal or Turbo Pascal programs.

In PROF-LP there are two ways to define an attribute
grammar.

In the Batch Version [6] of the system attribute grammar
description can be given in the metalanguage of the system
by using a usual text editor. In the first step the system
checks the correctness of the definition. After this the type
of the underlying CF grammar and the class of the attribute
grammar is determined by using the suitable modules of the
system.

In PROF-LP there are modules for generating LL(1) and
LALR(1) type parsers. The system is able to generate attribute
evaluators for L-attribute [2] and OAG [5] type attribute
grammars.

In the Interactive Version [7] of the system the attribute
grammar definition can be defined in an incremental way. The
user can give and improve the definition by using a comfortable
menu system. The complete definition of the attribute grammar
is a sequence of items. Each object of the grammar has an item
declaring it and one or more items applying it. If an item
including declarations is deleted or modified, then the other
items referring to the symbols declared in it becomes "uncertain"
and they are "ready" again only after reparsing. The tests
and codegenerators of the system can be called by using the
menu, but they do not start if one or more items are not
ready.

Several large language processors have been generated
by PROF-LP. The size of the generated programs were often
more than twenty thousands Pascal program lines. These large
applications raised some problems in the efficient using of
PROF-LP.

First of all it is very disturbing for a user, that
if he makes a little modification of the large attribute

grammar definition then the complete processor is generated and compiled again. This problem can be solved if the attribute grammar definition can be given in a modular way. So the new version of PROF-LP gives a possibility of the generation of modular compilers [8]. Unfortunately the modularity does not solve the problem of parsing table generation. If any rule in the grammar is changed then the complete parsing table of that module has to generate again. To solve this problem in the Interactive Version of PROF-LP we have developed an incremental method to test the LL(1) property and to make the parsing table. Using this method it is possible to generate parsing table for large grammars in a very short time.

PROF-LP has been used to generate language processors for natural language processing and syntactic pattern recognition too. However these problems can usually be defined by ambigous grammars so the system has been extended with a backtrack parser generator. The generated backtrack parsers use the LL(1) parsing table and thus a lot of useless backtracks can be eliminated. Further characteristic of the generated parsers is that the parsing can be influenced by the evaluated attributes. Calling the procedure corresponding to the start symbol of an ambiguous grammar repeatedly the all possible derivations of a given input can be constructed [4].

In the next section of this paper the Interactive Version of PROF-LP is described. In section 3 the incremental method for LL(1) parsing table generation is presented. Some general remarks can be found in the last section.

2. INTERACTIVE VERSION OF PROF-LP

The Interactive Version of PROF-LP supports the incremental writing of attribute grammar definitions and on the basis of this the generation of language processors. The functions required can be chosen by the help of menu system or by direct

typing of the commands. The textual writing of the attribute
grammar definition is supported by the internal "full screen"
editor. The main parts of the system are as follows:

AGDEF :   definition of an attribute grammar.

GENPART: generation of a compiler.

SERVICE: service routines.

In the part AGDEF an attribute grammar can be described.
So called "item"-s are used for the textual making of the
syntactic-semantic and lexical description of the attribute
grammar. An "item" involves an adjoining logically coherent
unit of the description. The "item"-s of an attribute grammar
description are as follows:

Syn-decl   : synthesized attribute declaration

Inh-decl   : inherited attribute declaration

Nont-decl   : nonterminal declaration

Token-decl : declaration of token class names

Term-decl   : declaration of terminal symbols

Prod-part   : production with the description of semantic
            activities belonging to it.

Lexs-part   : lexical description.

The "item"-s are usually handled as the elements of a sequence
with the exception of the "item"-s belonging to the functions
Token-decl, Term-decl and Lexs-part. Because of their
characteristics only one of them is necessary for the description of the given language. During the processing the state
of an "item" can be the following:

Wrong: indicating that the "item" is in a syntactically-
            semantically faulty state, or the "item" went
            wrong as a consequence of some other "item" parsing

Complete: the "item" is faultless from syntactical
            and semantical point of view.

Uncertain: the "item" got into an uncertain condition.
            This can happen if any other "item" has influence
            on this "item" and this influence does not
            inevitably spoil this "item".

Using the function GENPART if we have got a faultless
language description (all the "item"-s should be in Complete

state) the compiler generation can be started. The compiler generator commands to be chosen are as follows:

Finitest: the start of the module generating the finite automata of the lexical analyzer.

Lexgen: the start of the module generating the lexical analyzer.

LL(1)-test: the start of the LL(1) test and the parsing table generator module.

Codegen: the start of the codegenerator module.

Using the function SERVICE some useful service functions can be actived. These are as follows:

Profrest: it is used for the restoration of damaged language description in case of hardware error or others.

Agprint: this program provides possibility for listing the attribute grammar definition or for converting the description into "batch form".

Status: by the help of this function we can get information about the state of the attribute grammar under processing.

3. INCREMENTAL GENERATION OF THE LL(1) PARSING TABLE

The Interactive Version of PROF-LP system generates LL(1) type parsers. Although the generation of these parsers is fairly fast - usually few minutes are enough for large grammars - but even a short waiting may be disturbing for an "interactive user". This waiting is especially disagreeable for a user who modified only a single rule in a large attribute grammar description. In this case an interactive system is expected to generate the suitable parser very fast. The most time-consuming part of the LL(1) parsing table generator algorithm is the computation of the $FIRST_1$ and $FOLLOW_1$ sets. In the PROF-LP system the well-known iterative method [1] has been used to compute these sets.

We have developed a new, incremental algorithm to the more efficient computation. The main idea of this algorithm is that the computed $FIRST_1$ and $FOLLOW_1$ sets of a grammar are always saved in a file after the processing. When this grammar is modified these sets are used in the computation of the new $FIRST_1$ and $FOLLOW_1$ sets. More exactly, the iterative algorithm starts with the "old" $FIRST_1$ and $FOLLOW_1$ sets except for some modified nonterminals. The initial value of those sets which can be changed with the modification of the grammar is the empty set.

In the following we give a more detail description of the incremental computation of the $FIRST_1$ and $FOLLOW_1$ sets.

Iterative formulae are given in [1] for the computing these sets. These formulae are the following:

$FIRST_1$

$$F_0(X) = \emptyset$$
$$F_{i+1}(X) = F_i(X) \cup \{F_i(X_1) \oplus_1 \ldots \oplus_1 F_i(X_n)\} \quad (X \to X_1 \ldots X_n)$$

$FOLLOW_1$

$$H_0(X) = \left\{ \begin{array}{ll} \emptyset & X \neq S \\ \{\varepsilon\} & X = S \end{array} \right\}$$

$$H_{j+1}(X) = H_j(X) \cup \{FIRST_1(\beta) \oplus_1 H_j(Y) \mid \exists Y \to \alpha X \beta\}$$

In these formulae S, $\emptyset$ and ε denote the start symbol, empty set and empty word respectively.

If none of the sets $F_i(X)$ is changed in the i-th step, then $FIRST_1(X) = F_i(X)$ for the all nonterminals of the grammar. Similarly, $FOLLOW_1(X) = H_j(X)$ if the sets $H_j(X)$ are not changed in the j-th step.

Let us suppose that the $FIRST_1$ and $FOLLOW_1$ sets of a given grammar G have been computed. Denote $OFIRST_1$ and $OFOLLOW_1$ these sets, respectively. Let us modify the grammar G and denotes G° the modified grammar. Two cases are examined:

1. removing rules

2. adding new rules

The modification of a rule can be considered as the **removing of the old rule** and the adding of the modified one.

Let us define the sets FID(X) and FOD(X). For the non-terminals X and Y $Y \in FID(X)$ if the $FIRST_1$ set of Y "depends on" directly the $FIRST_1$ set of X. More exactly

$$FID(X) = \{(Y,k) \mid \exists Y \rightarrow \alpha X \beta \text{ with } \alpha \xrightarrow{*} \varepsilon\}$$

where k denotes the number of such rules for the nonterminal Y. Similarly

$$FOD(X) = \{(Y,k) \mid \exists X \rightarrow \alpha Y \beta \text{ with } \beta \xrightarrow{*} \varepsilon\}$$

The computation of the sets FID(X), FOD(X) is very simply by using the sets $FIRST_1$. (The conditions $\alpha \xrightarrow{*} \varepsilon$, $\underline{\beta} \xrightarrow{*} \varepsilon$ can easily be checked.)

Let us suppose that the sets FID, FOD have been computed for the given grammar G.

I. Removing of the rule $X_0 \rightarrow X_1 \ldots X_n$.
   Computation of the $FIRST_1$ sets
   a.) Let $OFIRST_1(X_0) = \emptyset$.
   b.) If the $FIRST_1$ set of a nonterminal X directly depends on the $FIRST_1$ set of the nonterminal X_0 then let $OFIRST_1(X) = \emptyset$.
   c.) Let us make the transitive closure of point b) by using sets FID.
   d.) By using these modified $OFIRST_1$ sets as the initial sets the new $FIRST_1$ sets are computed with the original iterative algorithm. But this computation is performed only for nonterminals the $OFIRST_1$ set of which changed. Of course the number of the iterative steps in this case is also less than in case of starting from empty sets.

After the new $FIRST_1$ sets are computed a set DEC is constructed. A nonterminal X is in this set if

$$FIRST_1(X) \subseteq OFIRST_1(X).$$

Computation of the $FOLLOW_1$ sets
a.) A set CH is constructed. A nonterminal X is in CH if the set $FOLLOW_1(X)$ is directly changed (or may be changed). More exactly:

$$CH = \{X \mid X = X_i \text{ for some } 1 \leq i \leq n \text{ or}$$
$$\exists Y \rightarrow \alpha X \beta Z \gamma \text{ and } Z \in DEC \text{ with } \beta \xrightarrow{*} \varepsilon\}.$$

b.) If $X \in CH$ then let $OFOLLOW_1(X) = \emptyset$.

c.) If $Y \in FOD(Z)$ and the set $FOLLOW_1(Z)$ is modified to the empty set then let $FOLLOW_1(Y) = \emptyset$ too.

d.) Let us make the transitive closure of the point c.).

e.) By using the modified $OFOLLOW_1$ sets and the new $FIRST_1$ sets the new $FOLLOW_1$ sets are computed with the original iterative algorithm.

After the sets $FIRST_1$ and $FOLLOW_1$ are computed the sets FID and FOD are modified.

If $X_i \in N$ $(1 < i \leq n)$ $X_1 \ldots X_{i-1} = \alpha \overset{*}{\to} \varepsilon$ and $(X_0,k) \in FID(X_i)$ and $k > 1$, then $(X_0,k-1) \in FID(X_i)$ and (X_0,k) is deleted from the set $FID(X_i)$. If $k = 1$ then $(X_0,1)$ is deleted from the set $FID(X_i)$.

If $X_i \in N$ $(1 \leq i \leq n)$ and $X_{i+1} \ldots X_n = \beta \overset{*}{\to} \varepsilon$ and $(X_i,k) \in FOD(X_0)$ and $k > 1$ then $(X_i,k-1) \in FOD(X_0)$ and (X_i,k) is deleted from $FOD(X_0)$. If $k = 1$ then $(X_i,1)$ is deleted from the set $FOD(X_0)$.

II. Adding a new rule to the grammar G.

This case is very simple. The initial value of the $OFIRST_1$ and $OFOLLOW_1$ sets of the new nonterminals is the empty set. The $OFIRST_1$ and $OFOLLOW_1$ sets of the old nonterminal are not changed. The computation of the new FID and FOD sets is also very simple, only the new dependences have to be saved.

Of course the time efficiency of this incremental algorithm strongly depends on the concrete modification of the grammar. The most time-consuming part of the algorithm is the transitive closure if the depth of the closure is large. In Figure 1. the computation time of the sets $FIRST_1$ and $FOLLOW_1$ using the original iterative method is presented for two programming languages. The depth of the transitive closure in the incremental algorithm depends on the sets FID and FOD. If these sets for many nonterminals are empty or have only one element then the computation of the new $FIRST_1$ and $FOLLOW_1$ sets are very fast.

In Figure 2. it can be seen that for example in COBOL a
lot of FID sets are empty (for more than half of nonterminals)
and only a few of FID sets have two or more elements.

4. CONCLUSIONS

In this paper the Interactive Version of the PROF-LP
software generator system is described. The attribute grammar
definitions of the given softwares can be defined in an
incremental way. An incremental algorithm for LL(1) parsing
table generation is also presented. Using this algorithm the
sets $FIRST_1$ and $FOLLOW_1$ of a given grammar can be computed
in a very short time.

REFERENCES

[1]   Aho-Ulmann: The theory of parsing, translation and
      compiling, Prentice Hall, Englewood Cliffs, N. J. 1973.
[2]   Bochmann, G.V.: Semantic evaluation from left to right,
      Comm. ACM 19. 55-62 (1976).
[3]   Gyimothy at al.: An implementation of the HLP, Acta
      Cybernetica, 6. 3 (1983) 315-327.
[4]   Gyimothy, T. and Toczki, J.: Syntactic pattern recogni-
      tion in the HLP/PAS system, Acta Cybernetica 8.1. (1987)
      79-88.
[5]   Kastens, U.: Ordered attribute grammars, Acta Inf. 13.
      229-256 (1981)
[6]   PROFLP User's guide - batch version,
      HLP-team of the Research Group on Theory of Automata,
      Rep., draft, Szeged 1986.
[7]   PROFLP User's guide - interactive version, HLP-team of
      the Research Group on Theory of Automata, Rep., draft,
      Szeged 1987.
[8]   Toczki et al.: Automatic compiler generation, Proc.
      of Symp. on Automata, Languages and Pr. Systems,
      Salgotarjan (1986).

	COBOL	FORTRAN
Number of nonterminals	175	109
Number of terminals	109	57
Number of syntactic rules	377	202
Number of $FIRST_1$ iteration steps	14	11
Number of $FOLLOW_1$ iteration steps	14	13
$FIRST_1$ computation time	27 sec	11 sec
$FOLLOW_1$ computation time	11 sec	5 sec

Figure 1.

	COBOL		FORTRAN	
	FID	FOD	FID	FOD
empty	104	37	52	26
1	45	46	49	47
2	9	56	7	32
3	12	24	1	1
more	5	12	∅	3

Figure 2.

Abstract Interfaces for Compiler Generating Tools

U. Kastens
University of Paderborn, FRG

1. Introduction

Compiler construction is supported by tools which generate modules for the main compiler subtasks. Different tools have to cooperate in order to produce a complete compiler. They are often developed stand-alone without consideration how to integrate the generated products. A considerable amount of engineering work is needed to configurate the whole compiler. Adaption of the generated modules often reduces the overall performance of the compiler.

A compiler tool generates a module for a compiler subtask from a formal specification. Problems of tool integration result from dependencies between the specifications for different subtasks and from integration of the modules. There are different strategies to simplify compiler development with tools: (1) A set of tools is developed together such that they fit together smoothly. (2) Independantly develpoed tools are embedded in a compiler construction environment which solves the integration problem for the user. Such a system is described in [WHK 88]. (3) Each single tool is designed with open interfaces which allow for easy integration and adaption of the generated products.

Strategy (1) is rather inflexible against exchange of single tools and adaption to implementation requirements. A compiler construction environment (2) can be composed for different tool sets. It embodies the know-how of tool integration. It can adapt the interfaces determined by a single tool but it cannot change them. The notion of the specification and the implementation of the modules are fixed. Hence we suggest in this paper to develop compiler generating tools according to (3). Such a tool takes an abstract representation of the specification as input and produces an abstract representation of the generated algorithm. Various frontends and backends can easily be derived to support suitable notions for the specifiaction and smoothly integratable implementations of the algorithm.

In Sect. 2 of this paper we dicuss the problems of compiler tool integration. Sect. 3 presents the suggested tool design concept. Two examples of tool design on that base are given in Sect. 4.

The ideas presented in this paper arose from the work on the development of compiler construction environments performed in cooperation with the group of W.M. Waite, University of Colorado, Boulder.

2. Integration of compiler tools

A task oriented compiler design refines the compiler task into a sequence of subtasks: lexical analysis, syntactic analysis, semantic analysis, code selection, and assembly. (Global optimization and peeephole optimization may be inserted before and after code selection.) The tasks are implemented by central compiler modules (scanner, parser, attribute evaluator, code generator, and assembler) which act as filters transforming one representation of the source program into another (character sequence, token sequence, structure tree, intermediate language, instruction sequence, object code). These filters use functions of additional modules which act as abstract data types, store properties of certain objects and provide access to them (e.g. identifiers, literal values, declared objects, ranges of declarations, registers). Such a compiler structure is well accepted, systematic methods for the solution of the subtasks are well known and can be found in most compiler texts [ASU 86], [WG 84].

Different compiler tools are in use to generate each of the central filter modules. (The ADT-Modules are usually not generated but adapted from precoined implementations.) Such a tool takes a specification of the subtask and generates the compiler module from it. The input to the tool specifies the translation step in some notion of a certain formal concept specific for that subtask, e.g. regular expressions for the scanner, a context-free grammar for the parser, an attribute grammar for the attribute evaluator, and tree patterns with associated instructions for the code generator. The compiler module generated by the tool is an algorithm of a certain class (e.g. finite state machine, stack automaton, etc.) implemented by a systematic technique (e.g. table driven) and expressed in a certain implementation language. Furthermore the module implementation includes interfaces to surrounding modules. Fig. 1 describes this situation for a set of tools graphically.

With such a set of generating tools a compiler is constructed mainly by developing the specifications. Additionally two classes of more technical problems have to be solved - often without help from the tools: The single specifications are interrelated and have to be ensured to be consistent. The generated modules must be integrated into the whole compiler.

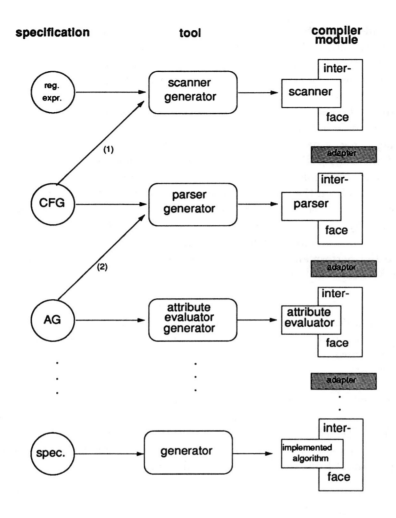

Fig.1: Tools generating compiler modules

As an example for relationships between specifications consider the scanner and parser generation steps: The symbols specified for the scanner are the terminal symbols of the context-free grammar for the parser. Usually the parser specification includes the notion of keywords and special symbols. Instead of specifying them twice (for the scanner and parser generator) they could be extracted from the CFG and directed to the scanner generator (arc (1) in Fig. 1). That leaves the scanner specification with regular expressions for identifiers and literals. A more subtle relationship exists between the specifications for the parser and the attribute evaluator: The attribute grammar is based on a CFG which describes the structure of the tree to be attributed. It is an abstraction of the derivation tree computed by the parser. Hence the concrete grammar for the parser specification has to be augmented by actions which construct that strucure tree (arc (2) in Fig. 1).

On the side of the generated products often a considerable amount of technical work is required for module integration: The modules may be generated in different implementation languages, e.g. a parser generated in C by YACC [Jo 75] and an attribute evaluator in Pascal from GAG [KHZ 82]. The interfaces of the modules may be based on different assumptions how information is passed from one module to the other (e.g. encoding and passing of tokens from the scanner to the parser, or execution of actions initiated by the parser). For both cases it might be necessary to adapt the interfaces. Since generated modules usually are not prepared for being modified additional procedures transforming the data structures or linking different languages have to be inserted. Such an adaption can reduce the performance of the compiler. It may even be impossible to adapt the modules reasonably. In the latter case a certain combination of tools must be discarded.

If each of the tools is used stand-alone the compiler developer has to adapt specifications and generated products for each compiler generated. The know-how for that work is not compiler specific but determined only by the combination of the tools. There are different strategies to reduce the amount of that work:

(1) Fixed tool sets: A certain set of tools is developed such that specifications and products easily fit together, e.g. LEX [Le 75] and YACC [Jo 75] or GAG [KHZ 82] and PGS [De 77]. If interfaces of the tools are hidden for the user such a toolset may even appear as a monolithic generator producing a readily integrated compiler (or part of it) from an integrated specification.

(2) Open compiler construction environments: The desired set of tools is combined under control of a tool mangement system. It takes care for relations between specifications, directs them to the tools and integrates the generated products. Hence it solves the tool integration problems for that specific tool combination. Such an environment is Eli [WHK 88] constructed with the tool mangement system ODIN [CL 88].

The integration problems discussed above will arise again in solution (1) if one of the tools in the set should be replaced by a generator with different characteristics, or if the set is completed by additonal tools. Such an exchange of single tools is usually impossible in monolithic systems. Environments like (2) support modifications of the tool set best of all: The know-how for the specific tool integration is embedded initially in the environment and can be modified when tools are changed. The management system applies that knowledge automatically for the construction of each compiler. We constructed several environments solving the integration problems for different tool sets. From that experience we learnt that tools should be designed with interfaces which simplify their integration.

3. Abstract tool interfaces

A main reason for the difficulties with the integration of compiler tools discussed in the previous section lies in the design of the tools themselves: Neither the notion of the input specification nor the implementation of the generated compiler module can easily be modified without rewriting large parts or all of the tool. Hence we suggest to develop tools according to the following design principle: The central task of a tool is the computation of an algorithm from a specification. The central part of the tool should be restricted to exactly that task. Its input and output interfaces both are abstract data structures instead of notions of the specification and implementations of the algorithm. Frontends and backends transform the notion and implement the algorithm. They can easily be modified without touching the central tool part in order to integrate the tool smoothly. Fig. 2 shows such a tool structure with the *abstract specification* and the *abstract algorithm* as its central interfaces.

The *abstract specification* is a data structure representing structure and information contents of a specification. Its data format is reasonably simple for any compiler tool due to the underlying formal specification concept, e.g. CFGs in the case of a parser generator. A frontend for the tool producing that format from some notion can easily be constructed or modified, e.g. in order to let a parser generator be used with the same input notion as that of YACC or PGS. Furthermore specification information can be exchanged between tools (as in Fig. 1) directly on the base of the abstract specification. Even interactive syntax directed editors can be adapted to the tool on that interface. Such a frontend should be restricted to transform the notion of the specification into the abstract representation. Any check for consistency or further transformation which is independant of the notion should be performed either in the central part of the tool or by additional modules with the abstract representation as both input and output interface.

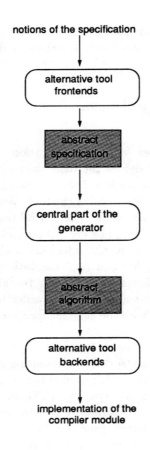

Fig. 2: Abstract tool interfaces

The central part of the tool generates an *abstract algorithm*. It is described by a data struture based on the underlying formal concept of the algorithm, e.g. the transition function of an automaton. It does not contain any implementation decision for the algorithm. Various backends can be developed for that interface implementing the algorithm using different techniques, e.g. either table driven or directly programmed, and using different implementation languages. Furthermore such a tool backend can easily be modified in order to produce compiler modules which fit to other modules without the need for explicit and costly adapters.

This general principle is applicable throughout all of the compiler generating tools because they are based on formal concepts for both the specification and the generated algorithms.

(It is of course applicable outside of compiler construction, too, where generation concepts have these characteristics. This generalization aspect is beyond the scope of this paper.) A scanner generator transforms representations of regular expressions (derived from character oriented or graphical notions) into a finite state machine described by its transition function. A parser generator takes a context-free grammar (with actions inserted), checks it for the required grammar class and produces an abstract parsing algorithm. It is represented by the grammar with inserted director sets in the case of an LL-parser, or by the transition function in case of an LR-parser. An attribute evaluator generator transforms a representation of an attribute grammar into a tree walking automaton. In the next section it will be shown how that algorithm can be represented easily. The generator of a code selector may take the description of tree patterns with associated actions for code generation and augments them by strategic information for pattern application.

4. Two Examples for Tool Design

In this section we briefly describe the design concepts of two projects for compiler tools where we applied the principles of abstract interfaces described in the previous section. In the first example a set of tools based on context-free grammars is presented. The second example refers to an attribute evaluator generator developed as a successor of the GAG system.

COMAR

COMAR is a data format for the representation of context-free grammars. It was developed for interfacing various tools which analyse and transform CFGs [HKPW 87]. It plays the role of abstract interfaces as introduced in Sect. 3, and is the base of an extensible set of CFG-tools.

The information structure of a CFG consists of objects which are terminals, nonterminals, productions and other objects which may augment the productions (e.g. actions, director sets, etc.). The abstract data structure of a CFG is a list of definitions of such objects. The productions in extended BNF are described by trees for their right hand sides. Additional application specific properties are associated to the objects: e.g. actions or first- and follow-sets associated to productions.

110

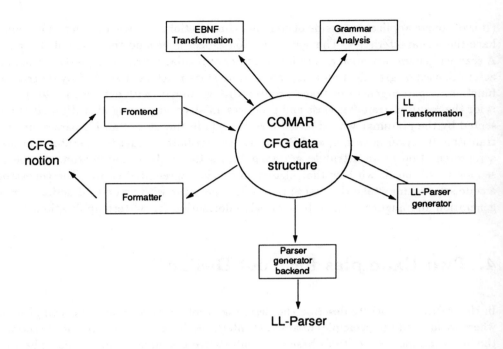

Fig. 3: COMAR Tool Set

The COMAR data format is defined in terms of the interface description language IDL [La 87]. From that definition the IDL-tool [SS 86] automatically generates an implementation of the data structure in C with access functions, and routines for reading and writing a standardized file representation of a COMAR structure. The development of a CFG tool can immediately concentrate on its specific task using such a complete implementation of the CFG representation. On this base we developed an initial, extensible set of CFG tools which cooperate via the COMAR structure, Fig. 3. Upto now it contains a frontend transforming a CFG notion into COMAR, a formatter for the opposite direction, tools for EBNF-transformation LL(1)-check, LL-transformations, and an LL(1)-parser generator [Bu 88].

The design of that LL(1)-parser generator follows the principle of abstract interfaces presented in this paper: Its input interface is a CFG in COMAR. The generator augments it by LL(1)-director sets. The result - again a COMAR structure - is an abstract representation of the LL(1)-parser. A backend of the generator implements it in C using a directly programmed non-recursive technique which yields fast parsers.

Another parser generator based on the LALR(1)-technique is being developed for CO-MAR. In this case the generated abstract algorithm of a LR-parser is not described by an augmented CFG as in the LL-case. It is a data structure specifying the transition function instead. Again suitable backends will implement it using a certain technique and implementation language.

LIGA

An attribute evaluator is the central module of the semantic analysis phase a compiler. The language independant generator for attribute evaluators LIGA is developed as a successor system for the well established generator GAG [KHZ 82]. Whereas the GAG system is fixed to a certain input language for AG specification (ALADIN) and the target implementation language Pascal, the design concept for LIGA is based on abstract tool interfaces, Fig. 4.

The information structure of an AG consists of objects which are symbols of a CFG with associated attributes, and CFG productions each with a set of attribute rules. An attribute rule specifies the context dependent computation of an attribute by a functional expression over other attributes. Similarly as for COMAR a data structure is defined for the abstract respresention of an AG. It consists of a list of the object definitions with the productions and the attribution expressions being represented by trees. (The meaning of operators and functions in the attribution is specificied outside the AG in terms of the implementation language.) Again that data structure is defined in IDL in order to take advantage of its automatic implementation.

In the AG the attribution of a production is a list of attribute rules in an arbitrary order. The LIGA system generates a tree walking attribute evaluator controlled by a visit-sequence for each production [Ka 80]. A visit-sequence is an ordered sequence of attribute rules with operations for tree movement (ancestor and descendant visits) inserted. Hence the abstract algorithm for such an attribute evaluator can be easily described by a slight extension of the AG data structure: For each production the LIGA system sorts the attribute rules according to the attribute dependencies and inserts visits at the appropriate positions. (How to compute the visit sequences and how to optimize attribute implementation is beyond the scope of this paper and can be found in [Ka 80], [Ka 87], and [Ha 87]. The central part of the LIGA system produces the abstract attribute evaluator as an augmented AG representation. Various backends may implement this evaluator using different trechniques (table driven, recursive procedures, directly programmed without recursion) and different implementation languages. The first existing backend applies the latter technique in C, which yields in general the fastest implementation.

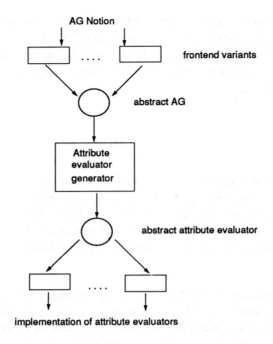

Fig. 4: LIGA system with abstract interfaces

5. Conclusion

The main tasks in compiler construction are solved by systematic algorithms. Tools are available which generate compiler modules from specifications. They are often developed as closed stand-alone systems difficult to combine with other tools. Integration of their products requires considerable engineering work and may loose efficiency because the tools fix all implementation decisions.

In order to improve the applicability of generating tools we suggest in this paper a modular tool structure: The central part of the generator translates an abstract representation of a specification into an abstract algorithm. These interfaces are open to meet the requirements of the tools environment by variations of the frontends and backends. Especially the implementation decisions for the generated products are separated from the generation of the abstract algorithm. We demonstrated this design principle applied to the development of a CFG toolset and an attribute evaluator generator.

Further work should be devoted to the development of other compiler tools on that base and to increase the variants of the existing tools. Furthermore we believe that the design principle is as well applicable to tools of areas different from compiler construction.

References

ASU 86   Aho, A.V., R. Sethi and J.D. Ullman, "Compilers", Addison Wesley, Reading MA, 1986

Bu 88   Budde, V., "Werkzeuge zur Grammatik-Transformation und LL-Parsergenerierung auf der COMAR-Datenbasis, Diplomarbeit, FB 17, Universität-GH Paderborn, 1988

Cl 88   Clemm, G.M., "The Odin Specification Language", in International Workshop on Software Version and Configuration Control '88, Teubner, Stuttgart, 1988, 144-158

De 77   Dencker, P. "Ein neues LALR-System", Institut für Informatik, Universität Karlsruhe, Diplomarbeit, 1977

Ha 87   Hall, M.L., "The Optimization of Automatically Generated Compilers", Ph.D. Thesis, Dept. of Computer Science, University of Colorado, Boulder, CO. 1987

HKPW 87   Heuring, V.P., Kastens, U., Plummer, R.G., Waite, W.M., "COMAR: A Data Format for Integration of CFG-Tools", University of Colorado, Boulder, ECE-Report 87/124, 1987, to appear in The Computer Journal

Jo 75   Johnson, S.C., "YACC - Yet Another Compiler-Compiler", Computer Science Technical Report 32, Bell Telephone Laboratories, Murray Hill, NJ, July 1975

Ka 80   Kastens, U. "Ordered Attributed Grammars", Acta Informatica 13, 229-256, 1980

Ka 87   Kastens, U. "Lifetime Analysis for Attributes", Acta Informatica 24, 633-651, 1987

KHZ 82   Kastens, U., Hutt, B., Zimmermann, E. "GAG - A Practical Compiler Generator", Lecture Notes in Computer Science 141, Springer, 1982

La 87   Lamb, D.A., "IDL: Sharing Intermediate Representations", TOPLAS, vol. 9, no. 3, 1987, 297-318

Le 75   Lesk, M.E., "LEX - A Lexical Analyzer Generator", Computer Science Technical Report 39, Bell Telephone Laboratories, Murray Hill, NJ, 1975

SS 86   Snodgrass, R., Shannon, K., "Supporting flexible and efficient tool integration", SoftLab Document No. 25, Computer Science Department, Universtiy of North Carolina, Chapel Hill, N.C., May 1986

WG 84   Waite, W.M., G. Goos, "Compiler Construction", Springer Verlag, New York, NY, 1984

WHK 88   Waite, W.M., Heuring, V.P., Kastens, U. "Configuration Control in Compiler Construction", Int'l Workshop on Software Version and Configuration Controll SVCC, Grassau, Januar 88

The INDIA Lexic Generator

Michael Albinus   Werner Aßmann*

1 Introduction

Because lexical analysis takes a conciderable amount of compilation time it is necessary
to build fast scanners. Generated scanners were brought into discredit because their
lack of efficiency, although finite automata are an appreciated method for generating
scanners. Some effort was made to improve the speed of generated scanners.

This paper describes the lexic generator of the INDIA system.

2 Lexical analysis in the INDIA system

The INDIA compiler generator, described in [Albinus86], is the basis for compiler construction in the INDIA system. It generates tables for all compiler components, which
contain the language specific informations. As presented in [Aßmann86], the compiler
can be viewed as a set of abstract machines associated by tables which contain the
abstract instruction codes to control the work. In this way we have a *lexical machine*
(scanner) that reads a sequence of input characters and fits them into a sequence of
lexical items, the smallest symbols known by the *syntactical machine* (parser). The
syntactical machine (based on LR(1) respectively LALR(1) mechanism) transforms this
sequence of lexical items into a sequence of meta symbols again, and so on. Therefore,
we have the following model:

*Academy of Sciences of the G.D.R.
Institute of Informatics and Computing Technique
Rudower Chaussee 5, Berlin, G.D.R.

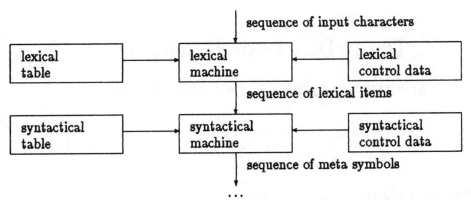

Figure 1: Principle of the lexical and syntactical machines

The other abstract machines of the compiler (tree constructor, table constructor, reparser, and code generator) are working in the same way. Every abstract machine is controlled by control data including options for list regime, production of test results and so on.

3 Generation of lexical table

The scanner has to construct the lexical items. There exists two kinds of lexical items, namely lexical items without "semantic" like '<', ':=' or 'BEGIN', and lexical items with a determined value like identifiers or numbers. We call them *terminal symbols* and *pseudoterminal symbols*, respectively. Keywords (like 'BEGIN') are ordinary *terminal symbols* from the viewpoint of syntactical analysis. Comments are special *pseudoterminal symbols*. Every lexical item is represented by an item number.

For generating the lexical table it is necessary to describe

- the text (string) of every *terminal symbol* and the item number belonging to,
- the syntactical structure of every *pseudoterminal symbol* and the item number belonging to,
- special features for handling of keywords, and
- special features for handling of comments.

The lexic generator transforms the description of lexical items into an deterministic finite automaton as described in [Aho77] and stores an abstract program, representing the automaton, into the lexical table. Some special features introduced in the next subsections are represented in the automaton.

3.1 Defining lexical items

The *terminal* and *pseudoterminal symbols* are defined during the generation of the syntactical table. Using extended BNF notation (described in [Aßmann85]), the syntax production

```
<Procedure Head>      ::= 'PROCEDURE' "Identifier" <Parameters> ';'   ||
```

defines the *terminal symbols* 'PROCEDURE' and ';' as well as the *pseudoterminal symbol* "Identifier". The item numbers belonging to are generated automatically. In a special part of the compiler generator it is possible to declare the item numbers explicitly. Nevertheless, in the most cases it is unnecessary.

Keywords are recognized by the property of being terminal symbols containing letters only. All these facts are available for the generation of the lexical table.

3.2 Syntactical structure of pseudoterminal symbols

The syntax of *pseudoterminal symbols* is described by using productions of regular grammars (instead of regular expressions as proposed in [Aho77]). The possibilities of description are derived from Alexis ([Mössenbeck86]) using the INDIA notation.

A typical production is

```
"Real_Number"        ::= [<Decimal Digit>]+ '.' [<Decimal Digit>]*
                         ['E' [('+'|'-')] [<Decimal Digit>]+ ]        ||
```

It defines the syntactical nature of real numbers (in MODULA-2). Elements of a production are simple character literals (like 'E') or previously declared character sets (<Decimal Digit>). Character sets are introduced in section 3.5. A non printable character literal can be written in its octal notation. For example, the character literal 36C stands for the EOL character.

Expressions are built using

- alternatives: ('+'|'-')

- options: [('+'|'-')]
  (repeat factor 0 or 1)

- optional iterations: [<Decimal Digit>]*
  (repeat factor 0, 1 or any more)

- iterations: [<Decimal Digit>]+
  (repeat factor 1 or any more)

It is possible to mark "redundant" character literals. These characters will be removed by the scanner from the string containing the *pseudoterminal symbol*. $\{\alpha\}$ describes removing a character.

3.3 Comments

Comments are treated as a special *pseudoterminal symbol*. The description contains
the leading and ending characters of an comment. It is possible to describe the nested
structure of comments with the keyword NESTED. This breaks the regularity of the expressions and will be handled in a special way.

The next productions describe nested MODULA-2 comments and unnested Ada comments.

"Comment"   ::= {'(*'} [ANY FOLLOWED BY '*)']* {'*)'} NESTED ||

"Comment"   ::= {'--'} [ANY FOLLOWED BY 36C]* {36C} ||

ANY stands for the character set containing all characters. FOLLOWED BY α is a construction that terminates the optional iteration [ANY]*, which never ends otherwise. It can
be used in other lexical declarations too for avoiding ambiguities, but requires multiple
access to characters and decreases the efficiency of the scanner.

3.4 Keywords

Keywords are sampled from the set of *terminal symbols* defined during the generation of
the syntactical table. Using the phrase EXCEPT KEYWORDS in the identifier production,
keywords and identifiers are distinguished.

"Identifier"   ::= <letter> [<extended letter>]* EXCEPT KEYWORDS ||

The lexic generator produces a perfect hash function h over the keywords. It uses the
(heuristic) approach from [Sager85]. This function is defined as

$$h : \mathcal{K} \to [0 \quad .. \quad N-1]$$

whereby $\mathcal{K}$ stands for the set of keywords and N is a cardinal number with $N \geq \|\mathcal{K}\|$.
h is called a perfect hash function if h proves as an injection (h is unique).

Perfect hash functions have the advantage that the decision for being a keyword (or
not) is very fast, because after computing the hash code of an identifier it needs only
one comparison with the keyword represented by this hash code.

A perfect hash function h is called minimal perfect hash function if $N = \|\mathcal{K}\|$.

The lexic generator realizes the hash function h as

$$h(k) = (h_0(k) + h_1(k) + h_2(k)) \quad \text{MOD} \quad N$$
$$h_0(k) = \text{ORD}(k[i_{01}]) + \text{ORD}(k[i_{02}])$$
$$h_1(k) = g_1[(\text{ORD}(k[i_{11}]) + \text{ORD}(k[i_{12}])) \quad \text{MOD} \quad r]$$
$$h_2(k) = g_2[(\text{ORD}(k[i_{21}]) + \text{ORD}(k[i_{22}])) \quad \text{MOD} \quad r]$$

whereas

- $k \in K$ is a keyword interpreted as a string (ARRAY OF CHAR)
- r is the smallest power of 2 with $r > \frac{\|K\|}{3}$;
- i_{xy} are array indices describing access to keyword characters;
- ORD is a function converting a character into its binary representation; and
- g_1, g_2 are arrays for parametrizing the hash function.

For details, see [Ernst87].

All these N, r, i_{xy}, g_1, g_2 are computed by the lexic generator and stored into the lexical table as parameters for the hash function used during lexical analysis. Appendix B contains the values computed for the keyword set of MODULA-2. By the way, all hash functions computed with this algorithm by the authors were minimal perfect hash functions. This holds for the compiler generator INDIA itself (22 keywords), MODULA-2 (40 keywords), PALM (our MODULA-2 extension, 51 keywords) and CHILL (86 keywords).

3.5 Character sets

Character sets are used in the productions of the lexic generator to allow the choice of one character from a set. It is in principle a simplified notation for a choice only. For example,

```
<octal digit>       ::= '01234567'                                        ||
"Octal_Number"      ::= [<octal digit>]+ 'B'                              ||
```

is equivalent to

```
"Octal_Number"      ::= [('0'|'1'|'2'|'3'|'4'|'5'|'6'|'7')]+ 'B'          ||
```

Definition of new character sets can use unions or differences of strings or already defined character sets, respectively.

```
<hexadecimal digit> ::= <decimal digit> + 'ABCDEFabcdef'                  ||
```

3.6 The generated automaton and its abstract program

The lexic generator samples all *terminal* and *pseudoterminal symbols* delivered by the syntax generator and builds an deterministic automaton from it. *Terminal symbols* (except keywords) are included into the automaton as chain, *pseudoterminal symbols* as partial automaton, derived from the affiliated production. Accepting any lexical item is done by using the longest chain. This technique is well known and described in [Aho77], for example.

The partial automaton for scanning the '<' symbol would be

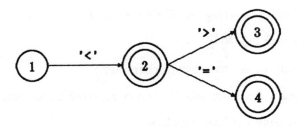

Figure 2: Abstract automaton

The lexic generator produces an abstract program using basic operations from this automaton. This abstract program is stored into the lexical table and interpreted by the scanner during the lexical analysis. The set of basic operations is described in appendix C. The resulting abstract program for state 2 above is

```
                         (* scan '<' *)
lex_accept
                         (* scan '>' and return item number of '<>' *)
lex_accept_and_return_if_next '>', 85
                         (* scan '=' and return item number of '<=' *)
lex_accept_and_return_if_next '=', 86
                         (* return item number of '<' *)
lex_return_code 72
```

4 Remarks on efficiency

4.1 Arrangements for increasing efficiency

- The approach of converting the deterministic finite automaton into program text of the scanner, favoured in the most lexic generators ([Horspool87], [Eulenstein88], [Grosch88], [Heuring86], [Mössenbeck86]), was not suitable for us, because the INDIA system is multilingual. Currently, it supports PALM (our MODULA-2 extension, see [Baum88]) and CHILL. Therefore, the scanner has to interprete the lexical table very efficiently. It tries to avoid multiple access to a character if possible.

  The main loop interpreting the lexical operations is a closed program part without any procedure calls (except keyword handling). The data structures inside the lexical table are optimized for this task and allow fast access to all parts of the lexical table.

- The length of a *terminal symbol* (except keywords) is restricted up to 2 characters. It results simple automata with short chains. *Terminal symbols* with the same start character decreases efficiency. For example, scanning '<' needs in MODULA–2 four operations instead of the simple lex_accept_and_return operation.

- Using character sets for transitions between states simplifies the automaton and allows shorter and faster operation sequences interpreting the automaton.

- The identifier automaton is optimized depending on the keywords:

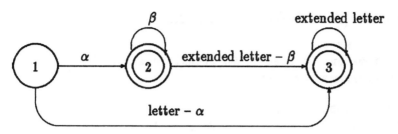

Figure 3: Abstract automaton for identifiers

α is the character set containing all start characters of the keywords. The character set β contains all characters occuring in keywords at any position but not the first. The check for being a keyword occurs only in state 2. Achieving state 3 an identifier cannot be a keyword, and the check would be absurd (and time consuming).

Therefore, if an identifier contains at least one character not included in the character set α or β, the check for being a keyword doesn't appear. In many programming languages it holds for all identifiers containing at least a small letter or a digit.

The abstract program for this automaton in respect of MODULA–2 keywords is

```
state 1:
 lex_goto_state_if_next_in_set
     ABCDEFILMNOPQRSTUVW, 2
 lex_goto_state_if_next_in_set
     GHJKXYZabcdefghijklmnopqrstuvwxyz, 3

state 2:
 lex_accept
 lex_accept_while_in_set
     ACDEFGHILMNOPRSTUVXY
 lex_goto_state_if_next_in_set
     0123456789BJKQWZabcdefghijklmnopqrstuvwxyz, 3
 lex_return_code_if_keyword
 lex_return_code 1
```

```
state 3:
  lex_accept
  lex_accept_while_in_set
      0123456789
      ABCDEFGHIJKLMNOPQRSTUVWXYZabcdefghijklmnopqrstuvwxyz
  lex_return_code 1
```

4.2   Results (for MODULA–2 lexic)[1]

```
lexic table: 2 KByte
  finite automaton: 54 states, 90 transitions
  abstract program: 159 operations

MODULA-2 mix:  2*25 modules
  1 116 525 characters              28 921 lines
    362 894 blanks/EOL             302 854 characters in comments

     99 456 lexical items            4 662 comments (4.7%)
     10 131 keywords (10.2%)        33 794 identifiers (33.98%)

runtime: 230 sec
      7 545 lines/min               4 854 characters/sec
    447 393 operations
      4 662 characters handled more than once (0.42%)
      5 308 identifiers were asked to be a keyword (15.71%)
```

---

[1]time measured on an 8 MHz IBM/AT

A Lexic definition part for MODULA–2

```
                                    (* Character set definitions *)
                                    (* ~~~~~~~~~~~~~~~~~~~~~~~~~~~ *)
<octal digit>        ::= '01234567'                                    ||
<decimal digit>      ::= <octal digit> + '89'                          ||
<hexadecimal digit> ::= <decimal digit> + 'ABCDEFabcdef'               ||
<letter>             ::= 'ABCDEFGHIJKLMNOPQRSTUVWXYZ' +
                         'abcdefghijklmnopqrstuvwxyz'                   ||
<extended letter>    ::= <letter> + <decimal digit>                    ||
<string1 character> ::= ANY - 36C - '"'                                ||
<string2 character> ::= ANY - 36C - 47C                                ||
                                    (* Pseudoterminal declarations *)
                                    (* ~~~~~~~~~~~~~~~~~~~~~~~~~~~~ *)
"IDENTIFIER"         ::= <letter> [<extended letter>]* EXCEPT KEYWORDS ||
"OCTAL_NUMBER"       ::= [<octal digit>]+ 'B'                          ||
"CARD_NUMBER"        ::= [<decimal digit>]+ [FOLLOWED BY '..']         ||
"HEX_NUMBER"         ::= <decimal digit> [<hexadecimal digit>]* 'H'    ||
"REAL_NUMBER"        ::= [<decimal digit>]+ '.' [<decimal digit>]*
                         ['E' [('+'|'-')] [<decimal digit>]+ ]         ||
"CHARACTER"          ::= {'"'} <string1 character> {'"'}                |
                         {47C} <string2 character> {47C}                |
                         [<octal digit>]+ 'C'                          ||
"STRING"             ::= {'"'} [<string1 character>
                         [<string1 character>]+ ] {'"'}                 |
                         {47C} [<string2 character>
                         [<string2 character>]+ ] {47C}                ||
"COMMENT"            ::= {'(*'} [ANY FOLLOWED BY '*)']* {'*)'} NESTED  ||
```

B Minimal perfect hash function for MODULA–2

The hash value must be computed by the following formula:
==

$h := (ORD(c_1) + ORD(c_0)$

$+ g_1[(ORD(c_3) + ORD(c)) \; MOD \; 16]$

$+ g_2[(ORD(c_2) + ORD(c)) \; MOD \; 16]) \; MOD \; 40$

Note: c_0 means length of terminal
      c means blank character (Code = 32)
      (can be eliminated by redefinition of g)

*** RESULTS ***

h	keyword	h	keyword	Nr	g1	g2
0	MOD	20	LOOP	0	0	0
1	NOT	21	FOR	1	9	26
2	FROM	22	VAR	2	27	29
3	MODULE	23	RECORD	3	8	0
4	OF	24	THEN	4	39	0
5	DIV	25	CASE	5	12	7
6	ARRAY	26	QUALIFIED	6	13	3
7	TO	27	IMPLEMENTATION	7	15	0
8	POINTER	28	AND	8	0	4
9	TYPE	29	BY	9	0	1
10	UNTIL	30	OR	10	0	0
11	WITH	31	DO	11	0	0
12	SET	32	END	12	0	32
13	BEGIN	33	ELSE	13	0	20
14	RETURN	34	ELSIF	14	2	1
15	REPEAT	35	CONST	15	19	1
16	WHILE	36	IN			
17	PROCEDURE	37	EXIT			
18	DEFINITION	38	IF			
19	IMPORT	39	EXPORT			

C Basic operations for a deterministic finite automaton interpreter

```
LexEndOfLine                (*                                      *)
LexEndOfFile                (*                                      *)
LexOverreadBlanks           (*                                      *)
LexOverreadUntil            (* <character>                          *)
LexOverreadUntils           (* <character>,    <character>          *)
LexOverreadIfCondUntil      (* <character>                          *)
LexOverreadIfCondUntils     (* <character>,    <character>          *)
LexReadComment              (* <character>,    <character>,         *)
                            (* <character>,    <character>,         *)
                            (* <nested>                             *)
LexAccept                   (*                                      *)
LexReturnCode               (* <lexical code>                       *)
LexAcceptAndReturn          (* <lexical code>                       *)
LexAcceptAndReturnIfNext    (* <character>,    <lexical code>       *)
LexReturnCodeIfNextNot      (* <character>,    <lexical code>       *)
LexAcceptWhileInSet         (* <class>                              *)
LexAcceptWhileNotInSet      (* <class>                              *)
LexReturnCodeIfKeyword      (*                                      *)
LexInsertCharacter          (* <character>                          *)
LexSkipCharacter            (*                                      *)
LexReturnCharacter          (*                                      *)
LexGotoInitialState         (*                                      *)
LexGotoStateIfNext          (* <character>,    <address>            *)
LexGotoStateIfNextNot       (* <character>,    <address>            *)
LexGotoStateIfNextInSet     (* <class>,        <address>            *)
LexGotoStateIfNextNotInSet  (* <class>,        <address>            *)
LexGotoState                (* <address>                            *)
LexError                    (* <error code>                         *)
```

References

[Aho77] Aho, A.V.; Ullman, J.D.:
Principles of Compiler Design
Addison Wesley 1977

[Albinus86] Albinus, M.; Aßmann, W.; Enskonatus, P.:
The INDIA Compiler Generator
Workshop on Compiler Compiler and Incremental Compilation,
iir-reporte 2(1986)12, Berlin 1986, pp. 58–84

[Aßmann85] Aßmann, W.:
Die Metasprache des Compiler-Rahmensystems INDIA
iir-reporte 1(1985)7, Berlin 1985, pp. 8–13

[Aßmann86] Aßmann, W.:
The INDIA System for Incremental Dialog Programming
Workshop on Compiler Compiler and Incremental Compilation,
iir-reporte 2(1986)12, Berlin 1986, pp. 12–34

[Baum88] Baum, M.:
PALM
internal material, IIR, Berlin 1988

[Ernst87] Ernst, Th.:
Eine Implementation des Minimalzyklen-Algorithmus zum Bestimmen
perfekter Hashfunktionen
internal material, IIR, Berlin 1987

[Eulenstein88] Eulenstein, M.:
The POCO Compiler Generating System
Workshop on Compiler Compiler and High Speed Compilation, Berlin
1988

[Grosch88] Grosch, J.:
Generators for High-Speed Front-Ends
Workshop on Compiler Compiler and High Speed Compilation, Berlin
1988

[Heuring86] Heuring, V.P.:
The Automatic Generation of Fast Lexical Analysers
Software — Practice and Experience 16(1986)9, pp. 801–808

[Horspool87] Horspool, R.N.; Levy, M.R.:
Mkscan — An Interactive Scanner Generator
Software — Practice and Experience 17(1987)6, pp. 369–378

[Mössenbeck86] Mössenbeck, H.:
Alex — A Simple and Efficient Scanner Generator
SIGPLAN Notices 21(1986)5, pp. 69–78

[Sager85]   Sager, T.J.:
                Polynomial Time Generator for Minimal Perfect Hash Functions
                Commun. ACM 28(1985)5, pp. 523–532

[Szwillus86]   Szwillus, Gerd.; Hemmer, W.:
                Die automatische Erzeugung effizienter Scanner
                University of Dortmund, Report Nr. 217, 1986

[Waite86]   Waite, W. M.:
                The Cost of Lexical Analysis
                Software — Practice and Experience 16(1986)5, pp. 473–488

ILALR:
AN INCREMENTAL GENERATOR OF LALR(1) PARSERS

R. Nigel Horspool
Department of Computer Science
University of Victoria, P.O. Box 1700
Victoria, B.C., Canada V8W 2Y2

Abstract

An incremental parser generator would be a desirable tool for use in compiler implementation projects or for experimental use in designing new languages. It would allow the tool user to incrementally add or remove production rules from a grammar while maintaining correct parse tables, and would report grammatical problems to the user at the earliest possible moment. ILALR is such an incremental parser generator for the LALR(1) class of grammars. It uses incremental algorithms for computing the LALR(1) parser tables.

Keywords and Key Phrases: parsers, LALR(1), compilers, incremental algorithms.

1. Introduction

In the bottom-up approach to compiler implementation, the compiler writer must create a grammar for the language and attach semantic actions to its production rules. The grammar is prepared in a computer file, typically using a notation based on BNF, and then the compiler writer uses a parser generator to create a parser from the grammar file. Different parser generators accept different classes of grammars. Examples of parser generators include *yacc* [9], *llama* [5] and *lalrgen* [3] which accept the LALR(1) class of grammars, and *llgen* [3] for the LL(1) class of grammars.

The compiler writer can rarely use a published grammar for the language — such a grammar is usually provided in a form more suitable for humans to read. The published grammar may suffer from ambiguities (resolved by separate written explanations), or it may not belong to a grammar class accepted by the available parser generators. Therefore, the compiler writer usually has to go through a process of *grammar debugging*. This is an iterative process of editing the grammar file, executing the parser generator to obtain error messages, re-editing and massaging the grammar rules to remove the problems and re-trying. A programming language designer might also like to ensure that he/she has an unambiguous grammar and this person would use a parser generator to check out and debug potential BNF grammar definitions. Grammar debugging can be a tedious and frustrating experience, especially for novices.

It would appear that the ideal solution to the grammar debugging problem would be an *incremental parser generator*. Such a software tool would operate interactively, permitting the user to modify a grammar one rule at a time and reporting problems to the user as soon as they become apparent. This tool would be more convenient because there is no need to alternate between separate editor and parser generator programs. It would also make it easier for the user to understand problems with the grammar, because the error would be reported immediately the user adds a rule that, for example, causes the grammar to become ambiguous.

There appears to have been little previous work on incremental generation of parsers. For the LR parsing methods, a doctoral dissertation [4] and a forthcoming technical report [6] exist. They are mentioned at the end of this paper. Also, some older work [7,12] has been published on incremental parser generation for the much smaller LL(1) class of grammars.

2. Basic Design Issues

An important issue to be decided is the unit of change for the grammar. At one extreme, we can imagine a tool that re-checks the grammar each time the user changes a single character in the grammar file. At the other extreme, the tool might re-check only after a complete set of production rules with a common left-hand side have been added or removed. We decided that the most convenient unit of change would be one production rule.

But if we re-check after each rule addition or deletion, our tool has to be prepared to accept (temporarily) an incomplete grammar. The symptoms of an incomplete grammar are that some rules may be unreachable and some non-terminal symbols may be useless. Algorithms for detecting (and removing) unreachable rules and useless non-terminals exist [1] and are often included in parser generators. In the case of *ilalr*, these algorithms are only applied at the explicit request of the user or when the user asks for the parser to be generated.

To make *ilalr* as flexible as is reasonably possible, the user is allowed to add or delete production rules in absolutely any order. Furthermore, the start symbol of the grammar can be specified at any time — or even be changed. Nor does *ilalr* require the user to specify which symbols are terminals and which are non-terminals. Why should it, when such information can be inferred from the complete grammar? (But *ilalr* will accept this information and use it for error-checking purposes if the user wishes to provide it.)

3. The General Approach

Suppose that the user has added the following rules to the grammar and has not yet specified a start symbol.

```
S       ::=    begin  SL   end
SL      ::=    SL  ;   STMT
ASMT    ::=    VAR  :=   EXPR
VAR     ::=    ident
```

In this example, S, SL, ASMT and VAR must be non-terminal symbols. But it is unclear whether STMT or even begin represents a terminal or non-terminal symbol. Therefore, *ilalr* assumes that any symbol which does not currently occur on the left-hand side of some rule must be a terminal symbol. To make any sense of the example grammar, we must consider it to define a language of *sentential forms* (as opposed to a language of *sentences* containing only terminal symbols). And in the absence of an explicit declaration, we must consider every non-terminal symbol as a potential goal symbol for the grammar. Thus, the example grammar describes a language that includes the sentential forms:

```
begin SL ; STMT end
begin SL ; STMT ; STMT end
ident := EXPR
etc.
```

In order to handle the multiple potential goal symbols, *ilalr* introduces a fictitious goal symbol S^*, which we call the *supergoal*. For each symbol N that is known to be a non-terminal, *ilalr* adds an implicit production rule

$$S^* \rightarrow \$_N \, N \, \$_N$$

where $\$_N$ represents a unique delimiter symbol. Normal grammar analysis techniques can be applied to the augmented grammar using S^* as the goal symbol. Unique delimiters are required around all the non-terminals because of potential conflicts during LR analysis.

While a grammar is incomplete, *ilalr* cannot know for certain whether a symbol is nullable or not. All the user has to add is one a rule like

```
X        ::=     <empty>
```

which causes X and, perhaps, several other symbols to suddenly become nullable. *Ilalr* assumes that all symbols are non-nullable unless nullability can be deduced from the grammar rules. The opposite approach of assuming all symbols to be nullable would cause many spurious error messages to be reported while a grammar is being developed.

4. Incremental LALR(1) Algorithms

Ilalr implements incremental forms of LALR(1) parser generator algorithms. At all times, it maintains the LR(0) sets of items for the grammar and a LALR(1) lookahead set for each item. To help compute the lookahead sets, *ilalr* also maintains a set *NULL* that contains all the symbols known to be nullable and it maintains starters sets for the symbols. The starters set for symbol X, *START(X)*, is defined as $\{ Y \mid X \Rightarrow^* Y \alpha \}$.

4.1. Addition of a New Rule

When a new rule, $A ::= X1 \, X2 \, ... \, Xn \, (n \geq 0)$, is added to a grammar G, a new grammar G′ is created. If we consider a grammar G to be defined by the quadruple <T, N, P, S>, then G′ is a modified quadruple <T′, N′, P′, S′>, where

$$
\begin{aligned}
N' &= N \cup \{ A \} \\
T' &= T \cup \{ \$_A, X1, X2, ..., Xn \} - N' \\
S' &= S^* \\
P' &= P \cup \{ A \rightarrow X1 \, X2 \, ... \, Xn, \ S^* \rightarrow \$_A \, A \, \$_A \}
\end{aligned}
$$

Note that G and G′ represent the grammars actually being analyzed by *ilalr* rather than the grammar as entered by the user. That is, G and G′ include the extra symbols and implicit goal production rules that are added by *ilalr*. If *ilalr* starts with an initially empty grammar, $<\phi, \phi, S^*, \phi>$, then the grammar held by *ilalr* after a sequence of rule additions is completely determined.

Algorithms for computing NULL, START and LALR lookahead sets are simplified by the observation that these sets grow monotonically when new rules are added to the grammar. However (unless some unnatural definitions are used), we cannot consider the graph of states for the LR(0) recognizer as growing monotonically.

In particular, *ilalr* can use a simple iterative algorithm for recomputing NULL, the set of nullable symbols, after a rule addition. (The algorithm is so simple that it is omitted.)

If it turns out that NULL' = NULL, there is a simple algorithm for updating the starters sets. It is expressed by the following equations:

$$\text{START}'(C) = \begin{cases} \text{START}(C) \cup \text{START}(X1\,X2\cdots Xn) & \text{if } A \in START(C) \\ \text{START}(C) & \text{otherwise} \end{cases}$$

where we use a definition of START extended by:

$$\text{START}(Y1\,Y2\cdots Yk) = \begin{cases} \text{START}(Y1) & \text{if } Y1 \notin NULL' \text{ and } k \geq 2 \\ \text{START}(Y1) \cup \text{START}(Y2\cdots Yk) & \text{if } Y1 \in NULL' \text{ and } k \geq 2 \end{cases}$$

We do not have such an efficient algorithm to handle the situation when NULL' ≠ NULL. In this case, *ilalr* uses a simple iterative algorithm, taking advantage of the monotonic nature of the problem.

Updating the LR(0) sets of items for the grammar is less trivial. The LR(0) recognizers for G' and G are closely related; in that for every state in G we can find one or more corresponding states in G'. But there does not appear to be an easy algorithm to tell when a state in G must map to two or more states in G'. Here is an example. Suppose that G is the grammar

```
S       : : =    C      |     D     |     E
C       : : =    a  A  b
D       : : =    a  e  c
B       : : =    e  d
E       : : =    f  D
```

Now, amongst about 20 other states, the LR(0) recognizer for G will include the states and transitions shown below.

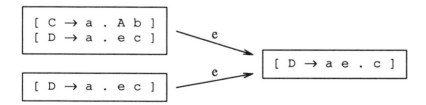

If we now add the rule, 'A ::= B', the corresponding states in the new LR(0) recognizer are

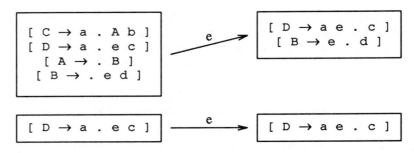

That is, the state on the right has split to become two states. But if the 'B ::= e d' rule had not been in the grammar, the state would not have split. This demonstrates that we cannot determine how to update the set of items for a state or whether to split that state unless we have already updated all the predecessor states.

The incremental algorithm implemented in *ilalr* begins by using an approximate method for modifying sets of items. It is approximate because it does not split states, implying that not all the states needed for the new recognizer are created, and it may create some sets of items that do not correspond to any states in the new recognizer. Missing states must be added by invoking a state closure algorithm. Extraneous sets of items are removed by a marking algorithm that checks to see which states are reachable from the start state. (Unless memory is in short supply, there is no need to invoke the marking algorithm after every rule addition.) As long as the mapping process performs a reasonably accurate job, the overall efficiency is not badly compromised by the creation of unreachable states. In essence, the mapping algorithm simply checks the item sets associated with each state and (incrementally) re-performs the item closure operation. Thus, if the set of items for some state contains an item of the form [X → α . A β], we add the new closure item [A → . X1 X2...Xn] (and more closure items if X1 is a non-terminal symbol). Addition of closure items is implemented by an iterative algorithm based on a worklist implementation.

Updating the LALR(1) lookahead sets is a difficult problem because these sets do not necessarily grow monotonically. After a rule addition, some sets may contract in size. Informally, this occurs when a state in the old recognizer is split — and then the old lookahead set is shared between the two new recognizer states. Our solution is to operate under the assumption that the lookahead sets cannot contract in size (but be prepared to correct the situation). *Ilalr* uses a simple worklist-oriented algorithm. In this algorithm, a change to the lookahead set for one item in a state ST causes that change to be propagated to closure items in the same state and causes affected states reached by transitions from ST to be added to the worklist (and thus they will later be updated themselves).

If a LALR(1) conflict is discovered in some state, this conflict may have been caused by our incorrect assumption, above. In this case, *ilalr* clears all the lookahead sets to empty and re-computes them correctly (using the worklist algorithm). The user is warned of a problem with the grammar only if the conflict still exists after the re-computation. It should be noted that this re-computation of lookahead sets is never required for a SLR(1) grammar.

4.2. Removing a Production Rule

Deletion of a rule from the grammar is a little harder to implement than addition, and the algorithms are also less efficient. But, since rule deletion is likely to be a less frequent occurrence than rule addition, the asymmetry in efficiency is not relevant. Here, in outline, are the methods used in *ilalr* to handle deletion of a rule, A → X1 X2...Xn, from the grammar. First, no update to the NULL set is required if A is currently non-nullable or if one of X1, X2, ... Xn is non-nullable. Otherwise, *ilalr* recomputes NULL from scratch.

Modification of the START sets can be performed reasonably efficiently if no symbols change their nullability because of the deletion. The updates are performed in two stages. First, if START(X) contains A, for any X, then the members of START(A) are all removed from START(X). However, this will usually remove too many elements and then an iterative algorithm (the same one mentioned for the action of adding a rule) is used to re-check the sets and add missing elements back.

Updating the LR(0) recognizer requires removal of some states and slimming many item sets down. Using an approach similar to that used for adding a rule to the grammar, we perform an approximate mapping process. The process considers kernel and completion items separately. Any kernel items formed from the deleted rule, with the marker in any position, are removed. All completion items formed from the deleted rule are deleted and any closure items for deleted items are themselves removed. As before, we must perform a state closure operation to add missing states and a reachability analysis is required to remove unreachable states.

The LALR(1) lookahead sets are computed only for items in new states that are added by the state closure step, above. This is likely to result in many lookahead sets containing extra elements (but not sets will be missing any elements). If the extra elements subsequently cause a conflict to be detected, the lookahead sets will be re-computed before any error is reported to the user.

5. The User Interface

The *ilalr* program includes interactive commands for these operations — rule addition; rule deletion; setting/changing the goal symbol; defining symbols to be terminals; reading commands from an external file; writing the current grammar and definitions to an external file; creating an external LALR(1) parse table file; checking the grammar for completeness; parsing a sample sentence; listing the grammar, its symbols, all rules with a particular left-hand side, the NULL set, the START sets, or the states of the LALR(1) recognizer.

As far as possible, the user commands adopt the notation used by the *yacc* parser generator on UNIX systems. Some features of *yacc*, such as declaratrion of operator precedences, are not supported by *ilalr*. But if the user avoids using the unsupported features, the same grammar file can be processed by either *yacc* or *ilalr*.

If the user adds a rule which causes a LALR(1) conflict, a brief message is generated which reports this fact. Although the conflict cannot go away if the user continues to add new rules, the warning message will not be repeated. However, as long as a conflict exists in the grammar, a different kind of input prompt is used to remind the user of the problem. The user can enter a special command at any time which asks *ilalr* to display example sentences that illustrate conflicts in the grammar.

The output from any command that generates more than a few lines of output is piped through the UNIX *more* pager program. Thus the user can, for example, easily scan forward to a particular state in a listing of the parser states. (If the *less* pager is used, backward scanning is also possible.)

If a grammar is complete and free of conflicts, the user can create an external file that contains a machine-readable representation of the LR recognizer. A separate program, *mkparser*, is provided for translating that file into an executable LALR(1) parser. This parser interfaces with scanners created by *lex*[10] or *mkscan* [8].

6. Experience

At the time of writing, *ilalr* has been in use for about one year and has already been used successfully by two classes of undergraduate students taking a compiler construction course. All the students found the incremental approach to grammar analysis easy to understand. Those students who had had experience with other parser generators (typically *yacc*) remarked on how much easier *ilalr* was to use.

In terms of machine resource consumption, *ilalr* is relatively inefficient compared to competing tools such as *yacc*. For the analysis of a complete grammar, *ilalr* consumes considerably more CPU time than *yacc*. And because sizes of internal tables cannot be determined by a pre-pass through the grammar, less memory-efficient data structures must be used by *ilalr*. Another point that becomes apparent to the user when rules are read in from a file is that the amount of CPU time needed to process a new rule grows with the size of the grammar. Empirically, the maximum time required to process one new rule is approximately proportional to the square of the grammar size, but most rules are processed quickly. A new rule that causes several symbols to become nullable is particularly slow to process. But, even with a moderately large grammar (say 200 productions), *ilalr* executing on a SUN 3/280 can process an additional rule faster than the user can type it. As an experimental observation, a grammar for the C language containing 219 production rules requires almost exactly three times as much CPU time with *ilalr* as with *yacc*.

The approximate procedure used to re-build the LR(0) recognizer after a rule addition turns out to be surprisingly effective. For example, when *ilalr* read 83 rules from a test grammar (a grammar based on Wirth's PL/0 language), a recognizer with 241 states was eventually constructed. But in the course of building the 83 different recognizers, a total of only 40 unreachable states were created. The unreachable states only had to be removed when the final version of the parser tables were output.

7. Comparison with Other Work

Heering, Klint and Rekers [6] have a Lisp implementation of an incremental parser generator. It is intended for use by language designers. Their implementation uses a 'lazy evaluation' approach which constructs the LR(0) states only as they are needed during a parse. Lookahead sets to resolve parser conflicts are not computed. Instead, a parallel parsing algorithm which attempts to follow all possible parses is used. For interactive testing of languages and grammars, this is an excellent approach. But it is unsuitable for use as a compiler construction tool because the complete set of parser states is not necessarily available and because the parallel parsing algorithm is too inefficient for use in a production compiler.

The PhD dissertation of Fischer [4] describes an incremental parser generator, implemented in PL/I, that is similar in nature to *ilalr*. In some respects, his parser generator is more powerful because it handles the full LR(1) class of grammars. It, too, uses an approximate technique for computing the lookahead sets, using the infamous NQLALR method [2] for this purpose. If a conflict is detected, the correct lookahead sets are re-computed using Pager's lane tracing method [11]. If the conflict still exists afterwards but can be eliminated by splitting states, the states are split (thus the full LR(1) class of grammars can be handled). Without access to his implementation, it is hard to make any comparisons between Fischer's methods and those used in *ilalr*. It certainly appears that Fischer did not provide an interactive interface for his implementation.

8. Conclusions

As computers become faster, it seems to be an inescapable (and desirable) trend for software to become interactive and incremental in nature. We have already seen text editing software progress from batch mode editors to interactive line editors to interactive screen-oriented editors like *vi* or *emacs*. WYSIWYG word processing is another example of this trend. *Ilalr* represents the first incremental and interactive software tool applied to grammar analysis and parser generation. The design of *ilalr* has raised some interesting issues and its implementation has required the invention of new algorithms for LALR(1) grammar analysis.

Further work is needed to improve the user interface — perhaps to integrate it with an intelligent editor like *emacs* so that more sophisticated editing operations than adding or deleting one production to/from the grammar can be supported (without the user having to learn a new editing language). Further investigation is needed into finding efficient incremental algorithms; some of the algorithms used by *ilalr* could be improved. Also, it might be worthwhile to investigate whether it would be easier and, if so, how much easier it would be to handle a smaller class of grammars, such as the SLR(1) or LL(1) classes.

References

[1] Aho, A.V., and J.D. Ullman. *The Theory of Parsing, Translation and Compiling.* Prentice-Hall, 1972.

[2] DeRemer, F.L., and T.J. Pennello. Efficient Computation of LALR(1) Look-Ahead Sets. ACM Trans. on Prog. Lang. and Systems, 4, 4 (Oct. 1982), pp. 615-649.

[3] Fischer, C.N., and R.J. LeBlanc Jr. *Crafting a Compiler.* Benjamin/Cummings, Menlo Park, 1988.

[4] Fischer, G. Incremental LR(1) Parser Construction as an Aid to Syntactical Extensibility. PhD Dissertation, Tech. Report 102, University of Dortmund, 1980.

[5] Hayes, I., and K. Robinson. A Tutorial on Llama: A Pascal Translator Generator. Dept. of Computer Science, Univ. of New South Wales, June 1985.

[6] Heering, J., P. Klint and J. Rekers. Incremental generation of Parsers. Technical Report (to appear), Centre for Mathematics and Computer Science,

Amsterdam, 1988.

[7]   Heindel, L.E., and J.T. Roberto. LANGPAK — An Interactive Language Design System. American Elsevier, New York, 1975.

[8]   Horspool, R.N., and M.R. Levy. Mkscan — An Interactive Scanner Generator. Software — Pract. and Exp. 17, 6 (June 1987), pp. 369-378.

[9]   Johnson, S.C. Yacc — Yet Another Compiler-Compiler. Computer Science Tech. Report 32, Bell Laboratories, 1975.

[10] Lesk, M.E., and E. Schmidt. Lex — A Lexical Analyzer Generator. Computer Science Tech. Report 39, Bell Laboratories, 1975.

[11] Pager, D. The Lane Tracing Algorithm and Ways of Enhancing Its Efficiency. Inf. Science 12, 1 (1977), pp. 19-42.

[12] Vidart, J. Extensions Syntaxiques dans une Contexte. PhD Dissertation, Département d'informatique, Université of Grenoble, 1974.

Type Checking in the Large

Michael R. Levy
Department of Computer Science
University of Victoria
P.O. Box 1700
Victoria, B.C.
Canada V8W 2Y2

1 Introduction

The larger a software system, the more important it is to maintain
consistency between module interfaces and the use of modules. Type
checking is an important technique for ensuring this consistency. Static
type checking (that is, type checking prior to run-time) is especially
attractive because it allows errors to be detected with no run-time cost. For
this reason, most program-language designers pay very careful attention to
their type system. The ideal is to design a type system which is flexible
enough to support algorithm development but which is secure. Secure
means that it is possible to guarantee that a procedure will not be given an
invalid type of data.

Type checking is straight-forward for most reasonable constructs if the
entire program source is available at type-checking time. However, in the
presence of separate compilation, this requirement is not reasonable. Some
languages therefore abandon any attempt to type-check across module
boundaries.

An alternative to supplying the entire source is to provide at least the
interface (and perhaps some type definitions) to the type-checker of the user
of a module. One of the disadvantages to this approach is the addition to
the system of an extra object to be maintained (the interface). Care has to
be taken to ensure that the user and the module itself agree on the interface.
Polymorphism introduces an extra complications which will be described
later in the paper.

We present here a new strategy for static type checking. This strategy ensures type security but removes from the programmer the need to include interface source in user programs.

2 A brief description of the strategy

A large piece of software can be represented as a directed, acyclic graph where nodes represent modules and edges represent a relationship between modules. The relationship is called 'uses' and the the edge is from the user to the used module. For example, if a module A contains calls to procedures in a module B, then this can be represented by the simple graph

$$A \rightarrow B$$

We say "A uses B". Objects such as variables within a module can be classified as being *free* or *bound*. Objects are bound in a module if there is a declaration of the type of the object within the module. All other objects are free. Given a module A it is simple to determine the set of free objects in the module. The types of the bound objects and the use made of the free objects impose constraints on the possible types of the free objects. For many programming languages there exists an algorithm that can infer the set of free objects in a module together with constraints on the types of each free object in the set. The output of this algorithm is called the **imports list** of the module. The type information about all bound objects within a module is called an **exports list**. Type checking is performed by attempting to unify the imports list of a module with the union of the exports list of all the modules it uses. Failure to unify is a type error.

This strategy is useful because it does not require the maintenance of common include files. It is also makes it possible to use type information for the purpose of creating software versions. It diminishes compile time because it can reduce the need to recompile modules that use modules that have been changed.

An algorithm for creating imports lists for Pascal has been previously reported[1]. Interesting questions are raised, however, by programming languages that support generic modules or polymorphic data types and modules.

It is not possible to compile generic modules efficiently because the size of the parameters is unspecified. However, it is reasonable to compile instances of a module, since any particular project is likely to use a manageable number of instances. The type checking algorithm therefore assumes that all 'imported' generic types are known before unification is attempted. In practice this is done by proceeding top-down from the top-level program.

3 A type description language

A **type description** is defined as follows:
There is a set of objects B called *base types*, a set of objects V *called Variables* and a set of objects U called *unknowns*. Each $b \in B$ and each $u \in U$ is a type description. If T_1 and T_2 are type descriptions and $t \in$ V then

$$T_1 \times T_2, \quad T_1 \to T_2, \quad \lambda t . T_1, \quad bt$$

are type descriptions.

λ-notation is used to denote the types of objects if they are generic (or polymorphic). For example,

$$f : \lambda t . \text{list } t \to t$$

is a proposition saying that f is a polymorphic function. *list* in this example is a type constructor.

4 Separate type checking without polymorphism

Type checking is performed at link time. Associated with each module is an imports list and an exports list. Type checking succeeds if each module's imports list can be unified with the exports list of all the modules it uses.

Example

Suppose that

$$A \rightarrow B$$

and that A has imports list

$$f : \alpha \times \beta \rightarrow char$$
$$g : int \rightarrow \alpha$$
$$g : int \rightarrow \beta$$

Also, suppose that the exports list of B is

f: int × int → char
g: int → real
g: int → char
g: int → int

Clearly the unifier is

$$\alpha \Leftarrow int$$
$$\beta \Leftarrow int$$

This algorithm is a simplified version of Milner's type-inference algorithm[2]. The differences are that
1. No inference is taking place - we assume that the types of routines are fully declared; and
2. The variables in Milner's algorithm are type variables. Here they are more like 'unknowns'. This distinction becomes more obvious when polymorphic procedures are allowed.

A key question is this: Can modules be compiled without access to complete type information of the imported procedures? If the answer to the question is no, then the language cannot properly support separate type-checking. For the programming language C, the answer to the question is yes. One construct in the programming language Pascal does create a problem, namely *var* parameters. The difficulty is that in expressions like *f(x)* it is not possible to determine whether *x* denotes an expression or a variable without access to the formal heading of *f*. One possible solution to this problem is to modify the syntax of Pascal so that call-by-variable is noted at the actual call, by using the keyword **var**, for example. This would in any case increase program readability.

The algorithm for determining the requirement is dependent on the grammar of expressions. For our purposes, assume

$$e ::= c \mid v \mid f(\ ) \mid f(e) \mid f(e,e)$$

where *c* is a literal constant, *v* an identifier and *f* a procedure name. Then we can define a procedure Req(e) as follows:

1. If *e* is *c* or *v* , then
    $$Re\ q(e) = \{e : \alpha\}$$

    where a is a variable ranging over type descriptions. The **result type** of *e* is a.

2. If *e* is *f()* , then
    $$Re\ q(e) = \{f : void \rightarrow \alpha\}$$

    The result type of *e* is a.

3. If e_1 is f(e_2) then
    $$Re\ q(e_1) = \{f : \alpha_0 \rightarrow \alpha_1\}$$

    where a_0 is the result type of e_2, and a_1 is a new unknown. The result type of e_1 is a_1.

4.

    $$Re\ q(f(e_1,e_2)) = \{f : \alpha_0 \times \alpha_1 \rightarrow \alpha_2\} \cup Re\ q(e_1) \cup Re\ q(e_2)$$

where a_0 is the result type of e_1, a_1 is the result type of e_2 and a_2 is new. The result
type is a_2.

The 'accuracy' of the type information determined by Req can be improved by using symbol table information.

5 Separate type checking with polymorphism

Our approach to polymorphic procedures is to regard them as templates for a family of possible instantiations. If $f:\lambda t.T$, and u is a type, them we will denote by f_u the instantiation of f of type $[u/t]T$. Only instances of polymorphic procedures are compiled. When a module is compiled, it is possible to determine which instances of its imported polymorphic procedures are required provided that the module being compiled has been fully instantiated. This suggests that initial compilation must proceed top-down, with instance requests being generated after each module compilation. Whenever a module is recompiled, new instance requests must be generated. Further instances may then need to be compiled. In practise, type parameter changes are not very common during software development, so there is not a frequent need for instance compilation.

If the requirement that only instantiated modules be compiled is met, then imports lists can be built using the algorithm given in the previous section. The unification step is, however, more complicated, because exported types may be polymorphic. For example, suppose that a module A has this imports list:

$f : list\ \alpha \rightarrow int$
$g : char\ \rightarrow \alpha$

and that a module B, used by A, has this exports list:

$f : \lambda t\ .list\ t \rightarrow t$
$g : char\ \rightarrow char$
$g : char\ \rightarrow int$

In this case, f must be instantiated to

$$f_{int} : list \ int \rightarrow int$$

before unification can be applied (getting $\alpha \Leftarrow int$).

The type-checking process can be described in the following way:

The **order** of a procedure p of type T is the number of outer-most λ-bindings of T. A non-polymorphic procedure has order 0. If p:T and p has order n, then it is possible to find an instance p' of order 0 of type $T(a_1,a_2,...,a_k)$ where each a_i is a type description.

If $E = (p_1 : T_1 ,...,p_n : T_n)$ is an exports list, then there is an obvious way to extend the notion of instantiation to the entire list. We will denote the instantiation of E that uses $(a_1,a_2,...,a_n)$ by $E(a_1,a_2,...,a_n)$.

A module is **type correct** with respect to an export list E iff there is an instance $I=E(a_1,a_2,...,a_n)$ of E such that the imports list of A unifies with I.

6 Abstractions

If a programming language supports an abstraction mechanism, such as **type** in Pascal, then each variable in a program has an abstract type and a concrete type. The above algorithms can be modified to deal with concrete types in a fairly simple way. The details are somewhat tedious, so the algorithm will only be outlined here. Firstly, the definition of type expressions is extended so that base types have two parts: an abstract type and a concrete type. For example

A: Matrix{Sparse}

Then we define a 'concretize' function on type expressions as follows: If $\rho : R \rightarrow T$ is an abstraction and t is a type description, then C_ρ is the function that extends

$$C_\rho (T \{ R \})= R$$

and

$$C_\rho (U \{ S \})= U \{ S \}$$

to arbitrary type descriptions.

Before seeking the match between a requirement and an environment, all procedures supplied by a module are concretized with respect to the abstractions they provide. The rest of the algorithm proceeds as before. It is also possible to look for an abstract match if the concrete one fails, thereby allowing a module to provide procedures that work at either the concrete level or the abstract level.

7 Conclusions

The algorithm presented here belongs to the class of type-inference algorithms. It is a very generous algorithm in the sense that it will allow type matches where most other systems would not. Consider the following example[3]: Suppose that

$$G : \lambda t . \lambda u . t \times (u \to int) \to int$$

Furthermore, suppose that the body of G contains the expression f(x) where x and f are the formal parameters of G. A system that validates the types of procedures independently of their use must fail because of a call such as G(3,g) where

$$g : char \to int$$

This call appears to satisfy the type requirement of G, but execution of G will fail since the actual call g(3) is not correct. In the system presented here, an instance of the module containing G is checked for each actual call of G. The instance for G(3,g) will fail because

$$f : char \to int$$

does not unify with

$$f : int \to int$$

However, if the type of the actual parameter g was

$$int \to int$$

the corresponding module instance would pass the type-checking test.

This strategy presented here is useful because it does not require the maintenance of common include files. It also diminishes compile time because it can reduce the need to recompile modules that use modules that have been changed.

Acknowledgement

This research was supported by a grant from The Natural Sciences and Engineering Research Council of Canada.

References

[1] Michael R. Levy Type checking, separate compilation and reusability. In *Proc. of the SIGPLAN '84 Conf. on Compilers*, pp 285-289, June 1984, Montreal.

[2] R. Milner. A theory of type polymorphism in programming. *J. Computer and Systems Sciencces, 17:348-375, 1978.*

[3] Sophia Drossopoulou. *Private Communication.*

A Compiler Generator
for Attribute Evaluation During LR Parsing

Jorma Tarhio

University of Helsinki
Department of Computer Science
Teollisuuskatu 23, SF-00510 Helsinki, Finland

Abstract

A compiler generator called Metauncle is introduced. Metauncle produces one-pass compilers in which all attributes are evaluated in conjunction with LR parsing. The description of a language is given to Metauncle as an L-attributed grammar, and the system transforms it before generation of an evaluator to another attribute grammar satisfying the requirements for evaluation. The transformed grammar belongs to the class of so-called uncle-attributed grammars. Besides general information about the system, the definition of uncle-attributed grammars, the idea of the grammar transformation and the default rules of the specification language are presented.

1. Introduction

The evaluation of inherited attributes is difficult in conjunction with LR parsing because the upper part of the derivation tree is incomplete during parsing and thus the tree structure cannot be used to convey values of inherited attributes. There are several methods [Wat77, JoM80, Tar82, Poh83, Mel84, SIN85] to cope with the situation. In the following, we will consider one of these, the uncle method introduced in [Tar82]. The uncle method requires that all the semantic rules for inherited attributes are copy

---

The work was supported by the Academy of Finland.

rules, which simplifies evaluation considerably, because then the attribute evaluator will be able to refer to the values of inherited attributes as copies of values of synthesized attributes associated with the roots of the completed subtrees.

We will introduce a new compiler generator Metauncle [Tar88b], which generates analyzers that evaluate all attributes during LR parsing according to the uncle method. The description of a language is given to Metauncle as an L-attributed grammar, and the system transforms it to another attribute grammar suitable for generation of an evaluator. The transformed grammar belongs to the class of so-called uncle-attributed grammars [Tar82, Tar88a].

The Metauncle system has been implemented using the compiler generator HLP84 [KNP88, KEL88]. A prototype of Metauncle was operational on a Burroughs B7800 in December 1986; the present version is now running on a VAX 8800/8300 under VMS.

The rest of the paper is organized as follows. In Section 2, general information of Metauncle is given. Default rules of the specification language are explained in Section 3. Uncle-attributed grammars are defined in Section 4, and the details of the grammar transformation are explained in Section 5. Finally, experiences of the system are described in Section 6.

2. General description

Metauncle consists of two processors: one performs the grammar transformation and the other generates an attribute evaluator from the transformed grammar. These processors have been implemented using the compiler generator HLP84 [KNP88, KEL88] by describing both of them as an attribute grammar. The implementation language of Metauncle and the generated compilers is Pascal.

The specification language for Metauncle has a traditional form. Attributes, grammar symbols and names of external types are declared before the attributed productions. Productions are given in the BNF-form. Present version of the specification language is slightly modified from the form presented in [Tar88b].

The example grammar in Fig. 1 is written in the specification language and it describes a simple block-structured language. A block consists of two lists: a declaration list and a use list. The function INIT initializes the symbol table, CONC stores a new identifier to the symbol table and CHECK examines whether a used identifier has been properly declared.

```
TYPES
    SYMBOLID;
    SYMBOLTABLE

ATTRIBUTES
    ID: SYNTHESIZED SYMBOLID;
    EI: INHERITED SYMBOLTABLE;
    ES: SYNTHESIZED SYMBOLTABLE

GRAMMAR SYMBOLS
    P; B(EI); DL(EI;ES); D(EI;ES); SL(EI); S(EI); IDENT(ID)

PRODUCTIONS
    P = B               RULES B.EI := INIT() END;
    B = 'BEGIN' DL ';' SL 'END'
                        RULES DL.EI := B.EI;
                              SL.EI := DL.ES END;
    DL = D              RULES D.EI := DL.EI;
                              DL.ES := D.ES END;
    DL = DL ',' D       RULES DL_2.EI := DL.EI;
                              D.EI := DL_2.ES;
                              DL.ES := D.ES END;
    D = 'DECL' IDENT    RULES D.ES := ADD(D.EI,IDENT.ID) END;
    SL = S              RULES S.EI := SL.EI END;
    SL = SL ',' S       RULES SL_2.EI := SL.EI;
                              S.EI := SL.EI END;
    S =  B              RULES B.EI := S.EI END;
    S = 'USE' IDENT     RULES CHECK(S.EI,IDENT.ID) END
```

Fig. 1. Example grammar.

When generating a compiler for a language, the user gives to Metauncle an attribute grammar, external declarations containing constants, variables and semantic functions (in Pascal) and a lexical description. From the attribute grammar Metauncle produces an attribute evaluator. While compiling of a target compiler, the evaluator and the external declarations are merged with a skeleton compiler, which is a modification of that one used for target compilers in the HLP84 system. A parser for the target compiler is produced with the same parser generator used in the HLP84 system. The default type of a parser is a table-driven LALR(1) parser, but the generator is also capable to make some other kinds of LR parsers, see [KEL88]. The lexical description is given in a separate file in the form used in HLP84 [KNP88].

In a compiler generated by Metauncle, attribute evaluation is directed by an LR parser. All evaluation actions are carried out in conjunction with reductions. To save space, storage areas for attributes are deallocated after the last reference to them.

3. Default rules

In the specification language, all copy rules of a grammar need not to be presented. So the list of productions with semantic rules in Fig. 2 is equivalent with the complete form given in Fig. 1. This is a new feature added to the latest version of Metauncle.

```
P = B                    RULES B.EI := INIT() END;
B = 'BEGIN' DL ';' SL 'END';
DL = D                   ;
DL = DL ',' D            ;
D = 'DECL' IDENT         RULES D.ES := ADD(D.EI,IDENT.ID) END;
SL = S                   ;
SL = SL ',' S            ;
S =  B                   ;
S = 'USE' IDENT          RULES CHECK(S.EI,IDENT.ID) END
```

Fig. 2. Productions without default rules.

The principles for default rules are based on the L-attributedness of the input grammar and on the following name convention. An inherited and a synthesized attribute symbol are assumed to represent the same global structure, if their names are the same except the last letter, which is i for an inherited symbol and s for a synthesized symbol. Thus inherited $envi$ and synthesized $envs$ are, for example, assumed to be used for the same purpose.

The right-hand side of a default copy rule for an output occurrence is the previous input occurrence of the same kind in the standard evaluation order for L-attributed grammars.

More formally, let us consider a production $X_0 \to X_1 X_2 ... X_n$. If X_k, $k > 0$, has an inherited attribute $X_k.$<a>i with no explicit semantic rule, the right-hand side of the default rule for $X_k.$<a>i is the first existing attribute occurrence of $X_{k-1}.$<a>s, ..., $X_1.$<a>s and $X_0.$<a>i. If X_0 has a synthesized attribute $X_0.$<a>s with no explicit semantic rule, the right-hand side of the default rule for $X_0.$<a>s is the first existing attribute occurrence of $X_n.$<a>s, ..., $X_1.$<a>s and $X_0.$<a>i.

In practical L-attributed grammars, the default rules seem to cover 75 % of all semantic rules.

4. Uncle-attributed grammars

The Metauncle system transforms an L-attributed input grammar to an uncle-attributed grammar from which an attribute evaluator is generated. We will define uncle-attributed grammars following mainly the notations of [Tar88a]. An introduction to the subject can be found in Section 3.1 in [Tar82].

In uncle-attributed grammars, the semantic rules for inherited attributes are restricted to copy rules, and then the values of inherited attributes are available as copies of values of synthesized attributes associated with the roots of the completed subtrees. Let us consider the situation described in Fig. 3. Just after the LR parsing of the subtree B has been finished, the nonterminal B will be in the parsing stack until the reduction by $A \to BC$ is performed, and the value of the synthesized attribute $B.b$ can be used for the values of inherited attributes $C.c$ and $E.e$ provided that the relevant semantic rules for $C.c$ and $E.e$ are copy rules. The synthesized attribute $B.b$ can be used even if B were not just on the top of the stack like in the situation described.

151

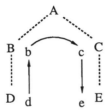

Fig. 3. Use of uncles.

We define a *copy relation*, denoted $\underline{C}$, on the set of the attribute symbols of the grammar as follows: $b\ \underline{C}\ c$, if there is a semantic rule $X_i.c :=$ $X_j.b$ in a production $X_0{\to}X_1...X_n$, where c is an inherited attribute symbol. When $b\ \underline{C}^+\ c$, we say that c is *copy-dependent* on b. Let b and d be inherited and s be synthesized. If $s\ \underline{C}\ d\ \underline{C}^*\ b$ and $X_i.d := X_j.s$ is a copy rule in $X_0{\to}X_1...X_n$, we say that the grammar symbol X_j is an *uncle symbol* of b and $X_j.s$ is an *uncle attribute* of b. In Fig. 3, the nonterminal B is an uncle symbol of the inherited attribute symbol e, and $B.b$ is an uncle attribute of e. In Fig. 3 an explanation can be seen for the term "uncle", for the uncle symbol of e is a left brother of an ancestor of the node with which e is associated.

The evaluation strategy can be described with these concepts. All the evaluation actions are applied to synthesized attributes and carried out in conjunction with the reductions. Let us study a parsing situation $(\beta\alpha, u)$, where the reduction by $A{\to}\alpha$ is the next parsing action. In conjunction with this reduction we will evaluate all the synthesized attributes of A using the values of the synthesized attributes associated with α (we assume those attributes have been evaluated before the current situation) and the values of the inherited attributes of A. The value of an inherited attribute $A.b$ is got from a synthesized attribute associated with the rightmost uncle symbol of b in β (i.e. the topmost uncle symbol of b in the parsing stack). Note that the inherited attributes themselves are never evaluated; their values are available only as copies of the values of synthesized attribute instances.

Definition. An L-attributed grammar G is *uncle-attributed*, if the conditions U1, U2 and U3 are satisfied.

U1. All semantic rules for inherited attributes are copy rules.

U2. If $X_0 \rightarrow X_1...X_n$ is a production with a copy rule $X_j.b := X_i.c$, where $0 \le i < j \le n$, then for every inherited attribute symbol d, such that $b \underline{C}^* d$, none of the grammar symbols $X_{i+1}, ..., X_{j-1}$ is an uncle symbol of d.

U3. An inherited attribute symbol is copy-dependent on only one of the synthesized attribute symbols associated with its uncle symbol.

The first condition fixes the form of semantic rules for inherited attributes, and the last condition ensures that we can use the values of uncle attributes unambiguously. The second condition deals with two kinds of copy rules for inherited attributes, where the right-hand side $X_i.c$ is either a synthesized attribute occurrence when $i > 0$ or an inherited attribute occurrence when $i = 0$. This condition guarantees that the topmost uncle symbol of d in the parsing stack will be used. In Fig. 4 there is a counter-example, where the grammar symbol B is an uncle symbol of d. The attribute $C.d$ gets its value from an uncle attribute attached to the occurrence of B which is not the topmost (rightmost) one.

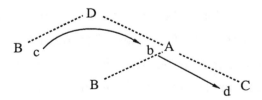

Fig. 4. Conflict against U2.

Theorem. All the attributes of an uncle-attributed LR(k) grammar G can be evaluated during LR parsing.

Proof. See [Tar88a].

5. Uncle transformation

An L-attributed grammar must be transformed to the uncle-attributed form before the generation of an evaluator. In this transformation called the uncle transformation, the conflicts against conditions U1, U2 and U3 are removed one at a time. This requires insertions of new marker nonterminals generating the empty string into the grammar.

Though the uncle transformation can make every L-attributed LR grammar uncle-attributed, it is not guaranteed that the grammar is any more LR after the transformation because of the marker nonterminals. For example, we cannot enter such a nonterminal in front of the right-hand side of a left-recursive production. However, the parsing conflicts do not seem to be very usual in the case of practical grammars. We will return to this subject later on.

The transformation consists of five phases. The first phase makes an L-attributed input grammar satisfy U1, i.e. all semantic rules for inherited attributes will be copy rules.. The technique used is well-known (see e.g. [ASU86]): a nontrivial rule for an inherited attribute is moved to a rule for a synthesized attribute associated with a marker nonterminal inserted in front of the nonterminal occurrence involved with the original inherited attribute. Let us consider an example. Let a semantic rule $C.c := F(A.a, B.b)$ be associated with a production $A \rightarrow BC$. The transformed structure will be:

$$A \to B\ X\ C$$
$$X.a := A.a$$
$$X.b' := B.b$$
$$C.c := X.c'$$
$$X \to \varepsilon$$
$$X.c' := F(X.a, B.b')$$

The example structure before and after transformation is described in Fig. 5. In the following we call this kind of a local transformation a *rule transfer*.

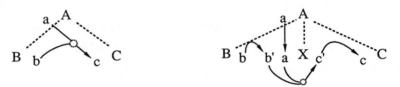

Fig. 5. A rule transfer.

The optional second phase eliminates a part of the conflicts against condition U2. This phase is explained in detail later.

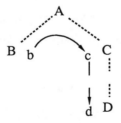

Fig. 6. A conflict against U3.

The third phase eliminates the conflicts against condition U3. Let us consider the situation in Fig. 6. If $c\ \underline{C}^*\ d$ for some inherited d, c is copy-dependent on b and B is an uncle symbol of d. There is a conflict against U3, if d is also copy-dependent on another synthesized attribute symbol associated with B. The solution is to perform a rule transfer for the copy rule $C.c := B.b$. The transformed production is shown in Fig. 7.

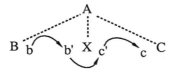

Fig. 7. A solution to the conflict against U3

The elimination of conflicts against U2 is trickier because it must be done in two phases. Let us consider an example where the semantic rule $C.c := A.a$ is associated with the production $A \to BC$, and B is an uncle symbol of c. In the fourth phase a rule transfer is performed for $C.c := A.a$. The modified structure is shown in Fig. 8.

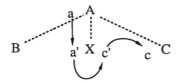

Fig.8. Rule transfer in the fourth phase

If B is not an uncle symbol of a, the conflict has been eliminated. However, the conflict may still be present like in Fig. 9 (a), where B is an uncle of a and a', and so the conflict against U2 is still present. This conflict will be recognized and eliminated in the fifth phase of the transformation where the rule $X.a' := A.a$ is transferred in front of B this time (Fig. 9 (b)).

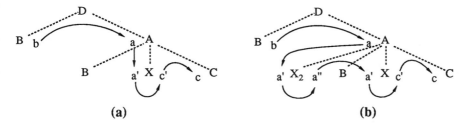

(a)   (b)

Fig. 9. Solution for an inherited conflict.

Now we return to the second phase. All the conflicts against condition U2 can be removed in the fourth and fifth phase of the uncle transformation, but this approach may produce parsing conflicts. For example, if we replace the nonterminal *A* by *B* in the example described in Figures 8 and 9, the resulting structure would cause a parsing conflict, because *B* is then left-recursive. In some cases a parsing conflict can be prevented by performing another kind of a transformation depicted in Fig. 10, where the uncle symbol *B* has been hidden.

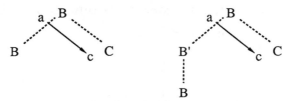

Fig. 10. Hiding of an uncle symbol.

This kind of hiding of uncle symbols does not, however, solve all the conflicts against U2. It is possible that the copy chain starts from the same production where the conflict against U2 is detected and then the hiding of an uncle symbol does not help.

It is easy to show that the uncle transformation removes all conflicts against U1 - U3 [Tar88a].

6. Experiences

To test the Metauncle system several attribute grammars have been processed. One of them describes a large subset of the static semantics of Pascal [Tuu87]. To give a view of the effect of the uncle transformation on the size of an attribute grammar, statistics of the L-attributed grammar for Pascal given as input and of the uncle-attributed form produced by the uncle transformation are given in Fig. 11.

	L-attributed	Uncle-attributed
Grammar symbols	148	183
Attribute symbols	19	47
Productions	297	332
Semantic rules	700	807

Fig. 11. Figures about two Pascal grammars

Evaluation conflicts appear always as parsing conflicts caused by marker nonterminals inserted by the uncle transformation. Because the changes made to the grammar are always local and they correspond to the conditions for uncle-attributed grammars, it is quite easy to infer the reasons for the conflicts by comparing the transformed grammar with the original one, because the transformed grammar is an ordinary attribute grammar written in the very same specification language as the original one. However, the conflicts are not very common in practical L-attributed grammars. In preparing the Pascal grammar mentioned above about ten evaluation conflicts were encountered. The solving of the conflicts took for a graduate student about 2 % of the total work time of the project.

The present version of Metauncle produces an analyzer of Pascal in 80 seconds of processor time on a VAX 8800 starting from the L-attributed description. The total time would be smaller, if the uncle transformation and the generation of an evaluator were merged. However, there are advantages in having two separate processors. Namely, the system is conceptually simpler to control and it is easier to understand reasons for evaluation conflicts as explained above. A separate transformation also offers flexibility and possibilities to make experiments. For example, a grammar may be only once augmented with the default rules (using an option of the first processor), and the augmented form is then developed further to optimize the coding time and to prevent possible errors in repeated augmentations.

To evaluate the overall efficiency of a compiler generated by Metauncle, the Pascal processor produced by Metauncle was compared on a VAX 8800 with a Pascal processor produced by HLP84. The processor generated by Metauncle was slightly faster than the other processor. As a comparison, the same tests were also run by the standard Pascal compiler of VAX (the times for this compiler include the code generation, too). The hand-written processor of VAX was typically about 2-3 times faster than the processor generated by Metauncle.

Another grammar written for Metauncle is a description of the specification language for input grammars [Ran88]. The processor generated from that grammar is used as a tool in developing new descriptions. One reason for making such a self description is the unsatisfactory error recovery of a processor generated by HLP84. The description could be easily extended so that the uncle transformation and the generation of a evaluator could be performed by processors generated by Metauncle itself.

One characteristic feature of the uncle method is the search for uncle symbols in the parsing stack. (Conceptually, it is slightly misleading to speak about a stack, because every item of the data structure should be accessible in our approach.) This feature is theoretically time-consuming, because the evaluation algorithm may need $O(n^2)$ time in the worst case for an input of length n [Tar82]. However, the uncle symbols are always close to the top of the parsing stack in the case of practical grammars. The search time was only 1 % of the total compilation time in experiments done with compilers generated by Metauncle.

The experiments support the fact that the uncle method combined with the uncle transformation offers an easy way to generate practical compilers for a large class of L-attributed grammars. This class is competitive with the classes accepted by related compiler generators [Tar88a]. The ease of implementing Metauncle using the HLP84 system was also a nice example of the power of compiler writing tools.

159

References

[ASU86]   A. V. Aho, R. Sethi and J. D. Ullman: *Compilers: Principles, Techniques, and Tools*. Addison-Wesley, Reading, Mass., 1986.

[JoM80]   N. D. Jones and C. M. Madsen: Attribute-influenced LR Parsing. In: *Aarhus Workshop on Semantics-Directed Compiler Generation* (ed. N. D. Jones), Lecture Notes in Computer Science 94, Springer-Verlag, Berlin-Heidelberg-New York, 1980, 393–407.

[KEL88]   K. Koskimies, T. Elomaa, T. Lehtonen and J. Paakki: TOOLS/HLP84 report and user manual. Report A-1988-2. Department of Computer Science, University of Helsinki, 1988.

[KNP88]   K. Koskimies, O. Nurmi, J. Paakki and S. Sippu: The design of a language processor generator. *Software Practice & Experience* **18, 2** (1988), 107-135.

[Mel84]   B. Melichar: Evaluation of attributes during LR syntax analysis. In: *Vorträge des Problemseminars Attributierte Grammatiken und ihre Anwendungen*, Pruchten. WPU Rostock, 1984.

[Poh83]   W. Pohlmann: LR parsing for affix grammars. *Acta Informatica* **20, 4** (1983), 283–300.

[Ran88]   O. Rannisto: Revisions for the Metauncle system (in Finnish). Draft. Department of Computer Science, University of Helsinki, 1988.

[SIN85]   M. Sassa, H. Ishizuka and I. Nakata: A contribution to LR-attributed grammars. *Journal of Information Processing* **8, 3** (1985), 196–206.

[Tar82]   J. Tarhio: Attribute evaluation during LR parsing. Report A-1982-4. Department of Computer Science, University of Helsinki, 1982.

[Tar88a]   J. Tarhio: Attribute grammars for one-pass compilation. Report A-1988-11. Department of Computer Science, University of Helsinki, 1988.

[Tar88b]   J. Tarhio: The compiler generator Metauncle. Report C-1988-23, Department of Computer Science, University of Helsinki, 1988.

[Tuu87]   H. Tuuri: An attribute grammar checking the semantics of Pascal for the Metauncle metacompiler (in Finnish). Report C-1987-59. Department of Computer Science, University of Helsinki, 1987.

[Wat77]   D. A. Watt: The parsing problem for affix grammars. *Acta Informatica* **8, 1** (1977), 1–20.

ATTRIBUTED TREE TRANSFORMATIONS WITH DELAYED AND SMART RE-EVALUATION

Henk Alblas

University of Twente, Department of Computer Science,
P.O. Box 217, 7500 AE Enschede, The Netherlands.

Abstract. Transformations of attributed program trees form an essential part of compiler optimizations. A tree transformation may invalidate attribute instances, not only in the restructured part of the tree but also elsewhere in the tree. To make the attribution of the tree correct again a re-evaluator has to be activated.

Criteria are formulated which allow a delay in calling the re-evaluator. These criteria allow a strategy of repeatedly applying alternate attribute evaluation and tree transformation phases. An attribute evaluation phase consists of a tree walk in which all attribute instances receive their correct values. A tree transformation phase consists of a tree walk in which as many tree transformations are performed as possible. The transformation phase is never interrupted to carry out a re-evaluation.

For re-evaluation purposes an incremental simple multi-pass evaluator is presented, which works optimally in the number of recomputations and in the number of visits to subtrees during each pass.

1. Introduction

In the classical theory [13] attribute grammars form an extension of the context-free grammar framework in the sense that information is associated with programming language constructs by attaching attributes to the grammar symbols representing these constructs. Attribute values are defined by attribute evaluation rules associated with the productions of the context-free grammar. These rules specify how to compute the values of certain attribute occurrences as a function of other attribute occurrences.

Compiler optimizations can be described by tree transformations, where complicated and non-efficient tree structures are replaced by equivalent but simpler and more efficient tree structures. For the specification of such tree transformations the classical attribute grammar framework has to be extended with conditional tree transformation rules [11, 15, 17], where predicates on attribute values (carrying context information) may enable the application of a transformation.

Traditionally, before the application of a tree transformation rule all attribute instances attached to the derivation tree are assumed to have correct values. A tree transformation may cause the values of some of the attribute instances within the derivation tree to become incorrect, which means that a renewed application of the attribute evaluation instructions will result in different values.

To make the attribution of a derivation tree correct again (which is generally needed in order to be able to test the predicates of subsequent tree transformations), a re-evaluation of the entire tree could be applied. However, a recomputation (after every application of a tree transformation rule) of all attribute instances attached to the tree is time consuming and should be avoided.

Instead, we formulate criteria which allow a delay in calling the re-evaluator until a sequence of tree transformations has been performed and several parts of the tree are assumed to be affected [4]. A delay in calling the re-evaluator requires a different view of the correctness of attribute values of a derivation tree. For a non-circular attribute grammar, the classical theory defines one single value to be correct for each attribute instance. This value is called the consistent value of the attribute instance. For the purpose of conditional tree transformations we extend the classical attribute grammar framework by allowing a set of values to be correct for each attribute instance. Such a value is called safe. Every safe value should be an approximation of the consistent value, which is therefore the optimal safe value. The set of safe values contains the consistent value.

Tree transformations based on safe attribute values should have the following characteristics.

1. If a tree transformation rule is applicable to a safely attributed tree, then it is also applicable to the corresponding consistently attributed tree.
2. A tree transformation applied to a safely attributed tree again yields a safely attributed tree.

These characteristics allow a tree transformation phase to perform without any interruption for re-evaluations anywhere in the tree.

The safety of the conditional tree transformation rules is the responsibility of the writer of these rules, i.e., their safety is not checked at compiler generation time. However, we do provide local criteria so that the writer can check the safety of his rules.

Practical examples show that, in general, after a sequence of transformations has been applied, continuation of the transformation phase is productive only after a complete re-evaluation of the entire derivation tree.

For such a "complete" re-evaluation we propose a "smart" simple multi-pass re-evaluator which keeps track of the attribute instances that need to be recomputed [2]. An attribute instance is marked as "needing recomputation" as soon as an argument of its attribute evaluation instruction has changed. Immediately after its recomputation this mark is removed. The tree traversal strategy can be improved by skipping unnecessary visits to subtrees. A subtree is "affected" for a certain pass if one of the attribute instances of one of its nodes needs to be recomputed during that pass. Otherwise the subtree can be skipped during that pass. For the pass-oriented approach this leads to an optimal incremental simple multi-pass evaluator that can be combined with any tree transformation strategy.

2. Basic Concepts

An *attribute grammar AG*, as defined in [13], is a context-free grammar G, which is augmented with attributes and attribute evaluation rules.

The underlying grammar G is a 4-tuple (V_N, V_T, P, S), where V_N and V_T denote the finite sets of nonterminal and terminal symbols, respectively, P is the finite set of productions and $S \in V_N$ is the start symbol, which does not appear in the right-hand side of any production. We write V for $V_N \cup V_T$.

Each symbol $X \in V$ has a finite set $A(X)$ of attributes, partitioned into two disjoint subsets $I(X)$ and $S(X)$ of *inherited* and *synthesized* attributes, respectively. For $X = S$ and $X \in V_T$ we require $I(X) = \varnothing$

The set of all attributes will be denoted by A, i.e., $A = \cup_{X \in V} A(X)$. Attributes of different grammar symbols are different. An attribute a of symbol X is also denoted by a **of** X. Each attribute a has a set $V(a)$ of possible values.

A production p is denoted as $X_{p0} \rightarrow X_{p1} X_{p2}...X_{pn}$. Production p is said to have the *attribute occurrence* (a, p, k) if $a \in A(X_{pk})$.

The set of attribute occurrences of production p can be partitioned into two disjoin sets of defined occurrences and used occurrences denoted by $DO(p)$ and $UO(p)$ respectively.
These subsets are defined as follows:

$$DO(p) = \{(s, p, 0) \mid s \in S(X_{p0})\} \cup \{(i, p, k) \mid i \in I(X_{pk}) \wedge 1 \leq k \leq n\},$$

$$UO(p) = \{(i, p, 0) \mid i \in I(X_{p0})\} \cup \{(s, p, k) \mid s \in S(X_{pk}) \wedge 1 \leq k \leq n\}.$$

Associated with each production p is a set of *attribute evaluation rules* which specify how to compute the values of the attribute occurrences in $DO(p)$. The evaluation rule defining attribute occurrence (a, p, k) has the form

$$(a, p, k) := f((a_1, p, k_1), (a_2, p, k_2), ..., (a_m, p, k_m))$$

where $(a, p, k) \in DO(p)$, f is a total function and $(a_j, p, k_j) \in UO(p)$ for $1 \leq j \leq m$. We say that (a, p, k) *depends on* (a_j, p, k_j) for $1 \leq j \leq m$.
For each sentence of G a derivation tree exists. The nodes of the tree are labeled with symbols from V. For each non-leaf node there is a production $p: X_{p0} \rightarrow X_{p1}X_{p2}...X_{pn}$, such that the node is labeled with X_{p0} and its sons with $X_{p1}, X_{p2}, ..., X_{pn}$, respectively. We say that p is the production (*applied*) at that node.
Given a derivation tree, instances of attributes are attached to the nodes in the following way: if node N is labeled with grammar symbol X, then for each attribute $a \in A(X)$ an instance of a is attached to node N. We say that the derivation tree has *attribute instance a of N*.
Let N_0 be a node, p the production at N_0, and $N_1, N_2, ..., N_n$ its sons from left to right respectively. An *attribute evaluation instruction*

$$a \text{ of } N_k := f(a_1 \text{ of } N_{k1}, a_2 \text{ of } N_{k2}, ..., a_m \text{ of } N_{km})$$

is associated with attribute instance *a of N_k* if the attribute evaluation rule

$$(a, p, k) := f((a_1, p, k_1), (a_2, p, k_2), ..., (a_m, p, k_m))$$

is associated with production p. We say that *a of N_k depends on a_i of N_{ki}* for $1 \leq i \leq m$.
For each derivation tree T a *dependency graph* D_T can be defined by taking the attribute instances of T as its vertices. Arc (*a of N_i, b of N_j*) is contained in the graph if and only if attribute instance *b of N_j* depends on attribute instance *a of N_i*.
A path in a dependency graph will be called a *dependency path*, for which the following notation will be used: $dp[a_1 \text{ of } N_1, a_2 \text{ of } N_2, ..., a_n \text{ of } N_n]$ for $n > 1$ stands for a path composed of the arcs (a_1 of N_1, a_2 of N_2), (a_2 of N_2, a_3 of N_3), ..., (a_{n-1} of N_{n-1}, a_n of N_n).
An *attributed derivation tree* is a derivation tree where all attribute instances have a value (which is not necessarily consistent). A *consistently attributed derivation tree* is a derivation tree where the execution of any evaluation instruction does not change the values of the attribute instances.
The task of an attribute evaluator is to compute the values of all attribute instances attached to the derivation tree, by executing their associated evaluation instructions. Initially, the values of all attribute instances attached to the derivation tree are undefined, with the exception of the instances of the imported attributes. For simplicity we assume that the imported attributes are the synthesized attributes of the leaves of which the values are determined by the parser. The output of the evaluator is a consistently attributed tree.

6. Conditional Tree Transformations

We restrict ourselves to attributed tree transformations which preserve the syntax, i.e., all intermediate trees are derivation trees in the same context-free grammar.

For the definition of a tree template we need the concept of a "possibly" incomplete derivation tree where arbitrary symbols may label the root and the leaves. Normally, when we refer to a derivation tree, we mean a "complete" derivation tree, i.e., a derivation tree whose root is labeled with the start symbol and whose leaves are labeled with terminal symbols only. By a subtree we mean a subtree of a complete derivation tree.

To define conditional tree transformations, we first need to recall the definition of a purely syntactical tree transformation rule [6], consisting of two tree templates.

A *tree template* is a possibly incomplete derivation tree. Multiple occurrences of the same symbol as the label of a node are distinguished by subscripts. So, in general, node labels are of the form X_i, where X is a terminal or nonterminal and i a subscript. Nonterminal symbols (possibly with a subscript) labeling the leaves are the *variables* of the tree template.

An *instance* of a tree template is created by substituting for each variable of the tree template a subtree whose root has the same nonterminal as the variable.

A *tree transformation rule* is a pair (*itt, ott*) of tree templates, such that all variables occurring in *ott* also occur as variables in *itt*; *itt* and *ott* are called the *input tree template* and the *output tree template*, respectively.

A tree transformation rule (*itt, ott*) is *applicable* to a subtree *IT* of a derivation tree *T1*, if *itt* matches the top of *IT*, i.e., if *IT* is an instance of *itt*. The fact that *IT* is an instance of *itt* establishes a relation between the variables of *itt* and subtrees of *IT*.

The application of tree transformation rule (*itt, ott*) consists of the creation of an instance *OT* of *ott* in which the relation between subtrees of *OT* and variables of *ott* is the same as established by matching *itt* with *IT*. The resulting subtree *OT* replaces subtree *IT* of *T1*, thus creating a new derivation tree *T2*. Note that by the definition of tree templates (the variables of *ott* must be different) duplication of a subtree of *IT* in *OT* is excluded.

The fact that *itt* and *ott* are (possibly incomplete) derivation trees in the same grammar guarantees that for each application of a tree transformation rule (*itt, ott*) the instance *IT* of *itt* and the corresponding instance *OT* of *ott* are in the same grammar.

To guarantee that *OT* correctly fits in the surrounding tree *T2* (i.e., that the production applied above *OT* preserves the syntax), it is necessary and sufficient to require that grammar symbol *A* labeling the root of *itt* may be replaced by grammar symbol *B* labeling the root of *ott*, at any occurrence of *A* in the right part of any production. However, for reasons of simplicity we impose an additional requirement on the transformation rules, namely that *itt* and *ott* have equally labeled roots (which also have the same index). Observe that it is always possible to extend *itt* and *ott* with an extra production so that their roots are labeled equally. Similarly, we require both the input template and the output template to consist of more than one node.

Syntactically (i.e., for attribute-free derivation trees), the applicability of a tree transformation rule to a subtree is confined by the above-mentioned matching criterion. It may be further restricted by contextual information, collected and distributed by attributes. For this we need to associate attributes with tree templates.

Let X_i be the label of a node of a tree template *tt*, where X is a grammar symbol and i denotes its subscript in *tt*. The subscript may be omitted in the case of a single occurrence of X in *tt*. We say that tree template *tt* has *attribute instance* (a, tt, X_i) if $a \in A(X)$. (a, tt, X_i) is an *inherited* instance if $a \in I(X)$, and a *synthesized* instance if $a \in S(X)$.

Let *(itt, ott)* be a tree transformation rule. Attribute instances in *itt* and *ott* are said t *correspond* if they are the same attribute of equally labeled nodes, i.e., they are of th form *(a, itt, Y)* and *(a, ott, Y)*. This notion is only relevant for attribute instances of th root and the leaves of *itt* and *ott*. Note that every attribute instance in *ott* of the root or th variables has a corresponding attribute instance in *itt*.

Having associated attributes with tree templates in a natural way, the transformatio rules can be extended by *enabling conditions* [11, 15, 17] which are predicates o attribute instances of the input template.

Next, we focus on the attribution of a derivation tree after the application of a tre transformation rule. The difference between the original tree and the restructured tree i effected by the replacement of the input template by the output template. No syntactica changes take place in the subtrees substituted for corresponding variables of *itt* and *ot* Notice also that the production above the restructured subtree remains unchanged, sinc we required *itt* and *ott* to have equally labeled roots. So, we assume that the attribut instances of the subtrees substituted for the variables of *itt* and *ott* keep their values afte a transformation. The same holds for the attribute instances of the tree part above *itt* an *ott*. Thus, to obtain a fully (but perhaps not correctly) attributed derivation tree we coul restrict ourselves to the evaluation of the attribute instances of *ott*.

The set of attribute instances of a tree template can naturally be partitioned into thre disjoint subsets of input, output and inner attribute instances.

Definition 3.1. With respect to a tree template, the *input attribute instances* are th inherited attribute instances of its root and the synthesized attribute instances of it leaves; the *output attribute instances* are the synthesized attribute instances of its root an the inherited attribute instances of its leaves; the *inner attribute instances* are the attribut instances of the inner nodes. □

Observe that the inner and the output attribute instances of *ott* are completel determined by the input attribute instances of *ott* and the ordinary evaluation rul associated with the productions applied in *ott*. It is assumed that corresponding inpu attribute instances of *itt* and *ott* keep their values. Explicit evaluation rules are, howevei needed for the synthesized attribute instances associated with the terminal nodes of *o* for which no corresponding node exists in *itt*. We propose these attribute instance (normally set by the parser!) to be defined, as part of the tree transformation rule, b *lexical evaluation rules* in terms of attribute instances of *itt*.

The synthesized attribute instances of terminal symbols of *ott*, for which corresponding terminal symbol exists in *itt*, are assumed to be copied from *itt*.

Having informally introduced the concept of a conditional tree transformation we ar now ready to give the following definition.

Definition 3.2. A conditional tree transformation rule is a 4-tuple *tr*: *(itt, ott, cond, eval* where

- *itt* and *ott* are the *input* and the *output tree template*, respectively. *itt* and *ott* mu have equally labeled roots (with the same subscript) and must contain more tha one node. All variables occurring in *ott* also occur as variables in *itt*.
- *cond* is the *enabling condition*, a predicate on attribute instances of *itt*.
- *eval* is the set of *lexical evaluation rules* which specify the computation of th synthesized attribute instances of the new terminal nodes of *ott* in terms c attribute instances of *itt* (in the case *cond* yields true). □

A conditional tree transformation rule *tr*: *(itt, ott, cond, eval)* is *applicable* to a subtre *IT* of a derivation tree *T*, if *itt* matches the top of *IT* and the evaluation of *cond* yield true.

The *application* of transformation rule *tr* consists of the steps (1), (2), and (3), and possibly (4):

(1)   Creation of an instance *OT* of *ott* (in which the correspondence between subtrees and variables, established by *IT*, is maintained) and the replacement of *IT* by *OT*, thus creating a (partially attributed) derivation tree *T2*.

(2)   Computation of the values of the synthesized attribute instances associated with the new terminal nodes of *ott*, using the rules specified by *eval*.

(3)   The local re-evaluation phase: evaluation of the attribute instances in the restructured area of *T2* (i.e., the area covered by *ott*).

(4)   The global re-evaluation phase: re-evaluation of all attribute instances of *T2* (except, of course, the synthesized attribute instances of the leaves).

The *full application* of *tr* consists of (1), (2), (3), and (4) and the *(partial) application* of *tr* consists of (1), (2), and (3). Note that both types of application result in a (completely) attributed derivation tree. The full application results in a consistently attributed derivation tree, whereas the attributed derivation tree resulting from the (partial) application of *tr* may contain inconsistencies.

Conditional tree transformation rule *tr*: (*itt, ott, cond, eval*) will be written as follows:

tr: **transform** *itt* **cond** *cond* **into** *ott* **eval** *eval* **end**.

It is allowed to leave out the part "**cond** *cond*" if *cond* is true and the part "**eval** *eval*" if *eval* is empty.

We illustrate the application of transformations with an example, taken from [17], which concerns constant folding. For the specification of tree templates we use the following linear notation for trees: within angular brackets the root is followed by its sequence of subtrees, comma symbols act as separators and we write *a* **of** *Y* for the attribute instance (*a, tt, Y*) of a tree template *tt*.

Observe that the notation *a* **of** *Y* for attribute instance (*a, itt, Y*) and (*a, ott, Y*) leads to the same notation for corresponding attribute instances in *itt* and *ott*.

Example 3.1. The conditional tree transformation rule

```
tr: transform <expr,ident>
        cond element (idno of ident) in: (pool of expr)
        into <expr,const>
            eval val of const :=
                value-of (idno of ident) in: (pool of expr)
    end
```

describes the replacement of an identifier by a constant, as depicted in Figure 1. Terminal symbol *ident* has a synthesized attribute *idno* indicating its number, assigned by the parser. Terminal symbol *const* has a synthesized attribute *val* representing its value. Inherited attribute *pool* **of** *expr* contains a pair (*idno, val*) for each variable whose value is known to have the same value whenever control passes through this point. Here, *idno* represents the identifier number of the variable and *val* its associated value.

The transformation of an identifier into a constant is enabled if its identifier number is found in the pool of constant variables. Its associated value will be assigned to synthesized attribute *val* of the newly created constant.

The function "element (*idno*: integer) in: (*p*: pool) **delivers** boolean:" checks whether a pair with first component *idno* is found in *p* or not. The function "value-of (*idno*: integer) in: (*p*: pool) **delivers** integer:" returns the value of *idno* in pool *p*. □

Fig.1. Replacement of a variable by a constant.

4. Delay of re-evaluation

In Section 3 we explained that the result of the partial application of a tree transformation rule on a consistently attributed derivation tree $T1$ will be a fully attributed tree $T2$, which may, however, contain inconsistencies. This is caused by the fact that, in general, the values of some of the output attribute instances of ott in $T2$ will differ from the values of their corresponding output attribute instances of itt in $T1$. Let a of $N1$ be an output attribute instance of ott whose new value differs from its old value. Then in $T2$, every attribute instance b of $N2$, such that the dependency graph D_{T2} includes a dependency path $dp[a$ of $N_1, ..., b$ of $N_2]$, may have a wrong value. A tree transformation may even cause the values of the input attribute instances of ott to be incorrect (and hence the inner and the output instances as well).

Hence, if a correct value is required for every attribute instance in $T2$, then the local re-evaluation phase has to be followed by a global re-evaluation phase, unless for every output attribute instance of ott in $T2$ its value is equal to the value of its corresponding output attribute instance of itt in $T1$.

We now discuss a strategy where the re-evaluation process after each tree transformation may be confined to the local re-evaluation phase, and where the global re-evaluation phase may be delayed. Thus, in the following we always assume the partial application of a tree transformation.

The classical theory on attribute grammars defines one single value to be correct for each attribute instance of any derivation tree (of which the values of the synthesized attribute instances of the leaves are given). For our tree transformation strategy, where re-evaluations may be restricted to ott, we extend the classical attribute grammar framework by allowing a set of values to be correct for each attribute instance. Each value of such set should be an approximation of the correct value according to the classical attribute grammar definition.

In [9, 10] the new correct values are called $safe$, whereas the old correct values are called $consistent$. We also use this terminology.

Hereafter, we assume that for each attribute a the set $V(a)$ of possible values of a is partially ordered, and we denote this partial order by $\leq$ (in fact, this is ambiguous because we should write $\leq_a$, but we want to keep our notation as simple as possible). For $x, y \in V(a)$, if $x \leq y$, we say that x is an $approximation$ of y, or that y is better ($\geq$) than x. For synthesized attributes of terminals we assume the partial order to be trivial, i.e., $x \leq y$ iff $x = y$. This is necessary, because these attributes are imported attributes for which no evaluation rules are defined. For all other attributes we assume that the partial order has a smallest element, denoted (again ambiguously) by $\bot$. As an example, $V(a)$ may be the set of all finite sets of identifiers, ordered by set-inclusion, with the empty set as the smallest element.

Informally, the value x of an attribute instance is called safe if $x \leq y$, where y is its consistent value.

For the comparison of safely and consistently attributed derivation trees, and for the expression of the requirements that guarantee the reliability of transformations based on safe derivation trees, we introduce the following notations and concepts.

Let T be an attributed derivation tree, then T^c denotes the result of a global re-evaluation of T. More precisely, T^c is the unique consistently attributed tree with the same underlying derivation tree as T, and the same values for the corresponding synthesized attribute instances of the leaves.

For attributed derivation trees $T1$ and $T2$, subtree IT of $T1$ and tree transformation rule tr: $T1 \, [IT] \longrightarrow tr \rightarrow T2$ means that tr is applicable to IT of $T1$, with $T2$ the result of the (partial) application. Note that $T2^c$ is the result of the full application.

The purpose of a set C of conditional tree transformation rules, for a given consistently attributed derivation tree T, is to produce another consistently attributed derivation tree T' such that T' is obtained from T by a sequence of full applications of rules of C. This is formalized as follows. T' is consistently derivable from T by C if

either $T' = T$

or   there is a subtree IT of T, a rule $tr \in C$, and an attributed derivation tree $T1$ such that $T \, [IT] \longrightarrow tr \rightarrow T1$ and T' is consistently derivable from $T1^c$ by C.

Of course, one would normally continue applying the rules of C until no rule of C is applicable anymore.

Note that if T' is consistently derivable from T then this can always be realized by a number of tree traversals, during which the rules are applied in their proper order.

We now want to define a condition on the transformation rules so that their partial application can be used rather than their full application. The idea is to use approximations of the consistently derivable trees rather than the consistently derivable trees themselves.

For attributed trees T and T' with the same underlying syntax tree, $T \leq T'$ means that the value of every attribute instance of T is an approximation of the value of the corresponding attribute instance of T'. Note that if $T \leq T'$ then $T^c = T'^c$.

We are now ready to formally define the safety of (the values of the attribute instances of) a derivation tree, and the safety of a tree transformation rule.

Definition 4.1. T is *safe* iff $T \leq T^c$. □

Note that T is consistent iff $T = T^c$; hence a consistent tree is safe.

Definition 4.2. A conditional tree transformation rule tr is safe if:
If $T1 \, [IT] \longrightarrow tr \rightarrow T2$, and $T1$ is safe, then
     a) $T1^c \, [IT] \longrightarrow tr \rightarrow T2'$, and
     b) $T2 \leq T2'^c$,
for some $T2'$. □

Part a) of this definition says that if tr is applicable to a subtree of a safely attributed tree, then tr is also applicable to that subtree of the corresponding consistently attributed tree. Part b) says that the result of the partial application is an approximation of the result of the full application. Note that it is also a safe approximation. In fact, from part b) we know that $T2 \leq T2'^c$, and from this it follows that $T2^c = T2'^c$, and so, $T2 \leq T2^c$. Thus we obtain the following fact: a safe transformation rule preserves safety of trees; this guarantees the reliability of subsequent transformations.

Using safety rather than consistency as the new definition of correctness we may conclude that during a tree walk, after the application of a tree transformation rule, the attribute instances may not have their best values, although their values are always safe. This means that during a walk where no global re-evaluations are performed, every tree transformation is correct, although an interrupt of the walk in order to perform a global re-evaluation (i.e., to compute the best values for all attribute instances) might have disclosed further opportunities for transformations during the continuation of the walk.

A tree $T2$ is safely derived from a consistently attributed input tree $T1$ if $T2$ is the result of a sequence of safe tree transformations applied to $T1$. It can easily be shown from Definition 4.2 that by a global re-evaluation of the safely derived tree $T2$ an output tree $T2^c$ is obtained which is consistently derivable from the input tree $T1$. This allows an attribute evaluation and tree transformation algorithm where the evaluation phase alternates with the transformation phase. This process is repeated until no more tree transformations are possible.

We now want to show that local restrictions can be imposed on the attribute evaluation and tree transformation rules that guarantee the safety of the tree transformation rules. First, we need the monotonicity of the evaluation rules and the enabling conditions.

A function $f(x_1, x_2, ..., x_n)$ of attribute values, whose result is an attribute value, is *monotonic* if:

$\quad$ if $a_i \leq b_i$ $(1 \leq i \leq n)$, and $f(a_1, a_2, ..., a_n), f(b_1, b_2, ..., b_n)$ are defined,
$\quad$ then $f(a_1, a_2, ..., a_n) \leq f(b_1, b_2, ..., b_n)$.

An attribute evaluation rule or a lexical evaluation rule is monotonic if the function in its right part is *monotonic*. Note that the monotonicity of a lexical evaluation rule means that if $a_i \leq b_i$ then $f(a_1, a_2, ..., a_n) = f(b_1, b_2, ..., b_n)$.

An enabling condition $f(x_1, x_2, ..., x_n)$ of a tree transformation rule is *monotonic* if:

$\quad$ if $a_i \leq b_i$ $(1 \leq i \leq n)$ and $f(a_1, a_2, ..., a_n) = \text{true}$,
$\quad$ then $f(b_1, b_2, ..., b_n) = \text{true}$.

(i.e., for false $\leq$ true f is monotonic).

Besides monotonic attribute evaluation rules, we also need for every tree transformation rule tr: $(itt, ott, cond, eval)$ that "ott is *better* than itt". By this we mean that for every possible choice of values for the input attribute instances of itt, the values of the output attribute instances of itt are approximations of the values of the corresponding output attribute instances of ott (if they exist). Intuitively, this means that application of tr "increases the amount of information".

Definition 4.3. A tree transformation rule tr: $(itt, ott, cond, eval)$ is *locally safe*, if:
$\quad$ a) $cond$ is monotonic,
$\quad$ b) all lexical evaluation rules in $eval$ are monotonic,
$\quad$ c) ott is better than itt. $\square$

In [4] it has been proved that, for monotonic attribute evaluation rules, every locally safe tree transformation rule is safe. These criteria may help the writer of the attribute evaluation and tree transformation rules to check the safety of his rules.

Practical examples show that, in general, after a traversal of an entire derivation tree, during which tree transformations are performed, a subsequent traversal is productive only after a global re-evaluation of the tree.

5. A smart re-evaluator

Throughout this paper we assume that the attribute evaluation strategy is *simple multi-pass*, which means that a fixed number of depth-first left-to-right traversals (called passes) are made over the derivation tree and all instances of the same attribute are evaluated during the same pass. From [1] we repeat some terminology and definitions concerning simple multi-pass evaluation.

A partition of the set of attributes A into a sequence of mutually disjoint subsets will be denoted by $\langle A_0, A_1, ..., A_m \rangle$, where A_0 includes all synthesized attributes of terminal symbols (whose values should be computed by the parser before the evaluator is started).

A partition $<A_0, A_1, ..., A_m>$ of the set of attributes A is *correct* if A_0 consists of the synthesized attributes of the terminal symbols and the instances of all attributes in set A_i $(1 \leq i \leq m)$ can be evaluated during the i-th pass of the simple multi-pass evaluator.

An attribute grammar is *simple m-pass* if a correct partition $<A_0, A_1, ..., A_m>$ of the set of attributes A exists. An attribute grammar is *simple multi-pass* if it is simple m-pass for some m.

For each partition $<A_0, A_1, ..., A_m>$ of the set of attributes A of an attribute grammar a *pass function* pass: $A \rightarrow \{0, 1, ..., m\}$ can be defined as pass$(a) = i$ if $a \in A_i$. The pass function is *correct* if the partition is correct.

The following tree-walk algorithm defines a simple multi-pass evaluator. Each call of "visit subtree ($root$, i)" corresponds to a pass. Node N is denoted by either "$N.0$" or "N" and "k-th son of N" is written as "$N.k$".

Algorithm 5.1. Simple multi-pass evaluation.
Input: an attributed derivation tree where only the synthesized attribute instances of the terminal symbols are defined;
a correct partition $<A_0, A_1, ..., A_m>$ of the set of attributes A.
Output: an attributed derivation tree where all attribute instances are defined.
Algorithm:

```
begin
    const m = ...;
    type node = ...;
         pass number = 1..m;
    var root: node;
    procedure visit subtree (N: node; i: pass number);
    begin {let p: Xp0 → Xp1Xp2...Xpn be the production at node N}
        for k from 1 to n
        do for all a ∈ I(Xpk)
            do if a ∈ Ai
                then evaluate a of N.k
                fi
            od;
            if Xpk ∈ VN
            then visit subtree (N.k, i)
            fi
        od;
        for all a ∈ S(Xp0)
        do if a ∈ Ai
            then evaluate a of N.0
            fi
        od
    end {of visit subtree};
    read (root);
    for i from 1 to m  {i: pass number}
    do visit subtree (root, i) od
end   □
```

Algorithm 5.1 describes the (re-)evaluation of all attribute instances attached to a derivation tree. Below we present a more efficient re-evaluator from [2], which does no unnecessary calculations and skips subtrees when possible.

To be able to mark the attribute instances that need to be evaluated, we associate with every tree node a variable *NeedToBeEvaluated* of type *set of attributes*. For *NeedToBeEvaluated* associated with node N we use the same notation as for attributes, namely *NeedToBeEvaluated* of N.

To update *NeedToBeEvaluated* properly, we introduce a global variable *Changed* of type *set of attributes*. During a pass, a node will be visited downwards and upwards. In a downward visit of a node the variable *Changed* includes those inherited attribute instances which have changed their value. Similarly, in an upward visit *Changed* includes those synthesized attribute instances whose values have changed during the current pass.

Attribute *a* is inserted in *NeedToBeEvaluated* of *N* as soon as an argument of the evaluation instruction of *a* of *N* has changed, as indicated by variable *Changed*. Deletion is done immediately after the recomputation of *a* of *N*.

We now try to improve the tree-walk strategy. A subtree is visited during the *i*-th pass if *Changed* is not empty and/or the instance of *NeedToBeEvaluated* attached to the root or one of its descendants includes attributes with pass number *i*.

We associate with every tree node labeled by a nonterminal symbol a variable *SubtreeAffected* of type *set of pass numbers*. Let N_0 be a node, $p: X_{p0} \rightarrow X_{p1}X_{p2}...X_{pn}$ the production applied at N_0 and $N_1, N_2, ..., N_n$ the sons of N_0 from left to right, respectively. *SubtreeAffected* of N_0 includes pass number *i* if and only if

either   a defined attribute occurrence (a, p, k) exists, such that pass(a of X_{pk}) = *i* and $a \in$ *NeedToBeEvaluated* of N_k, for some k ($0 \leq k \leq n$).

or $i \in$ *SubtreeAffected* of N_k, for some k ($1 \leq k \leq n$).

During re-evaluation passes, *SubtreeAffected* of N_0 will be updated at the following times:

1.   When N_0 is visited, pass number *i* will be inserted in *SubtreeAffected* of N_0 as soon as one of the requirements specified above is found to be fulfilled.

2.   Pass number *i* will be deleted from *SubtreeAffected* of N_0 when N_0 is visited for the second time during the *i*-th pass.

This guarantees a correct value for *SubtreeAffected* of N_0 whenever N_0 is visited during the re-evaluation process, provided that, when visiting a node, the instances of *NeedToBeEvaluated* and *SubtreeAffected* associated with all the nodes of its subtree (i.e., rooted in this node) are correct. At the end of the re-evaluation process *SubtreeAffected* of N_0 is empty for all N_0.

The re-evaluator starts at the root of the derivation tree. The moment the re-evaluator is activated, *NeedToBeEvaluated* of *N* and *SubtreeAffected* of *N* are required to be correct for any node *N* in the derivation tree. To explain the initialization of these variables we consider the effect of the partial application of a tree transformation.

The result of the partial application of a tree transformation rule *tr = (itt, ott, cond, eval)* to a fully and safely attributed derivation tree *T1*, is a fully and safely attributed tree *T2*. Observe that the local re-evaluation of attribute instances of *T2* stops at the border of *ott*, i.e., at the output attribute instances of *ott*. Let *a* of *K* be an output attribute instance of *ott* whose new value differs from its old value. This means that every attribute instance *b* of *N* such that D_{T2} contains an arc (*a* of *K*, *b* of *N*) has to be inserted in *NeedToBeEvaluated* of *N*. This holds for the attribute instances of the productions which "border on *ott*", i.e., the production applied immediately above the root of *ott* and the productions applied at the leaves of *ott*.

First, we treat the productions which border on a leaf of *ott*. Let N_0 be a node, $p: X_{p0} \rightarrow X_{p1}X_{p2}...X_{pn}$ the production applied at N_0 and $N_1, N_2, ..., N_n$ the sons of N_0 from left to right, respectively. Let N_0 be a leaf of *ott* and *a* of N_0 an output attribute instance of *ott* whose value has changed, then every attribute instance *b* of N_k ($0 \leq k \leq n$) such that (b, p, k) depends on $(a, p, 0)$ has to be inserted in *NeedToBeEvaluated* of N_k, and the associated pass number pass(b of N_k) has to be inserted in *SubtreeAffected* of N_0.

The variable *SubtreeAffected* of every non-leaf node *N* of *ott* must include all the pass numbers contained in the variables *SubtreeAffected* of all the leaves of *ott*. The values of these variables can be computed from the bottom up.

Next, we treat the production which borders on the root of *ott*. Let N_0 be a node, $p: X_{p0} \rightarrow X_{p1} X_{p2}...X_{pn}$ the production applied at N_0 and $N_1, N_2, ..., N_n$ the sons of N_0 from left to right, respectively. Let N_j $(1 \le j \le n)$ be the root of *ott* and a **of** N_j an output attribute instance of *ott* whose value has changed, then every attribute instance b **of** N_k $(0 \le k \le n)$ such that (b, p, k) depends on (a, p, j) has to be inserted in *NeedToBeEvaluated* of N_k, and the associated pass number pass(b **of** N_k) has to be inserted in *SubtreeAffected* of N_0.

All the pass numbers contained in *SubtreeAffected* of the root of *ott* (i.e., N_j) must be inserted in *SubtreeAffected* **of** N_0. Every ancestor of N_0 must include the same pass numbers as *SubtreeAffected* **of** N_0. The initialization of these instances of *SubtreeAffected* will be done during the bottom up moves of the tree walk to the root of the derivation tree.

Simple multi-pass re-evaluation using this scheme is defined in Algorithm 5.2. In this algorithm we use the statement "re-evaluate a **of** N", by which we mean the following steps:

```
old := a of N;
evaluate a of N;
new := a of N;
if old ≠ new then insert a in Changed fi;
delete a from NeedToBeEvaluated of N.
```

Procedure "visit subtree" in Algorithm 5.2 is an adapted version of the one presented in Algorithm 5.1. Procedure "propagate change" (with parameters k of type integer and p of type production number) inserts attribute instances, for which one of the arguments is found in *Changed*, in their corresponding sets *NeedToBeEvaluated* and updates the associated set *SubtreeAffected* accordingly. For $k = 0$, *Changed* contains inherited attribute instances associated with the left-hand side of a production, and for $k \ne 0$, *Changed* contains synthesized attribute instances associated with the k-th symbol of the right-hand side.

Algorithm 5.2. Simple multi-pass re-evaluation.
Input: an attributed derivation tree where all attribute instances have a safe value but some attribute instances may have an inconsistent value;
            sets *NeedToBeEvaluated* and *SubtreeAffected* associated with tree nodes;
            a correct partition $<A_0, A_1, ..., A_m>$ of the set of attributes A.
Output: an attributed derivation tree where all attribute instances have consistent values.
Algorithm:

```
begin
    const m = ...;
          EmptySetOfAttributes = [];
    type node = ...;
         production number = 1..r;
         pass number = 1..m;
         attributes = (... enumeration of attributes ...);
         set of attributes = set of attributes;
    var root: node;
        Changed: set of attributes;
```

```
procedure visit subtree (N: node; i: pass number);
begin {let p: X_{p0} → X_{p1}X_{p2}...X_{pn} be the production at node N}
    procedure propagate change (k: integer;
                                p: production number);
        begin {p: X_{p0} → X_{p1}X_{p2}...X_{pn} is the production with number p}
        if Changed ≠ EmptySetOfAttributes
        then for j from 0 to n
            do for all a ∈ A(X_{pj})
                do for all b ∈ A(X_{pk})
                    do if (a,p,j) depends on (b,p,k))
                        and b ∈ Changed
                        then insert a in NeedToBeEvaluated of N.j;
                             insert pass(a of X_{pj}) in
                                         SubtreeAffected of N
                    fi
                od
            od
        od
        fi
    end {of propagate change};
    {insertion of attributes in NeedToBeEvaluated of N.j (0≤j≤n),
     and pass numbers in SubtreeAffected of N}
    propagate change (0, p);
    for k from 1 to n
    do Changed := EmptySetOfAttributes;
       {recomputation of inherited attribute instances of N.k;
        deletion of these attribute instances
        from NeedToBeEvaluated of N.k;
        insertion of attribute instances in Changed}
       for all a ∈ I(X_{pk})
       do if a ∈ A_i and a ∈ NeedToBeEvaluated of N.k
          then re-evaluate a of N.k
          fi
       od;
       if X_{pk} ∈ V_N
       then if Changed ≠ EmptySetOfAttributes
               or i ∈ SubtreeAffected of N.k
            then visit subtree (N.k, i);
                 {insertion of attributes in
                  NeedToBeEvaluated of N.j (0≤j≤n),
                  and pass numbers in SubtreeAffected of N}
                 propagate change (k, p)
            fi
       fi
    od;
    Changed := EmptySetOfAttributes;
    {recomputation of synthesized attribute instances of N.0;
     deletion of these attribute instances
     from NeedToBeEvaluated of N.0;
     insertion of attribute instances in Changed}
    for all a ∈ S(X_{p0})
    do if a ∈ A_i and a ∈ NeedToBeEvaluated of N.0
       then re-evaluate a of N.0
       fi
    od;
    delete i from SubtreeAffected of N;
    for j from 1 to n
    do if X_{pj} ∈ V_N
       then SubtreeAffected of N :=
            SubtreeAffected of N ∪ SubtreeAffected of N.j
       fi
    od
end {of visit subtree};
```

```
   read(root);
   for i from 1 to m
   do if i ∈ SubtreeAffected of root
      then Changed := EmptySetOfAttributes;
           visit subtree (root, i)
      fi
   od
end  □
```

In [5] the approach of Algorithm 5.2 is adjusted to the visit sequences of ordered attribute grammars [12].

Algorithm 5.2 works optimally in the number of re-evaluations of attribute instances and the number of visits to subtrees. The space required for bookkeeping information (one bit for every attribute or pass number in every instance of *NeedToBeEvaluated* and *SubtreeAffected*) is linear in the size of the tree.

Observe that Algorithm 5.2 works in time linear in the size of the tree, but not in the size of its affected areas. Because of the recursive nature of Algorithm 5.2 every pass starts at the root of the tree and walks down to the affected areas. In [3], for the case where the re-evaluator is called after every tree transformation, an iterative version of Algorithm 5.2 is presented which works linear in the size of the affected area of the tree. This version of the re-evaluator starts its first pass at the root of the restructured subtree. This subtree is called the "subtree under consideration". If, at the end of a pass over the subtree under consideration, the value of *Changed* turns out to be non-empty, then the current subtree under consideration is widened, i.e., the father of its root becomes the root of the new subtree under consideration. The pass is then continued over the widened tree. This process of widening continues until the value of *Changed* is empty. Every subsequent pass starts at the root of the subtree under consideration.

A method similar to the iterative version is used by Engelfriet in [7] for l-ordered attribute grammars [8], although he does not make use of sets *NeedToBeEvaluated* and *Changed*. A tree node is marked to be affected for all coming visits after one of its attribute instances gets a different value. This may lead to unnecessary re-evaluations and superfluous visits to subtrees. Another solution for l-ordered attribute grammars is presented in [18].

Solutions for arbitrary non-circular attribute grammars are discussed in [14, 16]. Möncke et all. in [14] discuss the re-evaluation of attributes which become incorrect as a result of an optimizing tree transformation. Reps et all. in [16] give a solution for the updating of attribute values during an editing session.

References

1. Alblas, H.: A characterization of attribute evaluation in passes. Acta Informatica 16, 427-464 (1981).
2. Alblas, H.: Incremental simple multi-pass attribute evaluation. Proc. NGI-SION 1986 Symposium (1986), pp. 319-342.
3. Alblas, H.: Optimal incremental simple multi-pass attribute evaluation. Memorandum INF 86-27, University of Twente (1986).
4. Alblas, H.: Iteration of transformation passes over attributed program trees. Memorandum INF 87-28, University of Twente (1987).
5. Alblas, H.: Attribute evaluation methods. Memorandum, University of Twente, to appear (1988).
6. DeRemer, F.L.: Transformational grammars. In: Compiler Construction: An advanced course, F.L. Bauer, J. Eickel (eds.). Lecture Notes in Computer Science, Vol. 21. Springer 1974, pp. 121-145.
7. Engelfriet, J.: Attribute grammars: Attribute evaluation methods. In: Methods and tools for compiler construction. Cambridge University Press 1984, pp. 103-138.
8. Engelfriet, J., Filè, G.: Simple multi-visit attribute grammars, JCSS 24, 283-314 (1982).

9. Ganzinger, H. and Giegerich, R.: A truly generative semantics directed compiler generator. In: Proc. SIGPLAN 1982 Symposium on Compiler Construction, SIGPLAN Notices 17, 6 (1982), pp. 172-184.

10. Giegerich, R., Möncke, U., Wilhelm, R.: Invariance of approximative semantics with respect to program transformations. Informatik-Fachberichte 50, Springer 1981, pp. 1-10.

11. Glasner, I., Möncke, U., Wilhelm, R.: OPTRAN, a language for the specification of program transformations. Informatik-Fachberichte 34, Springer 1980, pp. 125-142.

12. Kastens, U.: Ordered attribute grammars. Acta Informatica 13, 229-256 (1980).

13. Knuth, D.E.: Semantics of context-free languages. Math. Systems Theory 2, 127-145 (1968). Correction in: Math. Systems Theory 5, 95-96 (1971).

14. Möncke, U., Weisgerber, B., Wilhelm, R.: How to implement a system for manipulation of attributed trees. Informatik-Fachberichte 77, Springer 1984, pp. 112-127.

15. Nestor, J.R., Mishra, B., Scherlis, W.L., Wulf, W.A.: Extensions to attribute grammars. Technical Report TL 83-36, Tartan Laboratories Inc., 1983.

16. Reps, T., Teitelbaum, T., Demers, A.: Incremental context-dependent analysis for language based editors. ACM TOPLAS 5, 449-477 (1983).

17. Wilhelm, R.: Computation and use of data flow information in optimizing compilers. Acta Informatica 12, 209-225 (1979).

18. Yeh, D.: On incremental evaluation of ordered attribute grammars, BIT 23, 308-320 (1983).

Incremental Attribute Evaluation with Side-effects

Görel Hedin

Lund Institute of Technology
Dept. of Computer Science
Box 118, S-221 00 Lund, Sweden
email: gorel@dna.lth.se

1. Introduction

Attribute grammars is a declarative formalism used to express context-sensitive constraints, e.g. the static semantic constraints on a program [Knuth 68]. Incremental attribute evaluators can be derived automatically from the grammar [Yeh 83], [Reps 84]. The incremental evaluator can be interfaced to a language-based editor, in order to give the user continuous feedback on static semantic errors during editing. It would also be desirable to be able to integrate other tools in the programming environment, e.g. code-generators and cross-reference tools, and let them utilize the attribute information.

However, there are drawbacks with the standard form of attribute grammars. One problem is that the incremental evaluation technique does not scale up for large programs. This is because reevaluation of complex attributes, such as symbol tables, triggers reevaluation in more places than is intuitively necessary. E.g. adding a new global procedure triggers reevaluation throughout the program, even if there are no calls to the procedure.

Another problem with attribute grammars is that the constraints are often unnatural to express and auxiliary attributes are needed which are only used to gather and propagate information between nodes. E.g. building up a symbol table must be done by propagating the partly built symbol table around the declaration nodes, possibly in several passes, depending on how the declarations are allowed to depend on each other. It would be more natural to put constraints on the final symbol table directly in terms of each of the declarations.

Several efforts have been made recently to solve these problems. E.g. Hoover and Reps have proposed mechanisms for incremental updating of aggregate attributes, and remote access to attributes [Hoover 86], [Hoover et al. 86], [Reps et al. 86]. Johnson & Fischer have proposed allowing non-local dependencies between attributes [Johnson et al. 82], [Johnson et al. 85]. Beshers & Campbell have proposed usage of maintained attributes which can be incrementally modified by automatically reversible operations during attribute evaluation [Beshers et al. 85]. Demers, Rogers & Zadeck have proposed using a scheme based on message-passing instead of attribute evaluation [Demers et al. 85]. Horwitz & Teitelbaum have proposed a combination of relations and attributes [Horwitz et al. 86].

In this paper we describe the technique used to perform incremental semantic analysis in the programming environment Mjølner [Dahle et al. 87]. Mjølner is a grammar-driven environment, supporting programming in statically typed object-oriented languages in the Simula tradition [SIMULA-67 68], [SIMULA 87]. Typed object-oriented languages have more complex scope rules than ordinary block structured languages such as Algol and Pascal. This is because of the type hierarchy introduced through inheritance. The technique used in Mjølner is based on attribute grammars, but also allows constraints to be expressed, which have side-effects when evaluated. The side-effects are automatically reversed when needed during incremental evaluation. The technique is thus similar to the one proposed by Beshers & Campbell. Mjølner includes a package for handling complex combinations of scope rules, allowing the scope rules of object-oriented languages to be expressed in an elegant way. The constraint facility is utilized to perform incremental updates and lookups in symbol tables, without having to copy information throughout the tree, as is normally done in attribute grammars. Since many non-local dependencies are handled directly rather than via the tree, the attribute dependencies become very simple, making it possible to use a simple and fast evaluator. Currently an ordered one-pass attribute evaluator is used in Mjølner. The evaluation technique has also been combined with demand attributes, and only very few attributes need to actually be stored in the tree. Default rules are elegantly expressed using an object-oriented grammar notation.

The rest of this paper is organized as follows: Section 2 describes the scope rules of object-oriented languages. Section 3 describes how scope-rules and symbol tables are represented in Mjølner. Section 4 describes the object-oriented grammar formalism. Section 5 describes the technique for incremental evaluation. Section 6 compares our technique to other proposed techniques. Section 7 concludes the paper.

2. Scope rules in object-oriented languages

In object-oriented languages in the Simula tradition, the normal scope rules for block structure are combined with scope rules for inheritance. In addition, via remote access ("dot-notation") and Simula's "inspect"-statement (similar to the "with"-statement of Pascal), attributes of an object can be accessed from the outside. This complexity of scope rules is not unique to Simula. Many new object-oriented languages combine block structure with inheritance, e.g. Beta [Kristensen et al. 87], Eiffel [Meyer 87], C++ [Stroustrup 86], and Trellis-Owl [Schaffert et al. 86]. There are also examples of procedural languages which use inheritance for records, e.g. PLANC [PLANC 79] and Oberon [Wirth 88]. Although inheritance is here restricted to data, such languages have scope rules similar to object-oriented languages.

2.1 Scope rules for Simula

In this section we briefly review the scope rules for Simula, and discuss the consequences of their combination.

Block structure

With *block* we mean a program construction which contains a local set of declarations. Simula has three kinds of blocks: *classes*, *procedures*, and Algol *block-statements*. In the Beta language, these constructions have been unified into one kind of block: the *pattern*. Both Simula and Beta allow full block structure, i.e. blocks may be nested to any level. Most other object-oriented languages have a simpler block structure allowing only three levels: Procedures nested inside classes, and classes nested inside a program module.

With *block-structured scope rules*, we mean the normal scope rules of Algol [Naur 63]. I.e. the scope of a declared identifier is the block it is declared in, and all inner blocks. Conversely the environment of a free identifier can be described as a search path, starting at the block in which the identifier occurs, and continuing in successively outer blocks.

Inheritance

In Simula, a class can be declared as a subclass of another class. The subclass will then inherit all the attributes of its superclass. The scope of a declaration in a class is thus the class itself, and all subclasses. In combination with block structure, we also have to add the inner blocks of the class and its subclasses. The environment of a free identifier now becomes more complex: It can be described as a search path, starting in the block, B, of the occurrence, continuing in the superblocks of B, then continuing in the enclosing block Bf of B, then continuing in the superblocks of Bf, and so on. E.g. in the figure below, the search path for free identifiers in class Rectangle's procedure Draw, will consist of the following blocks: Draw, Rectangle, Element, LINK, LINKAGE, GraphicPackage, SIMSET, and Main program.

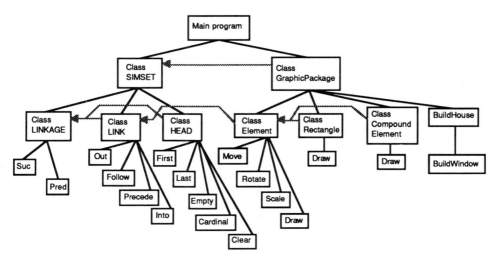

Figure 1. A block structured object-oriented program. The solid lines indicate block nesting. The dashed lines indicate subclass relationship. E.g. GraphicPackage is a subclass of SIMSET.

Remote-access

A declaration in a class may be accessed remotely, using "dot-notation". In Simula, this is used to call procedures in objects ("message-passing" in Smalltalk terminology) and to access data in objects. The environment of a remotely accessed declaration is a search path along the inheritance chain of the accessed object, starting at the static qualification of the object (the declared class of the object). E.g. in remote access to an object of class Rectangle, the search path will consist of: Rectangle, Element, LINK, and LINKAGE.

Inspect

Simula's inspect-statement "opens" an object, so the declared attributes of the object can be referenced by free identifiers. The search path for free identifiers inside an inspect statement is the inheritance chain of the inspected object, followed by the search path of the environment outside the inspect statement. E.g. if a Rectangle object is inspected in the procedure BuildWindow in figure 1, the search path will consist of the following blocks: Rectangle, Element, LINK, LINKAGE, BuildWindow, BuildHouse, GraphicPackage, SIMSET, and Main program.

It may of course be debated if the inspect statement is in agreement with object-oriented programming or not. Nevertheless, the inspect statement is widely used, and it is interesting to be able to handle it in an incremental environment.

2.2 Finding affected use sites

A problem in incremental semantic analysis is to quickly find affected identifier use sites, *IdUses*, after changes to declarations. With *affected* IdUses we mean those identifiers which refer to the added/removed/changed declaration either before or after the change. It is desirable that the affected IdUses are found in linear time, i.e. in time proportional to the number of affected IdUses. In the case of changing or removing a declaration, the problem is easily solved by maintaining cross-reference information at each of the declarations, e.g. a list of references to IdUses. However, when a new declaration is added, the problem is harder. There may exist IdUses which previously either were undeclared or referred to some other declaration, but will now refer to the new declaration.

Finding affected IdUses by checking traces

In Mjølner, a general method is used for finding affected IdUses after adding a declaration, by keeping track of *traces* when binding IdUses. This means that when we look for the declaration of an IdUse, the blocks are searched in the order prescribed by the environment of the IdUse, and in each block where the declaration is not found, a trace is left. A trace in a block thus means that there exists an IdUse which would rather refer to a declaration in that block than to whatever declaration it currently refers to. When a new declaration is added, the traces are checked to see if there are any IdUses which should be rebound, and information in the traces is used for efficient location of these IdUses.

Finding affected IdUses by searching environment

Another method for finding affected uses after adding a declaration is to search the environment of the declaration in order to find other declarations which will be hidden by the new declaration. This method is used e.g. in [Johnson et al. 82]. However, this method works only in simple cases, when the environment of an affected IdUse is a pure extension of the declaration's environment, e.g. in the case of pure block structure or pure inheritance. When block structure and inheritance is combined, or when environments are combined using the inspect-statement, this method fails.

3. Representation of symbol tables and scope rules

In a standard attribute grammar, symbol tables are built by propagating partly built symbol tables along the declarations and letting each declaration define a new symbol table value by concatenating its own information with an incoming symbol table. In the block bodies, the symbol tables are combined according to the scope rules of the language, and the appropriate combination of symbol tables is propagated to each IdUse.

We find the standard attribute-grammar approach unnatural, and it is also hard to implement efficiently. In Mjølner, each block has one symbol table attribute which is updated incrementally as the declaration information in the block is changed. Rather than propagating symbol tables to the IdUses, the appropriate symbol table *search path* is propagated to each IdUse.

The symbol table of a block contains an entry for each of the declared identifiers in the block. An entry contains information about the name, type, kind etc. of the declaration. Components of entries may contain references to other entries or to whole symbol tables. E.g. if the type of a variable is structured, the variable entry will contain a reference to the entry of the type. If a declaration is itself a block, the entry will contain a reference to the symbol table of that block. Each declaration has a binding-attribute which refers to the corresponding symbol-table entry. The declaration uses its binding-attribute to specify the component values of the entry. Each IdUse also has a binding-attribute which refers to the appropriate symbol-table entry, according to its search path. The IdUse can use the binding-attribute to look up information about its declaration, e.g. type and kind. Entries and components of entries are added, deleted, or changed as a consequence of changes to the declarations.

The scope-rules are represented by *search paths*. A search path is a list of references to symbol tables and other search paths. Each block has a number of search paths which define different kinds of accesses to the declarations of the block. E.g. local access, access from local blocks, access from subclasses, and remote access. In the syntax tree, these search paths are used to represent the environments of IdUses. Search paths of different blocks can be looked up and combined in order to form the appropriate environment for IdUses in different contexts. E.g. for Simula, the following search paths are used (see also figure 2):

The *static search path* defines the permitted access from local blocks. A Simula procedure has a static search path consisting of two elements: The first refers to the procedure's symbol table, and the second refers to the enclosing block's static search path. A Simula class has a three-element static search path: the class' symbol table, followed by the superclass' subclass search path, followed by the enclosing block's static search path.

The *local search path* defines the environment for free IdUses in the block. In Simula (and also in most other languages), the local search path coincides with the static search path.

The *subclass search path* of a class defines the permitted access from subclasses.

The *remote search path* of a class defines permitted remote access.

The subclass search path and the remote search path have the same structure. The reason for distinguishing between them is that Simula allows declarations to be "protected" or "hidden" from subclass and remote access respectively. It is e.g. often the case that local variables in a class should be hidden from remote access, but should be accessible from the subclasses. By associating filters with the search paths, individual declarations can be filtered out from a specific search path. Figure 2 gives a simplified view however, and does not distinguish between these search paths.

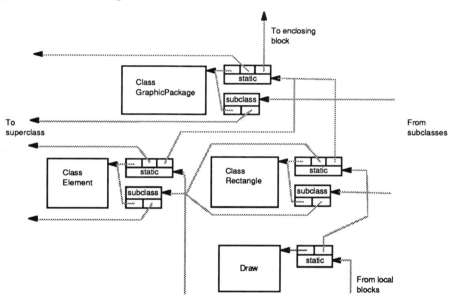

Figure 2. Search paths for some of the blocks in the program shown in figure 1.

4. Grammar formalism

In a standard attribute grammar, all attributes have functional values, defined by functional constraints. An attribution is said to be *valid* when all the constraints are satisfied. The above described symbol-table structure cannot be defined by functional constraints since it contains circular references both within and between individual symbol tables. Therefore, in addition to the functional constraints, we introduce *operational* constraints. In contrast to the functional constraints, the operational constraints may have side-effects when evaluated. Nevertheless, the formalism is still declarative, and we can use the same definition of a valid attribution.

In this section we describe the grammar formalism and give examples describing some aspects of the static semantics of Simula.

4.1 An object-oriented grammar notation

The grammar notation is object-oriented in that it supports abstract production specifications and specializations of these productions. The nodes follow the production description in a similar way as objects in an object-oriented language follow their class-descriptions.

The formalism supports four different kinds of productions: constructions, lists, lexemes, and abstract productions. Each production has a name, and defines a syntax node type. We will use the terms "production" and "node type" synonymously. Productions specify the node structure, the attributes of the node, and the constraints on those attributes. Construction productions specify that their nodes will have a specific number of son-nodes with certain names and types. List productions specify that their nodes can have an arbitrary number of sons of a specific type. Lexeme productions are used to model syntactic data such as identifiers and numerical constants. Each lexeme node has an attribute "string" which contains this data. Abstract productions model "un-expanded" nodes of a general type, e.g. statements, declarations, expressions. Any production may be a specialization of an abstract production. Specialized productions augment the definition of their super production. A constraint defining a particular attribute, will override constraints in super-productions defining the same attribute. The following notation is used for the node structure:

```
<cons-prod>:<super-prod> ::= {<son1:son1Prod>&<son2:son2Prod>&...}
<list-prod>:<super-prod> ::= <son:sonProd>*
<lexeme-prod>:<super-prod> ::= LEXEME
<abstract-prod>:<super-prod> ::= ABSTRACT
```

Attributes may be declared as synthesized, inherited, or local, with the usual meanings. An attribute defined by a functional constraint may also be specified "demand". This means that the attribute is not stored in the syntax tree, but instead evaluated each time it is accessed.

A kernel of pre-defined data types with associated operational constraints and functions are provided by the system. The implementation of the operational constraints is currently hand-coded, and new operational constraints cannot be defined within the grammar. Because of this, only a limited class of languages can be supported by the system in its present state.

4.2 Example: Variable declarations

The following example shows operational constraints that control a symbol-table entry for a variable declaration. Words in boldface are keywords in the grammar formalism. Words in italics are syntactic sugar for operational constraints. Two minus-signs at the end of a line indicates that the rest of the line is a comment.

```
-----------------------------------------------------------------
Production    <Node> ::= ABSTRACT
Attributes
     Inh     path : ref (SearchPath) demand
Constraints
     for all sons (x)
          Son(x) qua Node.path = path
-----------------------------------------------------------------
Production    <Decl>:<Node> ::= ABSTRACT
Attributes
     Inh     symTab : ref(SymbolTable) demand
     Loc     declBinding : ref(STentry)
     [declBinding] REPRESENTS THIS DECLARATION IN [symTab]       -- 1
-----------------------------------------------------------------
Production    <VarDecl>:<Decl> ::= {<varId:IdDecl>&<varType:Type>}
Attributes
     Loc     error : ErrorMarking
Constraints
     THE NAME OF [declBinding] IS [varId.string]                 -- 2
     THE KIND OF [declBinding] IS [VarKind]                      -- 3
     THE TYPE OF [declBinding] IS [varType.typeValue]            -- 4
     [error] MARKS THIS NODE WITH ["Double declared"]            -- 5
```

```
                   WHEN [DoubleDeclared(declBinding)]
-----------------------------------------------------------------------
Production    <IdDecl> ::= LEXEME
-----------------------------------------------------------------------
Production    <Type>:<Node> ::= ABSTRACT
Attributes
    Syn      typeValue : TYPE demand
Constraints
    typeValue = BottomType
-----------------------------------------------------------------------
Production    <IntegerType>:Type ::= {}
Constraints
    typeValue = IntegerType
-----------------------------------------------------------------------
Production    <RefType>:Type ::= {<classId:IdUse>}
Constraints
    typeValue = MakeRefType(classId.UseBinding)
-----------------------------------------------------------------------
```

The production Node is an abstract production whose only purpose is to establish a default rule for propagation of SearchPaths. I.e., the default is that a specialization of Node propagates its own search path to all of its children of production Node. See sections 4.3 and 4.4 for the usage of search paths.

Constraint 1 in production Decl expresses that the attribute declBinding in Decl refers to the declaration's entry in the symbol table symTab. VarDecl is a specialization of Decl, and constraints 2, 3, and 4 define the name, kind, and type components of the entry referred to by declBinding. The name depends on the identifier name in the IdDecl node. The kind is a constant, VarKind. The type of the variable depends on what specialization of production Type the son-node varType is. If varType is "unexpanded", i.e. of production Type, then typeValue is "BottomType", a general type compatible with everything. This default value is overridden in the specialized productions IntegerType and RefType. Constraint 5 expresses that the VarDecl should be marked on the screen, if there already exists another declaration with the same name. A message associated with the error-marking makes it possible for the user to interactively ask for an explanation of the error.

4.3 Example: Expressions and Identifier Uses

Identifier uses appear in statements, expressions, and also in some declarations (e.g. in the production RefType above). An identifier use is bound to the appropriate symbol-table entry by the operational constraint 1 in production IdUse as follows:

```
      -----------------------------------------------------------------
      Production    <Expr>:<Node> ::= ABSTRACT
      Attributes
          Syn      exprType : TYPE demand
          Syn      exprQual : TYPE demand
      Constraints
          exprType = BottomType
          exprQual = BottomClassType
      -----------------------------------------------------------------
      Production    <IdUse>:<Expr> ::= LEXEME
      Attributes
          Syn      useBinding : ref (STentry)
          Loc      error : ref (ErrorMarking)
      Constraints
          [useBinding] IS THE DECLARATION OF [string]              -- 1
              FOUND ON THE PATH [path]
          exprType = GetType(useBinding)                            -- 2
          exprQual =                                                -- 3
              if exprType.InLattice(BottomRefType, TopRefType)
              then exprType.Qualification
              else BottomClassType
          [error] MARKS THIS NODE WITH ["Not declared"]            -- 4
              WHEN [useBinding = NullEntry]
```

Constraint 1 expresses that useBinding will refer to the first symbol-table entry with the name
"string" which is found when following the search path "path". If no such entry is found, the
useBinding will refer to the constant "NullEntry". This is used in constraint 4 to decide if the
IdUse node should be marked with an error or not. Constraints 2 and 3 define the exprType and
exprQual attributes of the IdUse. These attributes are declared in IdUse's superproduction
(Expr), and are used for type-checking. ExprQual is only relevant when exprType is a reference
type, and will then be the appropriate class type. Types are arranged in a lattice in the following
style:

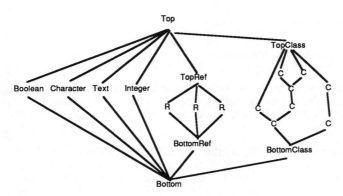

Figure 3. A type lattice.

BottomType is the least specific type. E.g. undeclared identifiers will have the type
BottomType. The higher up in the lattice, the more specific is the type. Lattice operations such
as InLattice, Above, Below, Meet, and Join, make it easy to specify type-checking.

4.4 Example: Overriding default search paths

Remote access (dot-notation) and inspect statements are examples when the default search paths
are overridden. This is specified as follows:

```
Production     <Dot>:<Expr> ::= {<receiver:Expr>&<selector:IdUse>}
Attributes
    Loc    error : ref (ErrorMarking)
Constraints
    selector.path =                                          -- 1
        if receiver.exprType.InLattice(BottomRefType, TopRefType)
        then RemoteSearchPath(receiver.exprQual)
        else NullSearchPath
    exprType = selector.exprType                             -- 2
    exprQual = selector.exprQual                             -- 3
    [error] MARKS THIS NODE WITH ["Prefix not defined"]     -- 4
        WHEN [not(receiver.exprType.Below(TopRefType)]
-----------------------------------------------------------------
Production     <InspectStmt>:<Stmt> ::= {<obj:Expr>&<do:Stmt>}
Attributes
    Loc    error : ref(ErrorMarking)
Constraints
    do.path =
        if obj.exprType.InLattice(BottomRefType, TopRefType)
        then Concatenate(RemoteSearchPath(obj.exprQual), path)
        else path
    [error] MARKS THIS NODE WITH ["Prefix not defined"]
        WHEN [not(obj.exprType.Below(TopRefType)]
```

Remote access in Simula (receiver.selector) is analogous to message-passing in Smalltalk [Goldberg et al. 83]. The "receiver" in production Dot thus represents the remotely accessed object, and "selector" represents the name of the accessed entity. The search path of the selector is the remote search path of the class of the remotely accessed object. This is expressed by constraint 1. In case the receiver is not a reference to an object, e.g. if it is an integer variable, the Dot-node will be marked on the screen, as defined in constraint 4. Constraints 2 and 3 express that the whole dot-expression has the same type as the selector.

The first constraint in production InspectStmt specifies that the search path of its interior statements (the do-part) is the concatenation of the remote search path of the inspected object and the search path of the inspect-statement itself.

4.5 Demand attributes

The high consumption of space is a well-known problem for attribute grammars, and the problem is even worse for incremental systems where the attribute values have to be saved in order to allow incremental update. Demand attributes have been used extensively in the examples above. Since demand attributes are evaluated each time they are accessed, no space needs to be reserved for them in the nodes. In combination with operational constraints, this allows the total space consumption for attributes to be kept very low. E.g. in the examples above, the only attributes which are actually stored, are one symbol table for each block, a binding for each declaration and for each IdUse, and error-marking attributes.

Using demand attributes instead of stored attributes need not slow down the evaluation. In many cases, an attribute is never accessed at all. E.g. the path attribute is propagated to all expressions. However, numeric constants (which are specializations of expressions) will not utilize the path information. If the path attribute was stored, this would take extra time both for evaluating it and for keeping it up to date.

The use of demand attributes thus makes it possible to define attributes which are used only in certain syntactic combinations, without penalizing the performance in other contexts. This is of course of most value when the attribute is used only in unusual syntactic combinations. E.g. test of assignability can be modelled as follows:

```
-----------------------------------------------------------------
Production    <AssignStmt >:<Stmt>::= {<to:Expr> & <from:Expr>}
Attributes
     Loc    error : ref (ErrorMarking)
Constraints
     [error] MARKS THIS NODE WITH ["Left of := cannot be assigned"]
          WHEN [not(to.assignable)]
-----------------------------------------------------------------
```

The left hand side of the assignment is here modelled as a general expression. However, the attribute "assignable" is only accessed in expressions on the left hand side of an assignment. Most expressions will not be in this context, and their "assignable" attribute will never be evaluated. Furthermore, most specializations of Expr are not assignable, e.g. all arithmetic, boolean, and relational expressions. By using default constraints, these productions need not include a constraint for "assignable".

Demand attributes may cause more reevaluation in an incremental system because old attribute values cannot be compared with new values in order to stop the evaluation. However, the time it takes to compare the attribute values is not necessarily less than what is won by stopping the evaluation.

Synthesized demand attributes are analogous to virtual procedures in object-oriented languages in that the "calling" node knows the general type of its son-node, but it does not know the actual type. To implement efficient access to demand attributes, the function defining the demand attribute must be located quickly. This is done by including a table of demand attribute functions in each production. In all specializations of a production, the function defining a particular demand attribute is located at the same offset. Accesses can then be done efficiently by indexing into the table. This technique is similar to the one used to implement virtual procedures in e.g. Simula and Beta.

For inherited demand attributes, the situation is not quite as simple, since a production says nothing about the father node's type. E.g. an IdUse-node may be the son of a Dot-node, an Add-node or a RefType-node. In our system we have solved this by actually including a constraint on the father node type of each production. This does not put any practical constraints on what kinds of grammars can be defined, since the inherited demand attributes can always be declared in the most general production class, which all productions are specializations of. Because a production now knows the general type of the father node, the functions defining inherited demand attributes can be looked up using the same technique as for synthesized demand attributes.

The inherited demand attribute "path" is e.g. actually specified as follows:

```
------------------------------------------------------------------
Production     <SuperNode> ::= ABSTRACT
Attributes
    Exp     path
Constraints
    for all sons(x)
        son(x) qua Node.path = NullSearchPath
------------------------------------------------------------------
Production     <Node>:<SuperNode> son of <SuperNode> ::= ABSTRACT
Attributes
    Inh     path : ref(SearchPath) demand
Constraints
    for all sons(x)
        son(x) qua Node.path = path
------------------------------------------------------------------
```

SuperNode defines the behavior of being able to "export" the demand inherited attribute "path" to its sons of type Node. It also defines a default value for this attribute. Typically, the root node of a syntax tree is a specialization of SuperNode.

Node is the general production for nodes which have an inherited demand attribute "path". It also specializes the behavior of SuperNode by overriding the value it propagates to its sons. Typically, all nodes in the syntax tree, except for the root node, are specializations of Node.

5. Incremental Evaluation

The incremental attribute evaluator is activated after each of the user's editing actions. The evaluator is similar to an incremental evaluator for a standard attribute grammar, following evaluation orders derived from the attribute dependencies. The main differences are that 1) the side-effects introduced when evaluating an operational constraint have to be undone properly when needed, and 2) the attribute evaluation can spread to distant locations in the syntax tree during evaluation of an operational constraint.

5.1 Undoing side-effects

Each operational constraint has two associated operations: one *evaluation* operation for establishing the constraint, and one *de-evaluation* operation for cancelling the side-effects introduced by the previous evaluation operation. E.g., when evaluating the constraint defining the useBinding attribute, trace-information will be inserted into the symbol tables as described in section 3. When the constraint is de-evaluated, that trace-information is removed. This makes it possible to *re-evaluate* an operational constraint simply by de-evaluating it and then evaluating it. For efficiency reasons one may also define a re-evaluation operation which has the same net effect as a de-evaluation followed by an evaluation. It is also necessary that the (de-)evaluation of one constraint does not interfere with the (de-)evaluation of other operational constraints. I.e. the order of (de-)evaluation must only depend on the attribute dependencies in the grammar.

These properties make it possible to let the incremental evaluator treat operational and functional constraints in the same way. The evaluator can evaluate, re-evaluate, and de-evaluate a constraint. For functional constraints, re-evaluation is the same thing as evaluation, and de-evaluation of functional constraint is an empty operation.

In order to do a proper de-evaluation of an attribute defined by an operational constraint, one may need access to the arguments used at the previous evaluation. E.g. when de-evaluating the useBinding attribute, the old search path is needed in order to find the appropriate symbol tables where trace-information should be removed. Thus although it is not directly visible in the grammar, the old search path is actually stored in the node together with the useBinding attribute.

There are four basic editing actions: *subtree replacement*, when an old subtree is removed from the syntax tree and replaced by a new subtree. *Subtree insertion*, when a new subtree is inserted as a son to a list node. *Subtree deletion*, when a son of a list node is removed. Finally, *lexeme-string replacement*, when the string attribute of a lexeme node is replaced.

After a subtree replacement, the attribute evaluator goes through three phases: In the first phase, *monolithic de-evaluation*, all attributes of the old subtree are de-evaluated to remove side-effects. New subtrees are considered unattributed, so in the second phase, *monolithic evaluation*, the inherited attributes in the root of the new subtree are given values, and all attributes in the new subtree are evaluated. The third phase, *incremental re-evaluation*, re-evaluates all attributes dependent on the synthesized attributes in the root of the new subtree.

The subtree insertion/deletion actions can be seen as special cases of subtree replacement, with one of the monolithic phases missing. The lexeme-string replacement action will trigger incremental re-evaluation of attributes dependent on the string attribute.

5.2 Propagation to distant nodes

During the (de-)evaluation of operational constraints which add, remove, or change symbol-table entries, affected IdUses are located as described in section 3 and incremental re-evaluation is started in these nodes. In general, such re-evaluations must be queued until ongoing evaluations are completed. This is in order to avoid conflicts by incrementally re-evaluating constraints whose arguments are not yet initialized, or are no longer relevant.

Our system supports incremental evaluation of L-attributed grammars [Lewis et al. 74], but because of the possibility to incrementally update symbol tables, and to propagate evaluation to distant nodes, a larger class of languages can be handled, than is normally the case with L-attributed grammars. E.g. in Simula, a declaration may depend on any other declaration in the same block. In a standard attribute grammar for Simula, the declarations in the block need to be traversed in three passes: one pass for gathering information about the class hierarchy, a second pass for gathering information about individual classes, and a third pass for propagating the information to the variables. In our system, only one pass is needed. However, when evaluating one declaration, all information may not yet be available in the symbol table. Through the propagation to distant nodes, the evaluation will then return to that declaration when the needed information is added to the symbol table. E.g. suppose the following two declarations are inserted at once:

```
ref (A) rA;
class A;
begin
end;
```

The declaration for the variable rA will be added first to the symbol table. Since A is not yet in the symbol table, the type component of rA will be set to a reference to an unknown type. When the class A is inserted into the symbol table, evaluation will propagate back to the rA variable declaration and the type of rA will be re-evaluated. This evaluation scheme is clearly sub-optimal, but in an incremental system where the user edits small increments at a time, adding several declarations at once is probably very unusual. Also, the sub-optimal behavior will only occur when the declarations are in the "wrong" order, with uses before declarations.

5.3 Circular dependencies

Because of the possibility in operational constraints to propagate the evaluation to distant nodes, there are attribute dependencies which are not visible in the grammar. In fact, these dependencies may give rise to circularities. However, rather than to prohibit circular dependencies, we allow them to exist, and instead break the circular evaluation by other means. One example of circular dependencies is the following:

```
ref (B) A;
ref (A) B;
```

This example is an erroneous program fragment since A ans B are variables, and the qualification of a reference variable must be a class. If no special precaution was taken in this case, the evaluation would continue for ever as follows:

```
 1. add A-entry
 2. set type of A-entry to ref(BottomType) since B is not in symbol table
 3. add B-entry
 4. set type of B-entry to ref(A)
 5. since the type of B is changed, reevaluate IdUses referring to B
 6. reevaluate the type of A (set it to ref (B))
 7. since the type of A is changed, reevaluate IdUses referring to A
 8. reevaluate the type of B (set it to ref (A))
 9. same as 5
10.same as 6
...
```

This circularity was broken by changing the evaluation operation for setting the type of a symbol-table entry. A check was added to see if the new type was the same as the previous one. In that case, the re-evaluation of distant nodes was stopped.

Another example of a circularity is when the inheritance chain is circular (this is also an illegal program fragment), e.g. as follows:

```
A class B;
begin
end;

B class A;
begin
end;
```

If the symbol table would reflect this circular structure, this would lead to loops in the search paths, and endless searching when binding IdUses. To avoid this, a check was inserted into the constraint defining the superclass of a class declaration as follows:

```
-----------------------------------------------------------------
Production    <ClassDecl>:<Decl> ::=
    {<superId:IdUse> & <classId:IdDecl> &...}
Attributes
Constraints
    THE SUPERCLASS OF [declBinding] IS
        [if superId.exprType.Above(GetType(declBinding))
         then BottomClassType
         else superId.exprType]
-----------------------------------------------------------------
```

If the intended super-class is already a subclass to the ClassDecl (subclasses are above their superclasses in the type lattice), the superclass of ClassDecl's entry will instead be set to BottomClassType, the most general class type.

6. Related Work

In related work on making incremental evaluators more useful in practice, all examples are given for very simple block-structured languages. It is unclear if the proposed techniques are sufficiently efficient for object-oriented languages.

Hoover [Hoover et al. 86] and Reps [Reps et al. 86] introduce aggregate valued attributes which can be incrementally updated and are thus suitable to represent symbol tables. New symbol tables can be constructed from other symbol tables in order to represent concatenated scopes in a space efficient way, and usage information is maintained in each symbol table about attributes depending on it as a whole, or on specific elements in it. This makes it possible to do selective propagation to use sites, so only those use sites which are actually affected by the change will be visited. However, when changing a symbol table, all dependent symbol tables have to be updated. This may prove to be very expensive for object-oriented languages. E.g. if the environment of each selector in each remote access is represented by an individual symbol table, adding a new procedure in a class would cause updating of the symbol tables of all remote accesses to that class. Another problem is that the proposed aggregate values may not be part of other attributes [Hoover 87]. This will probably make it hard to combine symbol tables to represent e.g. inheritance.

Demers et al. propose a declarative message-passing formalism as an alternative to attribute grammars [Demers et al. 85]. It allows a natural modelling of information similar to ours, in that symbol table information is maintained locally in the block and not propagated to all use sites. Identifier use sites send messages to the symbol tables to find out typing information. However, messages can only be propagated according to the syntax tree structure. This would probably make it hard to propagate messages along an inheritance search path as would be needed for an object-oriented language.

The technique we use of augmenting attribute grammars with constraints which have side-effects when evaluated, is very similar to the work of Beshers and Campbell [Beshers et al. 85]. In their terminology, our symbol tables would be classified as "maintained attributes", and our operational constraints as "constructor attributes".

Our use of demand attributes solve similar problems as do the copy rules of Hoover [Hoover 86] and the remote attributes of Reps [Reps et al. 86]. However, due to our object-oriented notation, identity constraints need not be repeated in all intervening nodes as in the copy-rules of Hoover, and son-nodes do not need to know the exact type of their remote father node as in Reps. Also, the demand attributes are more general than copy rules and remotely accessed attributes, since they may refer to information which is not explicitly stored in other attributes. The Cornell Synthesizer Generator also includes a mechanism for demand evaluation of attributes, but it differs from our demand attributes in that the attributes are stored when they have been evaluated the first time [Reps et al. 85].

Our use of default constraints for general productions also solve similar problems as the default message propagation orders of Demers et al. [Demers et al. 85], in that information can be propagated via nodes without having to add propagation rules in each individual node type. However, their approach is different in that they associate the propagation order with the messages (the attributes) rather than with the node types.

7. Conclusion

We have demonstrated how an attribute grammar, augmented with operational constraints, can be used to specify the static semantics of an object-oriented language. The operational constraints have side-effects which make it possible to incrementally update attributes. This makes it possible to represent symbol tables in a natural and efficient way. A tracing technique is used to efficiently locate all affected identifier use sites after changes to symbol tables. The technique is general enough to handle the various combinations of scope rules which appear in object-oriented languages.

A mechanism for demand attributes is used, which together with the operational constraint allows the total space consumption for attributes to be kept very low. This is extremely important in order to be able to represent large programs. An object-oriented notation has been introduced which allows default definition of constraints. This gives a high degree of flexibility in the grammar specification, and is particularly useful in combination with demand attributes.

Acknowledgements

This work has been carried out within the Mjølner project. I would like to thank the other participants in this project, especially Lars-Ove Dahlin who has designed and implemented the search path mechanism, and with whom I have had many constructive discussions.

The Mjølner project is partially financed by the Nordic Fund for Technology and Industrial Development (Nordisk Industrifond) and by the Swedish national board for Technical Development (STU).

References

[Beshers et al. 85]   Beshers G., Campbell R.: *Maintained and Constructor Attributes*. In Proceedings of the ACM SIGPLAN 85 Symposium on Language Issues in Programming Environments. Seattle, June 1985.

[Dahle et al. 87]   Dahle, H.P., Löfgren, M., Madsen, O.L., Magnusson, B., *The MJØLNER Project* Proceeding of the Conference held at Software Tools, Online Publications, London 1987.

[Demers et al. 85]   Demers A., Rogers A., Zadeck F.K.: *Attribute Propagation by Message Passing*. In Proceedings of the ACM SIGPLAN 85 Symposium on Language Issues in Programming Environments. Seattle, June 1985.

[Goldberg et al. 83]   Goldberg A., Robson D.: *Smalltalk 80. The language and its implementation*. Addison-Wesley 1983.

[Hoover 86]   Hoover R.: *Dynamically bypassing copy rule chains in attribute grammars*. In Conference Record of the 13th Symposium on Principles of Programming Languages, St. Petersburg, Fla. Januray 1986.

[Hoover et al. 86]   Hoover R., Teitelbaum T.: *Efficient Incremental Evaluation of Aggregate Values in Attribute Grammars*. Proceedings of the SIGPLAN '86 Symposium on Compiler Construction, Palo Alto, June 1986.

[Hoover 87]   Hoover R.: *Incremental Graph Evaluation*. PhD Thesis. Cornell University, Dept. of Computer Science, May 1987.

[Horwitz et al. 86]   Horwitz S., Teitelbaum T.: *Generating Editing Environments Based on Relations and Attributes*. ACM TOPLAS, Vol 8, No 4, October 1986. Pages 577-608.

[Johnson et al. 82]   Johnson G. F., Fischer C. N.: *Non-syntactic attribute flow in language based editors*. In Conference Record of the 9th ACM Symposium on Principles of Programming Languages, Albuquerque, N.M., January 1982. 185-195.

[Johnson et al. 85]   Johnson G. F., Fischer C. N.: *A meta-language and system for nonlocal incremental attribute evaluation in language-based editors*. In Conference Record of the 12th ACM Symposium on Principles of Programming Languages, New Orleans, La. January 1985. 141-151.

[Knuth 68]   Knuth D. E.: *Semantics of context-free languages*. Math. Syst. Theory 2:2, June 1968, 127-145.

[Kristensen et al. 87]   Kristensen B. B., Madsen O.L., Møller-Pedersen B., Nygaard K.: *The BETA Programming Language*. In Shriver B., Wegner P. (eds.) *Research Directions in Object-Oriented Programming*. The MIT Press, 1987.

[Lewis et al. 74]   Lewis P.M., Rosenkrantz D.J., Stearns R.E.: *Attributed translations*. J. Computer and Systems Sciences 9:3, 279-307.

[Meyer 87]   Meyer B.: *Eiffel: Programming for Reusability and Extendibility*. SIGPLAN Notices, Vol. 22, No. 2, Feb 1987.

[Naur 63]   Naur P.: *Revised report on the algorithmic language ALGOL 60*. Comm. ACM 6:1, 1-17.

[PLANC 79]   PLANC Reference Manual. Norsk Data A.S. Oslo, Norway, 1979.

[Reps 84]   Reps T.: *Generating Language-Based Environments*. The MIT Press, 1984.

[Reps et al. 85]   Reps T., Teitelbaum T.: *The Synthesizer Generator. Reference Manual*. Cornell University, Dept. of Computer Science. 1985 (revised 1987).

[Reps et al. 86]   Reps T., Marceau C., Teitelbaum T.: *Remote attribute updating for language-based editors*. In Conference Record of the Thirteenth ACM Symposium on Principles of Programming Languages, St. Petersburg, Florida, January 1986. pp 1-13.

[Schaffert et al. 86] Schaffert C., Cooper T., Bullis B., Kilian M., Wilpolt C.: *An Introduction to Trellis/Owl*. In *Proceedings of OOPSLA '86*. The 1986 Conference on *Object-Oriented Programming Systems, Languages and Applications*. SIGPLAN Notices. Vol 21 No 11, Nov 1986.

[SIMULA 87]   Data Processing - Programming Languages - *SIMULA*. Swedish Standard SS 63 61 14. SIS. Stockholm, Sweden, June 1987.

[SIMULA-67 68]   Dahl, O.-J., Nygaard, K.: *SIMULA 67 Common Base Language*. Norwegian Computing Center, Oslo, 1968. Revised 1970, 1972, and 1984.

[Stroustrup 86]   Stroustrup B.: *The C++ Programming Language*. Addison-Wesley, 1986.

[Wirth 88]   Wirth N.: From Modula to Oberon. Tech. Rep. ETH, Zurich, 1988.

[Yeh 83]   Yeh D.: *On Incremental Evaluation of Ordered Attribute Grammars*. BIT 23:3, 1983.

Optimizing Implementation of Aggregates in the Compiler Specification System MAGIC [1]

A. Poetzsch–Heffter

Technische Universität München
Institut für Informatik
Arcisstraße 21
8 München 2
Federal Republic of Germany
poetzsch@lan.informatik.tu–muenchen.dbp.de

Abstract

The paper describes the implementation concept including optimizing transformations of the aggregate handling in the MAGIC System. The MAGIC System is a system for specification and rapid prototyping of compilers developed at the Technical University of Munich. One of its main features is a powerful functional specification language based on an extension of attribute coupled grammars [GaG84]. For the specification of structured symboltables, the language provides the generic abstract datatype *aggregate*.

As the user may handle aggregates like any other values, the system must provide the mapping of aggregate values to objects in the storage and of functions to storage changing procedures. This optimizing implementation mapping consists of three parts. First, all aggregate occurrences are determined and their dependencies are analysed. Then the algorithm tries to refine the attribute dependencies, so that reading operations to an aggregate–valued attribute preceed writing operations to this attribute. Finally, the functions are replaced by the corresponding operations that operate on a shared hashtable.

1. Introduction

The paper describes the implementation concept including optimizing transformations of the aggregate handling in the MAGIC System. The MAGIC System is a system for specification and rapid prototyping of compilers developed at the Technical University of Munich. Its main features (compared with other compiler generating systems) : It has a graphical user interface to support the specification process and to visualize compilations, a functional specification language based on an extension of attribute coupled grammars [GaG84], and an interpreter to allow high–level debugging. A short overview of the system (as far as needed for this work) is given in chapter 2; a more detailed description can be found in [KLP88].

---
[1] Support for this research was provided by the Siemens AG München ZTI SOF 2

1.1. The Problem

The major task in the development of a compiler front end is the design of a suitable symboltable; this especially holds for big languages like Ada or Chill where the front end is about half of the whole compiler (c.f.[Bjö80] p.IX) and a high-level specification with an efficient implementation of symboltables is particularly necessary. The existing compiler generating systems don't provide special means for the specification of symboltables:

- Either the user has to program imperative semantic actions getting efficient but very complex solutions which often even violate the paradigm of the specification formalism (cf.[BaT84])

- or the user specifies the symboltable by using functional list structures loosing efficiency (cf.[UDP82]).

The MAGIC Specification Language provides the generic abstract datatype *aggregate* with functions like enter, lookup, etc.. Aggregates are mainly used to specify structured symboltables (e.g. in a block structured language, the symboltable is a list of aggregates). As the user may handle aggregates like any other values (figure 1 shows a typical situation, where an aggregate value is used for the calculation of two attributes), the system must provide the mapping of aggregate values to objects in the storage and of functions to storage changing operations (implementation mapping).

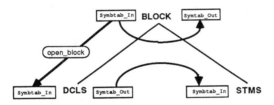

figure 1

The paper describes this implementation mapping and demonstrates how to use and refine attribute dependencies during generation time to get efficient implementations.

1.2. Informal Outline of the Approach

The user specifies the symboltable as a structure of aggregate types and uses the symboltable values as any other values in a purely functional manner. The system implements the aggregates by a shared datastructure with hashed lookup. In contrast to functional languages like ML [Har86], where the dynamic behaviour of a program is in general unknown, so that copy actions can't be avoided, functional attribute grammars allow effective optimization : The attribute flow can be calculated and even be influenced; and as the main application of aggregates is known, we can use heuristics where necessary.

The optimizing implementation mapping consists of three parts. First, all aggregate occurrences are determined and their dependencies are analysed. Then the algorithm tries to refine the attribute dependencies, so that reading operations to an aggregate-valued attribute preceed writing operations to this attribute. Finally, the functions are replaced by the corresponding operations that operate on a shared hashtable. Aggregate values are represented by access information to the hashtable. The algorithm for the implementation mapping is presented in chapter 3.

1.3. Related Work

The work is related to different papers in the area of functional languages and attribute grammars. Especially, four aspects in the treatment of attribute grammars have influenced our work, namely storage optimization [Gan79], nonlocal attribute handling [Räi86], lifetime analysis for attributes [Kas87], and incremental evaluation for aggregate values [HoT86].

2. The MAGIC System and its Specification Language

2.1. The MAGIC System

The MAGIC System is a tool for the interactive specification and development of compilers. Compared with other compiler generating systems, it stresses the specification and testing process. For this purpose, the MAGIC System provides :

- a modular and powerful high-level specification language based on attribute grammars (introduced in section 2.2).
- a graphical and interactive user interface to most components of the system supported by a consistency check mechanism.
- generator, interpreter and a graphical debugger enabling fast and high level testing of the specification as well as a rapid prototype implementation of the compiler.

The following figure gives a rough overview of the system:

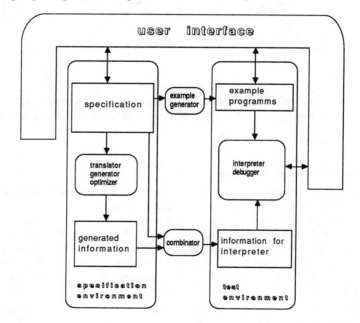

The user interface supports the specification process by enabling users to directly edit graphical representations of attribute grammars and the testing phase by debugging attribute evaluation on the same level. The main aspects of the graphical representation of attribute grammars will be introduced together with the specification language in the following section.

2.2. The MAGIC Specification Language

This section introduces those features of the MAGIC Specification Language (*MS*) needed for the following central chapter of this paper; a complete description can be found in [Poe88].

2.2.1. The Type Concept

MS has a uniform type concept to describe syntax trees and attribute values. Besides standard types and subtypes thereof, there are structured types (for the description of syntactical productions and variant records resp.), list types, and aggregate types. To illustrate the usage of types and their values, we stepwise introduce a miniature programming language minPL and specify a function *simple_sem_analyse*. This function computes a table that records the number of all occurences of an identifier where it was not visible. The following figure gives the abstract syntax of minPL :

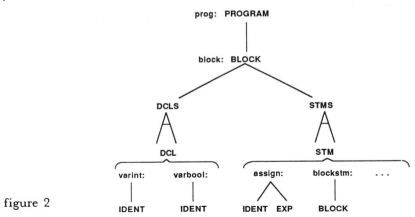

figure 2

As shown in the figure, a minPL program consists of a block that itself consists of a declaration list and a statement list. minPL provides integer and boolean variables. Every used identifier must have been declared as in known block structured languages. For brevity, we ommit other statements and the specification of expressions.

Figure 2 defines the grammar types PROGRAM, BLOCK, DCL, STM, and the list types DCLS and STMS, as well as the constructors (in figure 2 prog,varint,varbool,..) to construct the trees/terms of those types, to name the productions, and as discriminators of the defined type.

2.2.2. Lists and Aggregates

As shown in figure 2, the abstract syntax of a programming language can be defined by grammar types and list types. The manipulation of lists is done by functions like emptylist (denoted by <>), concatenation (.+.), and makelist (<.>).

For the specification of symboltable mechanisms and comparable tasks, the system provides aggregate types [BaW81]. E.g. to specify the function *simple_sem_analyse*, we
need a symboltable that records the declarations. Figure 3 shows the definition of the
type SYMTAB. Values of type SYMTAB are lists of aggregates of type
LOCAL_SYMTAB. Each local symboltable is an aggregate with keytype IDENT and
entrytype VARTYPE. VARTYPE is a type with the two constants vint and vbool to
record the type of the found declaration.

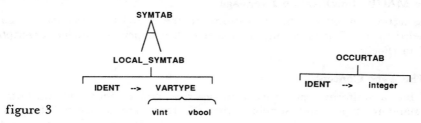

figure 3

Aggregates are constructed and handled by the following functions: empty_grex
(denoted by []), enter (. &(.,.)), lookup (.[.]), isdefined, etc.. Their usage is illustrated in the following section.

2.2.3. Functional Abstraction

In the MAGIC Specification Language, there are four kinds of functions:

- Standard functions: They are provided by the language to handle the standard
  and generic datatypes.

- External functions: They are an interface to the programming languages C and
  Pascal. They are not further discussed in this paper (c.f.[Poe88]).

- Applicative functions: They are recursively defined functions as *rec_isdefined* in
  the example below.

- Attributive functions: They are defined by means of an attribution as the function *simple_sem_analyse* in the example. They are an generalization of attribute
  coupled grammars [GaG84].

To continue the example and the illustration of aggregates, the following figure
shows the specification of the function *simple_sem_analyse* consisting of the functionality and the corresponding attributions:

function simple_sem_analyse (PROG p) OCCURTAB:

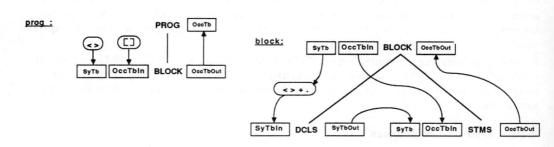

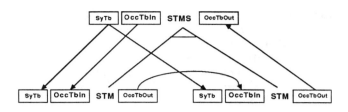

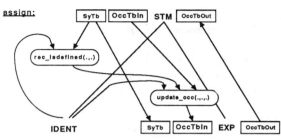

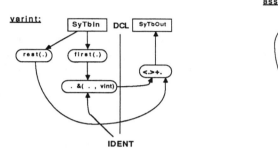

figure 4

For brevity, the trivial attribution schemes for DECLS and blockstm are left out; the attribution scheme for varbool is like that for varint.

By this kind of functional abstraction, attribute grammars become a flexible means for modular function specification. They can be used in all places where syntax–directed computation is needed: For the specification of a whole compiler phase as well as for the specification of semantic actions (not shown in the example).

Finally, we give the definitions of the predicate *rec_isdefined* that checks whether an identifier has been declared and the function *update_occ* that updates the occurrence table if the is_decl parameter is true:

```
function rec_isdefined ( SYMTAB st; IDENT id ) boolean:
    if    is_< >(st)
        then     false
        else if  isdefined( first(st), id )
                then     true
                else     rec_isdefined( rest(st), id )
                end
    end
```

```
function  update_occ ( boolean is_decl; OCCURTAB ot; IDENT id ) OCCURT
     if    is_decl
        then      ot
        else if   isdefined( ot, id )
              then     ot &( id, ot[id]+1 )
              else     ot &( id, 1 )
           end
     end
```

3. Implementation of Aggregates

The following four sections describe the implementation of aggregates in the MAGIC–System. First, the target datastructure for aggregates is presented. Then, we explain the analysis of attribute equations and the algorithm for a slightly restricted language. Finally, we show the extensions for the unrestricted case.

3.1. Implementing Functions by Storage Changing Procedures

To implement the specification language of MAGIC, each function expression in an attribute equation has to be substituted by a storage changing procedure or function call and additional operations. Furthermore, datastructures must be given for the types of the language.

We implement aggregates by a shared hashtable. The following dependency graph gives an idea of what can be shared and motivates the chosen datastructure.

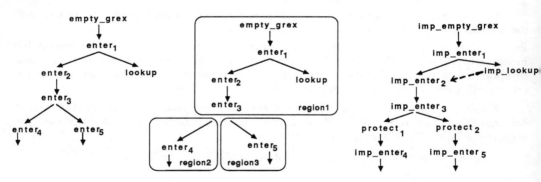

figure 5

As illustrated in figure 5, every aggregate value is computed by the function *enter* starting from an initial value (here *empty_grex*). If we can execute the *lookup*–operation before the $enter_2$–operation, then $enter_1$, *lookup*, $enter_2$, and $enter_3$ can operate on the same table, whereas the resulting table has to be protected from the entries of $enter_4$ and $enter_5$ in order to get correct tables after these entries; i.e. son nodes always share the table of their father. Figure 5 shows the corresponding partition of the dependency graph reflecting the sharing. E.g. the table after $enter_4$ consists of region 1 and region 2. The third part of figure 5 shows the dependency graph with the corresponding imperative procedures. Before we give their definitions, we describe the underlying datastructures and functions :

197

- A global hashtable HashTable and a global region counter RegCount
- A injective function *code_key*: KEY_DOMAIN x NAT --> HASH_KEY that codes the aggregate key and the region number into a key for the hashtable
- For each aggregate value a record AGGR with two components: One that records the corresponding list of region numbers (RegList); the other holds the boolean value IsProtected that records whether the aggregate value is protected (see below)

The functions are implemented by the following imperative procedures:

```
enter:
  procedure imp_enter ( AGGR a; KEY k; ENTRY e ) AGGR:
    if   a.IsProtected
      then    hash_tab_enter( code_key(k,RegCount) , e );
              var AGGR  avar := new(AGGR);
              avar.RegList    := append( RegCount, a.RegList );
              avar.IsProtected := false ;
              RegCount      := RegCount + 1 ;
              avar                          top(a.RegList)
      else    hash_tab_enter( code_key(k,RegCount) , e );
              a
    end

empty_grex:
  procedure imp_empty_grex () AGGR:
    var AGGR avar := new(AGGR);
    avar.RegList    := make_list( RegCount );
    avar.IsProtected := false ;
    RegCount      := RegCount + 1 ;
    avar
    end

lookup:
  procedure imp_lookup ( AGGR a; KEY k ) ENTRY:
    imp_rec_lookup( a.RegList, k ) ;

  procedure imp_rec_lookup ( REG_LIST regl; KEY k ) ENTRY:
    if   isempty( regl )
      then  not_found
      else var e : ENTRY_TYPE;
              e := hash_tab_lookup( code_key(k,first(regl)) );
              if  e == not_found
                then    imp_rec_lookup( rest(regl), k )
                else    e
              end
    end
```

The operation to protect hashtable states:
```
  procedure protect ( AGGR a ) AGGR:
    a.IsProtected := true ;
    a
```

3.2. Analysis of Attribute Equations

The aim of the approach is to replace the expressions on the right hand side of the attribute equations by the corresponding operations of the previous section and to refine the attribute and functional dependencies. As we want to perform static optimizations (i.e. at generation time), the actual dependency graph of the aggregate values is not available. But in contrast to functional programming languages like ML (cf.[Har86]), we posssess a very good approximization of it, namely the patterns it consists of: The dependency graphs of the grammar productions.

To concentrate on the main ideas, we introduce some simplifications; the general case will be discussed in section 3.4 :

- nested expressions in attribute equations are assumed to be broken off by using auxiliary attributes
- output attributes may not be used in the production
- structured types based on aggregate types are not allowed (e.g. a type like SYMTAB (see figure 2) is then forbidden)

With these restrictions, we get the following central definition :

Definition:

The *production dependency graph* (PDG) G_P = (V,E) of an attributed grammar production P consists of a set V of labelled vertices, a set E of labelled edges, and the functions

$source, target$: E --> V

to denote the incidence relation:

- V equals the set of attributes labelled by:
    $attr\_kind$: V --> { in, out, aux } , telling the kind of the attribute;
    has_aggr_type : V --> boolean , telling whether the
    attribute will hold an aggregate value or not;

- E, *source*, and *target* express the attribute dependencies; E is labelled by:
    $dependency\_kind$: E --> { i/o_attr_dep, aggr_passing_dep,
                                    aggr_using_dep, other_dep } ,
    in the following way:

i) $dependency\_kind(e)$ = i/o_attr_dep
    if *source*(e) is an output attribute and
        target(e) is an input attribute of the same nonterminal.

ii) $dependency\_kind(e)$ = aggr_passing_dep
    if $has\_aggr\_type($ *source*(e)) and
       $has\_aggr\_type($ *target*(e)) and
       the value of *source*(e) is passed to *target*(e)
       either without change or by an *enter* operation.

iii) $dependency\_kind(e)$ = aggr_using_dep
    if the function that yields the value of *target*(e) has the aggregate valued attribute *source*(e) as a parameter and performs only *lookup* and/or *isdefined* operation on it.

iv) $dependency\_kind(e)$ = other_dep   in all other cases.

□

With the restrictions given above and because of strong typing in MS, the computation of V, *attr_kind*, and *has_aggr_type* is straightforward. The computation of E, *source*, *target* and *dependency_kind* proceeds as follows:

- compute the functional dependencies local to the production, and label the corresponding edges as described in the definition of PDG's. This is no problem for functions like *enter, lookup,* etc. or user defined functions that are not recursive. For recursive or attributive functions we compute a simple, but effective and of course correct static approximation of the dynamic dependencies:

   i)   If the function has parameters and results of the same aggregate type, then label the corresponding edges by aggr_passing_dep.

   ii) If the function has parameters of aggregate type but the result is of another type, then label the corresponding edges by aggr_using_dep.

   iii) If the function has no parameters of aggregate type, then label the corresponding edges by other_dep.

   (cf. the discussion in chapter 4).

- compute the input/output–graph of the production as described in [KeW76] and label the resulting edges by i/o_attr_dep;

The production dependency graph is the abstract notation of the information that we need for the "value"–flow analysis in the following section.

3.3. The Algorithm

The algorithm has two parts. First, it refines the partial order given by the PDG in order to place aggregate using functions before aggregate passing functions with the same input aggregate (cf. *lookup* and *enter$_2$* in section 3.1.). The second part of the algorithm labels those edges of the PDG where the procedure *protect* has to be inserted. Finally, the global frame of the algorithm will be discussed.

3.3.1. Refining the production dependency graph

The refinement of the PDG's is done to minimize the number of protect operations, i.e. to keep the region lists as short as possible. The refinement of one PDG proceeds as follows:

Let "<" be the partial irreflexive order implied by the PDG, i.e. v<v' if there is a sequence of edges that starts at v and ends at v';

1. Compute the set
   S^1_{refine} = { (v,e,U) ∈ V x E x (set of E) |
                                    has_aggr_type(v)
                     and   (e is the only edge with *source*(e) = v
                              and *dependency_kind*(e) = aggr_passing_dep)
                     and   e' ∈ U <==> (*source*(e') = v
                              and *dependency_kind*(e') = aggr_using_dep) }

2. Delete all tuples from S^1_{refine} where at least one element of the using set U depends on the value produced by the passing edge:
   S^2_{refine} = { (v,e,U) ∈ S^1_{refine} | there is no e' ∈ U: *target*(e) < *target*(e') }
   (In these cases the protect operation can't be avoided.)

3. Reduce the using sets in the tuples as follows:
   S^3_{refine} = { (v,e,U) ∈ V x E x (set of E) | there exists a (v',e',U') ∈ S^2_{refine} :
                  v = v' and e = e' and   U contains exactly the edges of U'
                  that have maximal target vertices in *target*({e}∪U') w.r.t. "<" }
   (As we want to add dependencies between target vertices of the using edges and the target vertex of the passing edge e, we only have to consider "independent

edges").

4.   Take *one* element (v,e,U) from S^3_{refine} and add other_dep edges between the vertices in $target(U)$ and the vertex in $target(e)$.

5.   Delete the chosen element (v,e,U) from S^3_{refine} and proceed with step 2 until S^3_{refine} is empty.

$\square$

Remarks:

i)   The refinement process seems perhaps quite costly; but it is not, as even in big compiler front end specifications S^3_{refine} and the using sets rarely contain more than two elements.

ii)   The choice of the element in step 4 is guided by heuristics which partially depend on issues concerning the extensions of the outlined algorithm (see section 3.4.). The main idea is to minimize the number of added dependencies. So we prefer elements with small using sets if a choice is necessary at all (cf. (i) above).

iii) Correctness of step 4: We have to show that adding dependencies doesn't destroy the partial order. This is proved by the following two lemmata:

Lemma 1
For each element (v,e,U) of S^3_{refine} holds that the targets of $\{e\}\cup U$ are not mutually comparable w.r.t "$<$", i.e.:
for all $v, v' \in target(\{e\}\cup U)$: $\neg\ v<v'\ \wedge\ \neg\ v'<v$.

Proof: Let v, v' be two targets of $\{e\}\cup U$ with $v < v'$;
Case $v = target(e)$:   contradicts step 2.
Case $v = target(U)$:   contradicts the reduction of the using set in step 3.

$\square$

Lemma 2
Let $PO(<)$ be a partial irreflexive ordering of V, $U\subset V$, and $p,u\in V\backslash U$ so that the elements of $U\cup\{p,u\}$ are mutually incomparable
(for all $v,v' \in U\cup\{p,u\}$: $\neg\ v<v'\ \wedge\ \neg\ v'<v$);
let $PO'(<)$ be the transitive closure of $PO(<)\cup\{(u,p)\}$, i.e. the refinement of $PO(<)$ by putting u before p.
Then $PO'(<)$ is a partial irreflexive ordering of V and for all $v,v' \in U\cup\{p\}$:
$\neg\ v<v'\ \wedge\ \neg\ v'<v$;

Proof: i) $PO'(<)$ is transitive by construction;
ii) $PO'(<)$ is irreflexive: Suppose there is an element v with $v < v$; this implies $p < v$ and $v < u$; so we have $p < u$ in contradiction to the presupposition of this lemma.
iii) Suppose there are $v,v' \in U\cup\{p\}$ with $v < v'$; this implies $v < u$ and ($p = v'$ or $p < v'$) , which again contradicts the presupposition of this lemma.

$\square$

Finite induction over U yields the desired result.

3.3.2. Insertion of the Protection Operation and Global Frame of the algorithm

After the refinement of a PDG, protection operations (see section 3.1.) have to be inserted where an aggregate value is passed to different attributes or where an aggregate value is possibly passed before it is used. In our formalism, we denote the insertion as the set of edges in question:

Let $\mathbf{G}_{refine}$ be the refined PDG; the set $E_{protect}(\mathbf{G}_{refine})$ is defined as follows:

$$E_{protect}(\mathbf{G}_{refine}) =$$
$$\{ e \in E \mid dependency\_kind(e) = aggr\_passing\_dep$$
$$\wedge (\exists e' \in E: source(e') = source(e)$$
$$\wedge ((dependency\_kind(e') = aggr\_passing\_dep \wedge e \neq e')$$
$$\vee (dependency\_kind(e') = aggr\_using\_dep$$
$$\wedge \neg target(e') < target(e)))) \}$$

Finally, the refined and augmented PDG is translated back to attribute equations whereby the functions of the functional specification are replaced by the corresponding imperative procedures, the protection operations are inserted, and control statements are added to respect the refinements.

Thus far, we have only discussed the treatment of single productions. It remains the problem, how to process the production list. As the refinement of one PDG causes a refinement of the i/o–graphs of the other productions, an efficient algorithm would be needed to incrementally recompute these i/o–graphs and to choose the next production to be refined.

Up to now, we can't give a really satisfactoring answer to this problem. We tackle it by starting with the root production, continuing with the productions of the sons, while recomputing the i/o–graphs as usual.

3.4. Raising the Restrictions

In section 3.2, we restricted the problem in order to concentrate on the main issues. The described algorithm is powerful enough to master aggregates like the occurence table in the example of chapter 2 : As it is never necessary to open a new region, the resulting occurence table implementation is as almost efficient as a hand coded implementation. But so far the algorithm can't deal with lists of aggregates like the symboltable of the example.

Whereas the first two restrictions are merely chosen to avoid technical overhead, the restriction to plain aggregates is a real simplification. In the general case, the PDG becomes quite more complex, as the attributes may contain several aggregates – in most cases a list of aggregates – so that the "value"–flow analysis has to keep track of sets of aggregates. To illustrate this, we shortly discuss two different cases:

i)   In the *varint* production of the example, the incoming aggregate list is splitted in its first element and its rest; so the aggregate sets belonging to the *first* vertex and the *rest* vertex are disjoint and no protection operation has to be inserted.

ii) The following figure shows an attributed production where the first and last element of a list of aggregates are passed through. In this case, the aggregate values have to be protected, as they could be the same.

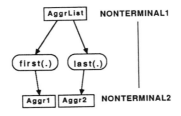

A more detailed and formal treatment of this problem can be found in [Ple88]. However, we expect further optimizations by using a more powerful "value"–flow analysis.

4. Conclusion

4.1. Summarizing Epilogue

We described the usage and implementation of aggregates in the compiler development system MAGIC and pointed out that having aggregates in the specification language has two seemingly contrary advantages:

- a convenient and powerful high–level specification facility
- efficient implementation

By closing this gap, we again realized the importance of a carefully designed typing mechanism for good language implementation.

Many details and improvements of the presented algorithm could not be discussed in this paper. Some of them should at least be mentioned:

- further optimization to avoid even more *protect* operations by taking advantage of the expression nesting
- treatment of *enter* operations in expressions that only "temporarily" change aggregates
- treatment of *delete* operations
- improvements to the analysis of recursive and attributive functions, especially if they have more then one aggregate as parameter
- storage management

4.2. Future Work

For the future, we envisage three other related topics:

- A better integration of this approach and other optimization techniques (and where possible a statistical support to guide the decisions).
- A careful analysis of the dependency between attribute evaluation strategy and aggregate optimization.
- A combination of this approach and globalizing transformations as described in [Räi86]. This would be particularly interesting to isolate certain classes of linearly behaving aggregate computations. For such classes, even more efficient implementations could be provided.

Acknowledgements

Thanks are due to A. Liebl and J. Knopp for helpful discussions, to Prof. J. Eickel for initiating and supporting the MAGIC Project and to F. Plenk; his diploma thesis was the basis for this work.

References

[BaT84] G. Bartmuß, S. Thürmel: MUG–Tutorial; Internal Report; Technical University of Munich; 84

[BaW81] F.L. Bauer, H. Wössner: Algorithmische Sprache und Programmentwicklung; Springer Verrlag; 81

[Bjö80] D. Björner: Towards a Formal Description of Ada; LNCS 98; Springer Verlag; 80

[Gan79] H. Ganzinger: On Storage Optimization for Automatically Generated Compilers; LNCS Vol. 67, pp 132–141

[GaG84] H. Ganzinger, R. Giegerich, et al.: Attribute Coupled Grammars; SIGPLAN 84 Symp. on Compiler Construction; 84

[Har86] R. Harper: Introduction to Standard ML; Dep. of Computer Science, University of Edingburgh; Technical Report ECS–LFCS–86–14

[HoT86] R. Hoover, T. Teitelbaum: Efficient Incremental Evaluation of Aggregate Values in Attribute Grammars; ACM Proc. of the 86 SIGPLAN Symposium on Compiler Construction

[Kas87] U. Kastens: Lifetime Analysis for Attributes; Acta Informatica 24; 1987, pp.633–651

[KeW76] K. Kenedy, S. Warren: Automatic Generation of Efficient Evaluators for Attribute Grammars; 3rd ACM Symposium on Principles of Programming Languages, Atlanta; 76

[KLP88] J. Knopp, A. Liebl, A. Poetzsch–Heffter: MAGIC – An Interactive Compiler Specification System; Internal Report; Technical University Munich; 88

[Ple88] F. Plenk: Optimierende Implementierungstransformation für funktionale Attributgrammatiken; Diplomarbeit; Technical University of Munich; 88

[Poe88] A. Poetzsch–Heffter: Report on the MAGIC Specification Language; to appear december 88

[Räi86] K.–J. Räihä: A Globalizing Transformation for Attribute Grammars; ACM Proc. of the 86 SIGPLAN Symposium on Compiler Construction

[UDP82] J. Uhl, et al.: An Attribute Grammar for the Semantic Analysis of Ada; LNCS 139; Springer Verlag; 82

Code generation for a RISC Machine

Petr Kroha

1. Introduction

An important part of the whole development in computers comes from the idea of a new computer architecture based on processors with a simplified instruction set.To date, two prominent approaches to designing CPUs and their instruction sets have emerged - reduced instruction set computer (RISC) and complex instruction set computer (CISC) designs.The primary difference between these strategies is whether to use a small number of fast-executing primitive instructions or to use more complicated instructions that make writing programs easier.

From the first projects at IBM (IBM 801) and at Berkeley and Stanford [1] we can follow the development of the RISC idea to the current RISC machines. From the software point of view we can see the difference in number of machine instruction (CISC about 200, RISC about 30).Because of the simplicity of a hardware construction we can achieve the same performance much cheeper or we can realize the chip on GaAs technology and increase the speed of computing considerably.

In the following paragraphs we shall briefly show the structure of our RISC machine, general principles and interesting programming techniques used for engineering of a RISC compiler and using them for modifying of the UNIX C compiler for purposes of our RISC machine.

2. Structure of the used RISC machine

The detailed description of our RISC machine is given in [5].We shall present here only information needed for understanding of the following parts of our contribution.From the same reason we shall not describe the possibilities of parallelity and reconfigurability.

The most instructions of our RP-RISC machine (Reconfigurable Parallel RISC machine) have three operands. Every instruction is 32 bits long.The most significant 8 bits are used for the operation code, but only 5 bits really serve as code of operation, whereas the other 3 bits contain the information about the number of clock cycles needed for the instruction execution. The greatest number of clock periods is needed for CALL-instruction (6 cycles).Due to the fast execution of this instruction was used the windowing on a register field.The usually used stack concept for the CALL and RETURN instructions doesn't satisfy the condition of the LOAD-STORE access as the only access to the memory.Using procedures involves two groups of time-consuming operations: saving or restoring registers on each call and return, and passing parameters and results to and from the procedure.In the window concept each procedure call allocates a new "window" which is a subset of the large register field.This windows are overlapping for nested procedure calling(see Fig.1).

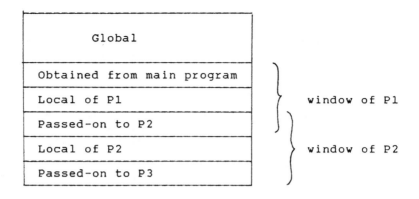

Fig. 1 Register windowing

        The CALL and RETURN instructions are then only moving the
window pointer on the field of registers.To the obvious
programming techniques in RISC programs we can count the placing
of the mostly used constants (e.g. zero, one) into the global
registers.From the 32 global registers in our RP-RISC machine
there are 12 registers used for saving constants and for some
optimization purposes and 20 registers are used for purposes of
evaluation of expressions as usual.The user can access in every
moment only 56 registers - 32 global and 24 registers of the
window.The total amount of registers is 288.The window pointer is
incremented by CALL instruction and decremented by RET
instruction. Each window has three parts:
 - 8 registers for parameters obtained from previous subroutine
 - 8 registers for local variables
 - 8 registers for passed-on parameters.
Stack in memory and stack pointer are used automatically by
hardware means only if subroutine nesting is too deep.
        The relevant instructions are shown in the following table.

                Machine instruction for the RP-RISC machine

        Instruction   Function

ADD   R1,R2,R3   R1 + R2   --> R3
ADC   R1,R2,R3   R1 + R2 + C   --> R3
SUB   R1,R2,R3   R1 - R2   --> R3
SBC   R1,R2,R3   R1 - R2 - C   --> R3

AND   R1,R2,R3   R1 and R2   --> R3
OR   R1,R2,R3   R1 or R2   --> R3
XOR   R1,R2,R3   R1 xor R2   --> R3

SRL   R   shift right logical with carry

ICR   R,n,const   insert constant into nth cell
                                     of register R

ICA   addr. in page   insert 16-bit constant into the

		address register
ICP	number of page	insert 8-bit constant into the prefix register
LMR	[direct address]	load contents of given address into the register RP (one of the global registers).If no direct address is given, addressing is indirect,i.e.by means of address register
SMR	[direct address]	store contents of the register RP into the given address (as in LMR)
CJZ CJC CJN	[direct address]	conditional jump in accordance with flags ZERO,CARRY,NEGATIVE (if set), addressing identical with LMR, SMR
CALL RET	[direct address]	subroutine call addressing like LMR,SMR return from subroutine

Tab. 1 Instruction set of RP-RISC machine (the relevant subset)

3. Special programming techniques used in a RISC compiler

A RISC machine provides primitive hardware functions rather than bundling functionality into complex instruction, allowing the compiler to optimize below the level of other architectures.The compiler can generate optimal code for a simple machine more easily since the architecture provides fewer alternatives in performing a given function.This allows the compiler to focus its attention on other aspects of optimization, including global optimization and an efficient run-time environment.It must, of course, support a reduced instruction set by providing for function not present in the hardware.Each compiler phase usually performs optimizations.After local optimization will be done the peep-hole optimizations and architecture-dependent pipeline scheduling.
Procedure call, entry and return must be designed as fast and simple as possible, because there are often called the procedures and the functions of the run-time support standing for the complex instructions of CISC.It was discovered that 95% of the calls pass fewer than four parameters [3].
Using of pipelining improves performance by 20% on average [4], but brings problems because the next instruction will be started before the current instruction has completed its activity.We speak about data conflicts and branch conflicts and solve this by load delay and branch delay methods.A load delay

occurs when one instruction loads a value into a register and the
next instruction uses that register.It is necessary to change the
instruction order so that the instruction following the load does
not depend on the load.This permits one instruction to access
memory in parallel while executing another instruction.An other
effect in pipeline reorganization is called a delayed branch.When
a branch instruction is executing the logical order and the
physical order of instructions are different.The logically next
instruction should be prepared but the physically next
instruction is.The basic solution is to insert so many NOP-
instruction how many are needed for elimination of the branch
conflict.

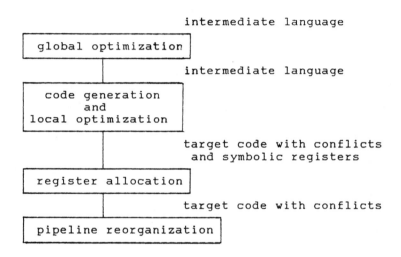

intermediate language

global optimization

intermediate language

code generation
and
local optimization

target code with conflicts
and symbolic registers

register allocation

target code with conflicts

pipeline reorganization

Fig.2   Scheme of a back-end of a RISC compiler

        The first phase of the code generation is the global
optimization and substitution of small procedures by sequences
of instructions.In the following process a naive code will be
generated which uses unlimited set of registers and doesn't worry
about data and branch conflicts caused by pipelining.During this
process are complex instructions of the intermediate language
substituted by sequences of the RISC primitive instructions and
a local optimization is provided.Register allocation will be
organized by help of a method for coloring graphs [2].The last
phase of the code generator deletes data and branch
conflicts.Some algorithms are given in [4].

4. Features of the UNIX C compiler

        The version of the UNIX C compiler [6] we have got in the
source form doesn't use a machine-independent intermediate
language, but it is not important for our purposes.Each
intermediate file is represented as a sequence of binary numbers
without any explicit delimiters.It consists of a sequence of
logical lines, each headed by an operator, and possibly
containing various operands (numbers or strings).Expressions are
transmitted in a reverse-Polish notation; as they are being read,

a tree is built which is isomorphic to the tree constructed in the last phase.

The reader maintains a stack; each leaf of the expression tree (name, constant) is pushed on the stack;each unary operator replaces the top of the stack by a node whose operand is the old top-of -stack; each binary operator replaces the top pair on the stack with a single entry. When the expression is complete there is exactly one item on the stack.Following each expression is a special operator which passes the unique previous expression to the optimizer and to the code generator.

The optimizer tries to modify and simplify the tree so its value may be computed more efficiently and conveniently by the code generator.Each interior node will be marked with an estimation of the number of registers required to evaluate it.This register count is needed to guide the code generation algorithm.The common subexpression are not discovered and used for optimization.The basic algorithms the depth-first scan of the tree,but the code generation is in principle independent of any particular machine.It depends largely on a set of tables.It could seem to be easy to modify this tables for producing code for other machines, but:
- structure of these tables is machine-dependent
- it is non-trivial to prepare such tables.

The basic code generation procedure works with a pointer to a tree representing an expression, with the name of a code generation table, and returns the number of the register in which the value should be placed.There are four code generation tables:
- REGTAB actually produces code which causes the value represented by the expression tree to be placed in a register.
- CCTAB is used in the case, when we need not the value of the expression, but instead the value of the condition code resulting from evaluation of the expression.This table is used to evaluate the expression after IF.
- SPTAB is used when the value of an expression is to be pushed on the stack(e.g. an actual argument).
- EFFTAB is used when an expression is to be evaluated for its side effects, not its value.This occurs mostly for expressions which are statements, which have no value.It doesn't need to leave the value in a register.

All of the tables besides REGTAB handle a relatively few special cases.If one of these tables does not contain an entry applicable to the given expression tree, the table REGTAB will be used and perhaps a redundant code will be generated.Parts of the items in the REGTAB can be macros which are expanded during the generation.

The processing of register allocation during the code generation is based on Sethi-Ullman algorithm.

The main code generation tables consist of entries each containing an operator number and a pointer to a subtable for the corresponding operator.A subtable consists of a sequence of entries, each with a key describing certain properties of the operands of the operator involved;associated with the key is a code string.Once the subtable corresponding to the operator is found, the subtable is searched linearly until a key is found such that the properties demanded by the key are compatible with the operands of the tree node.A successful match returns the code string; an unsuccessful search returns a failure indication.

5. Modification for the RISC target code

Because the global optimization is running on the program in the intermediate language it wasn't changed.This means the first we have to change is the target code to be generated.The main part of it is generated by help of the table REGTAB.The table CCTAB isn't relevant for our purposes because we have the operands evaluated in registers for testing anyway (the LOAD-STORE access to the memory).The SPTABLE isn't relevant too because we have no instructions working with stack.The table EFFTAB we needn't for the same reason as the table CCTAB, because we always obtain a value in a register.

The REGTAB table is organized hierarchically.The first level is built on the operator of the tree node representing the operation to be translated (has about 50 entries).The second level is built on the types of operands in the compile stack (total about 120 entries).Because of many possibilities of addressing in the PDP 11 instruction set there are many cases to distinguish.For the PDP 11 code will be the operator of indirection translated not immediately.Its operand in the compile stack will be only signed and the operation of indirection will be generated in the most cases by help of possibilities of the addressing modes of the PDP 11.In operands in the REGTAB for the PDP 11 is distinguished between operand *X and *(X+c) because of addressing modes (R) and X(R).For the RP-RISC machine we have only one way, how to translate the indirect addressing.It simplifies the tables because the number of cases is therefor considerable smaller (about 4 times).

The power of expression of the RP-RISC code is illustrated in the following table.

Instruction set of PDP 11			Instruction set of RP-RISC	
CLR	R	(clear)	ADD	RO,RO,R
COM	R	(complement)	SUB	RO,R,R
INC	R	(increment)	ADD	R1,R,R
DEC	R	(decrement)	ADD	R-1,R,R
NEG	R	(negate)	XOR	R,R-1,R
ASR	R	(arith. shift right)	SRA	R
ASL	R	(arith. shift left)	ADD	R,R,R
MOV	Ra,Rb	(Rb <- Ra)	ADD	RO,Ra,Rb
ADD	Ra,Rb	(Rb <- Ra + Rb)	ADD	Ra,Rb,Rb
SUB	Ra,Rb	(Rb <- Rb - Ra)	SUB	Rb,Ra,Rb
BIS	Ra,Rb	(Rb <- Ra or Rb)	OR	Ra,Rb,Rb
BIC	Ra,Rb	(Rb <- Ra and Rb)	SUB	RO,Ra,RP
			AND	RP,Rb,Rb
BIT	Ra,Rb	(Ra and Rb)	AND	Ra,Rb,RP
TST	R	(R ? O)	SUB	R,RO,RP
CMP	Ra,Rb	(Ra ? Rb)	SUB	Ra,Rb,RP
JMP	address	(jump)	ADD	RO,RO,RP
			CJZ	address
JSR	PC,address	(jump to subr.)	CALL	address
RTS	PC	(ret. from subr.)	RET	

Tab. 2 Comparison of some instruction of PDP 11 and RP-RISC.

To have a scale for comparing the branching of tables we will not take in account the operations in the float and double arithmetic. Than we become the following table.

Operator	Number of distinguished cases of operands	
	PDP 11	RP-RISC
JUMP	2	1
CALL	3	1
LOAD	6	2
ASSIGN	7	1
PLUS	12	3

Tab. 3   Number of cases of operands to be distinguished

The structure of generated code we can see on the following example compared with the code for PDP 11.
First of all we shall show a function without a local field.

Example 1:

In C language:

```
getnum (ap)
  char *ap;
  {
  register char *p;
  register int  n,c;
    p=ap;
    n=0;
    while ((c=*p++) >= '0' && c<= '9')
          n = n*10 + c - '0';
    if ( *--p !=0 )
          return(o);
    return(n);
  }
```

In code for PDP 11:

```
_getnum:
        jsr     r5,csv
        mov     4(r5),r4
        clr     r3
:3:
        movb    (r4)+,r2
        cmp     r2,#60
        blt     .2
        cmp     r2,#71
        bgt     .2
        mov     r3,r0
        asl     r0
        asl     r0
```

```
        add     r3,r0
        asl     r0
        add     r2,r0
        sub     #60,r0
        mov     r0,r3
        br      .3
.2:
        tstb    -(r4)
        beq     .4
        clr     r0
        br      .1
.4:
        mov     r3,r0
.1:
        jmp     cret
```

In code for RP-RISC:

```
        ICR     R43,0,48
        ICR     R44,0,57
        ADD     R32,R0,R40      ... p=ap
        ADD     R0,R0,R41       ... n=0
L3:
        ADD     R40,R0,RA
        LMR
        ADD     RP,R0,R42       ... c=*p++
        SUB     R42,R43,RP
        CJN     L2
        SUB     R44,R42,RP
        CJN     L2
        ADD     R41,R0,R20
        ADD     R20,R20,R20
        ADD     R20,R20,R20
        ADD     R41,R20,R20
        ADD     R20,R20,R20     ... 10 * n -> R20
        ADD     R42,R20,R20
        SUB     R20,R43,R20
        ADD     R20,R0,R41
        SUB     R0,R0,R0
        CJZ     L3
L2:
        SUB     R40,R1,R40
        ADD     R40,R0,RA
        LMR
        SUB     RP,R0,RP
        CJZ     L4
        ADD     R0,R0,R40
        SUB     R0,R0,R0
        CJZ     L1
L4:
        ADD     R41,R0,R40
L1:
        RET
```

Example 2:

Using of a local field presumes to have a run-time support
function for location of the field in memory and storing its
address in the local variable with the same order as the local
field has.

In C language:

```c
int a[100];
move ()
{
   int i,b[50],j;
      j=5;
      for ( i=0;i<50;i++)
          b[i]=a[i*2]+1;
      i=0;
      }
```

For PDP 11 we obtain:

```
_move:
          jsr     r5,csv
          sub     #146,sp
          mov     #5,-156(r5)
          clr     -10(r5)
          br      .4
.5:
          mov     -10(r5),r4
          asl     r4
          asl     r4
          add     #_a,r4
          mov     (r4),r4
          inc     r4
          mov     -10(r5),r0
          asl     r0
          add     r5,r0
          mov     r4,-154(r0)
.3:
          inc     -10(r5)
.4:
          cmp     -10(r5),#62
          blt     .5
.2:
          clr     -10(r5)
.1:
          jmp     cret
```

For RP-RISC we obtain:

```
       ICR      R10,0,50
       ADD      R10,R0,RP
       CALL     Loc-field
       ADD      RP,R0,R41
       ICR      R42,0,5        ....j=5
       ADD      R0,R0,R40      ....i=0
       SUB      R0,R0,R0          jmp L1
       CJZ      L1
L2:    ADD      R40,R40,R43    ....i * 2 -> R43
       ICA      _A
       ADD      RA,R43,RA      ....A[i*2]
       LMR                     ....A[i*2] -> RP
       ADD      R1,RP,RP       ....A[i*2] + 1 -> RP
       ADD      R41,R0,RA
       ADD      R40,RA,RA      ....B[i]
       SMR                     ....RP -> B[i]
       ADD      R1,R40,R40     ....i=i+1
L1:    SUB      R40,R10,RP     ....i < 50
       CJN      L2
```

We can see that we obtained:
19 instructions a 4 byte for RP-RISC   ... 76 byte
18 instruction of variable length for PDP 11 ... 60 byte.
If we make a summa of the time needed for execution of instructions in one sequence we obtain:
-for RP-RISC: 20 microsec. (about 100 cycles for 5 MHz clock)
-for PDP 11 : 71.94 microsec.
The tables are not the only one place, where the machine dependent code occurs.For example for a conditional branch there is in the UNIX C compiler a procedure:

```
   branch (label,aop,c)
   {
    register op;
    if (op=aop) PRINS(op,c,branchtab);
            else   printf("jbr");
    printf('\tL%d\n',label);
   }
```

The dependent code occurs on about 70 places.The number of registers used for evaluation is in the UNIX C compiler defined as 3, we extended to 20 (only through changing a constant).

6. Conclusions

The algorithms of the UNIX C compiler was used to prove some properties of a Small C compiler for a RISC machine.Because of lack of the most addressing modes many tables and many procedures were becoming much more simple.The problem of data and branch conflicts we hadn't to solve because our machine doesn't use pipelining.This is due to the motivation of the machine in control of parallel processes, where the greatest part of the processor activity can be spent by waiting for an asynchronous event.That's why it didn't seem to be important to use pipelining.On examples we showed that the increase of number of instructions of the generated code when compiling a program isn't so considerable as will be usually proposed.

References

[1] Patterson,D.A.,Sequin,C.: A VLSI RISC. Computer,15,No 9,1982.
[2] Chaitin,G.J.: Register Allocation and spilling via graph
                 coloring.Proceedings of the SIGPLAN'82
                 Symposium of Compiler Construction,
                 SIGPLAN Not. 17, 1982.
[3] Chow,F.: Engineering RISC compiler system. Compcon Spring
             1983.
[4] Gross,T.R.: Code optimization technique for pipelined
               architecture. Compcon Spring 1983.
[5] Blazek.Z.,Kroha,P.: Design of a reconfigurable parallel
                       RISC machine. EUROMICRO'87,Portsmouth.
                       reprinted in:
                       Microprocessing and microprogramming 21(1987),
                       North-Holland.
[6] Ritchie,D.M.: A Tour through the UNIX C Compiler.
                 Bell Laboratories,documentation of UNIX.

[7] Blazek,Z.:A reconfigurable processor with RISC features.
             Thesis,Czech Technical University,
             (to appear on Czech)
[8] PDP 11 Processor Handbook.Digital Equipment Corporation,1978.

TWO TREE PATTERN MATCHERS FOR CODE SELECTION

Beatrix Weisgerber*, Reinhard Wilhelm

FB 10 - Informatik
Universität des Saarlandes
D - 6600 Saarbrücken
Federal Republic of Germany

ABSTRACT

A bottom up- and a top down pattern matching algorithm for code selection are presented. The setting is the same as in [AhGa84]. First all covers of the intermediate representation (IR) are computed, and cheapest ones are determined by dynamic programming. Then code selection proper is performed. While Graham-Glanville-like code generators ([GlGr78],[Glan77]) use dynamic targeting, i.e. by selecting appropriate productions at reduction time, and while Aho- Ganapathi shift the targeting task to the semantic attributes and functions, the two algorithms presented in this paper use static targeting. Targeting rules, i.e. rules with patterns of depth 1, are simulated in the states of the recognizing automata. Therefore, all covers found for an IR are adequate as far as no semantic constraints are concerned. The bottom up approach suffers from the theoretical worst case complexity, i.e. the (static) size of the automata may grow exponentially with the size of the machine description. The top down approach has a linear (static) size of the automaton, but a dynamic size, i.e. the size of additional data structures, of |IR| * |machine description|. The bottom up approach has been implemented as a modification of the OPTRAN bottom up pattern matcher generator [Weis83].

1. Introduction

In recent years, there has been done a considerable amount of research on the generative approach to code generation. A survey is given in [Lune83]. This approach automates the generation of code generators and facilitates retargeting. In the area of code selection, works based on pattern matching has been proved to deliver reasonable results ([Glan77], [Henr84]). For a comparison of different approaches on an algebraic basis see [GiSc88] [Gieg88].

In the pattern matching approach, machine instructions are selected according to patterns of the intermediate representation (IR). Each (input) pattern models a target machine instruction. A second (result) pattern describes, where the result of the corresponding instruction will be available. Leaves in the input pattern and the single node result pattern correspond to registers, memory cells etc. Input pattern, result pattern, machine instruction and a cost statement estimating the amount of memory and machine cycles necessary for the machine instruction, form a kind of a "annotated" reduction rule. See figure 1.

---

present address: Standard Elektrik Lorenz AG, Forschungszentrum, Lorenzstr. 10, D-7000 Stuttgart 40

Machine instruction :

add const reg

Add the content of a memory cell, the address of which is given by "const" to the content of the register "reg". The result is written into the register "reg". The subpatterns of the left-hand side pattern are numbered for later reference.

Figure 1

For every given IR tree, a pattern driven code generator has to find at least one sequence of instructions corresponding to the tree. Such sequences are issued as indicated by covers of the IR tree by input patterns. A cover is found by plastering the tree with input patterns, such that every node of the tree has to be covered by exactly one node of one pattern and such that the patterns "fit together". This means, that the result pattern of the input pattern is or can be transferred to a leaf of another input pattern. The problem corresponds to the targeting problem: the result of the corresponding machine instruction has to be in the place where the next instruction expects it to be. An example is given in figure 2.

On the other hand, addressing modes may be factorized by special rules. Then, each result pattern of such rules symbolizes a certain addressing mode (indirection, indexing etc.) which can be used within other patterns without explicitly repeating the possible huge address pattern. "Fitting together" means in this context insuring that the appropriate addressing mode can be used.

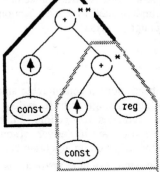

The pattern of figure 1 matches at node * and delivers a result 'reg', so that the pattern matches again at node **. Every node of the original tree is covered by exactly one pattern. The result of the first reduction produces a leaf of the second pattern.

Figure 2

A tree pattern matcher finding covers of trees should simulate the "pasting" process. This means in terms of rewrite systems to simulate the reduction of the input pattern by the result pattern. If the input pattern of a rule matches a subtree, this subtree is replaced by the result pattern. The process continues until no more pattern matches and only one node results. See figure 3.

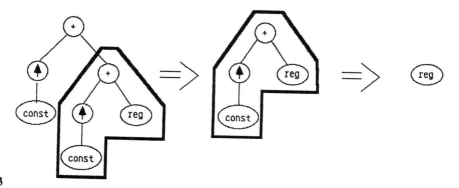

Figure 3

In general, there is more than one cover for a tree by real (non RISC) machine descriptions. A code generator should be able to select one with minimal costs, i.e. sum of the costs for the instruction sequence issued.

The Graham/Glanville approach ([Glan77], [GlGr78]) reduced the problem of tree pattern matching to the problem of recognizing words of a (string) language. The IR tree is linearized according to a preorder traversal. Each reduction rule is represented by a production of a context-free grammar.

Example: REG -> + ↑ const REG,

A LR-type parser is generated from this grammar. Each reduction in the parsing process corresponds to a tree reduction. Certain heuristics and backtrack mechanisms had to be built in to find a cover, because the grammars are ambiguous in general. But there is a left bias due to the preorder traversal and the employed heuristics. Early selection decisions and the one pass approach preclude the generation of even locally optimal code.

The approach of Ganapathi/Fischer [GaFi82] provides further attribution mechanisms and formulation of predicates for more flexible conflict resolution.

As [Henr84] indicates, the context-free approach to the problem has been driven to its inherent limits. Tree pattern matching technology promises to overcome these limitations. However, tree analysers like those of Kron [Kron75] or Hoffman/O'Donnell [HoDo82] cannot be used unchanged for this purpose. They can determine whether and where in a tree patterns from a set of patterns match, but they don't simulate the reduction process as described above.

Aho/Ganapathi [AhGa85] propose a solution for this problem. The leaves of their patterns and the result patterns are parameter nodes which match every tree. So, they can use conventional pattern match automata. A suitable attribution has to provide the targeting task. These computations give rise to additional costs at run time.

The approach presented in this paper will overcome this problem by adapting the well-known tree pattern matching automata to simulate the reduction process. For every given tree, the automata will provide all possible covers according to a set of reduction rules. Dynamic programming ([AhJo76]) performed in parallel will then find a locally cheapest code sequence.

2. The bottom up tree analyser

Bottom up tree analysers have the great advantage, that their analysis time costs are linear in the number of the nodes of the subject tree. The bottom up tree analyser of Kron and Hoffmann/O'Donnell works as follows: With every node in the tree a set of subpatterns is associated which match the subtree at this node. These match sets are computed bottom up.

The match set of a node can be determined, if all subtrees of this node are already analysed. A subpattern matches at a node if and only if its root has the same label as the node and if every child pattern matches the corresponding child tree of the node. The latter fact can be determined by inspecting the match sets of the children. If the child pattern can be found in the match set of the corresponding child tree, then the child pattern matches the child tree.

subject tree

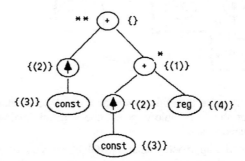

Figure 4

In figure 4 the subject tree to be analysed is shown together with its match sets. At node *, the full pattern matches. This fact is represented by associating match set {(1)} with *. The root label of the pattern is the label of the node, at the first child the first subtree of the pattern ((2)) matches and at the second child the second subtree of the pattern ((4)) matches. We can see, that at node ** no pattern matches, because at its second child no match can be found for subpattern <reg>. This subpattern would be produced by reduction at node *. We can simulate this rewrite rule. Every time, a full pattern occurs in a match set, all occurrences of the result pattern (as input subpatterns) are added to the match set. Figure 5 shows the result for our example.

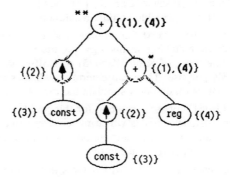

Figure 5

At node *, we now have the additional information that subpattern (4) matches. This has the effect, that the main pattern is recognized at node **. Each match set now reflects the actual situation of the tree and additionally each situation which could arise by reductions of the tree.

An example for more complex rules as shown in figure 6 is given in figure 7.

At this point, we can observe several properties of the analyser. Chains of so-called transfer rules (rules having an input pattern consisting of a single node, modelling for example

transformation rules (represented by the top node of the left—hand side pattern)

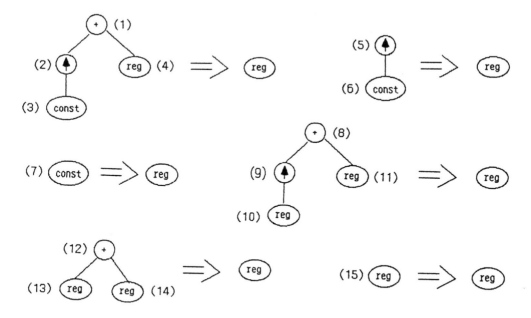

Figure 6   subject tree

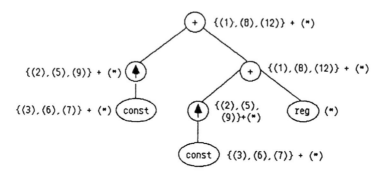

Figure 7   (*) = {(4),(10),(11); (13),(14),(15)}

register-to-register transfers or memory-to-register transfers or factorizing rules) are enclosed in one match set. If the input pattern of a transfer rule is contained in a match set, then at the same time the input subpatterns having the same label as the result pattern of the rule can be added to this match set. See for example rule (7) and (15). If (7) is contained in a match set, then set (*) can be added immediately. For rule (15) nothing is added, because the results are already considered. The effects of such chains of transfer rules are computed simultaneously. There are no problems with possible loops in transfer rule chains. In the Graham/Glanville approach, such possible infinite reduction sequences have to be detected and broken explicitly.

The second observation concerns the kind of information provided: The simulating analyser only states, that certain patterns match, if certain transformation rules are applied at certain subtrees or possibly no transformation rule is applied. But the information about the different covers found is not immediately available. The approach of Möncke [Moen85] provides more exact information in this respect, but it will probably produce larger automata.

Thus, we have to collect further information at run time to determine an actual instruction sequence corresponding to the covers found by the automaton. A possible solution is to construct the graph representing all covers for an individual tree. An example for such a graph, called history graph, is shown in figure 8. Reduction rules are associated with those nodes in the tree to which they can be applied. If a reduction at node n depends on other reductions at descendent nodes, then an edge is drawn from the history graph of the descendent node to the history graph of n. This shows which result of which reduction is responsible for the existence of an appropriate leaf of another pattern.

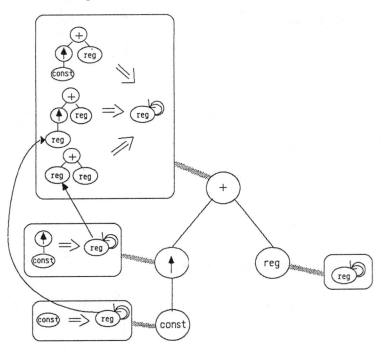

Figure 8

3. The generator of the bottom up analyser

Naturally, it is possible to compute the match sets at analysis time. But it will be much more efficient to precompute them as the states of a finite tree automaton from the machine description. We are then able to compute encoded match sets and the associated partial history graphs for IR trees by means of this automaton. Pure analysis costs are linear in the number of nodes of the subject tree to be analysed.

Hoffmann/O'Donnell [HoDo82] developed a generator for conventional tree analysers producing a n-dimensional matrix $M[op]$ for every operator op, where n is the rank of op. Each entry $M[op][f_1,...,f_n]$ supplies the match set for a tree node labelled op, where every child i, from 1 to n, is already analysed by match set f_i. Realistic pattern sets will result in huge sparse matrices, i.e. most entries will denote the empty match set. Table compression methods will produce reasonable automata representation [MWW85].

Kron's generator [Kron75] (see also [Weis83]) produces finite bottom up tree automata. Match sets (or states in the finite automata terminology) are computed for a subtree by successively regarding the root label (op), the match set of the first child (f_1), the match set of the second child (f_2),...and the match set of the last child (f_n). $init[op]$ yields the start state containing all subpatterns having root label op. Let the rank of the operator op be greater than zero. Then $trans(init[op],(1,f_1)) = z_1$ denotes the state containing all the subpatterns of $init[op] = z_0$ which agree with the tree in the root label and the first child. All those subpatterns of z_0, whose first child cannot be found in f_1, are not contained in z_1. $trans(z_{i-1},(i,f_i)) = z_i$ encodes the subpatterns of z_i which match the tree regarding the root label and the match sets $f_1,...,f_i$ of the children 1,...,i. Compared to z_{i-1}, all those subpatterns are removed, whose child is not contained in f_i. At last, the final state $z_n = trans(z_{n-1},(n,f_n))$ denotes the match set of patterns agreeing with the whole subtree. An example of a tree analysis process on the basis of the rule set of figure 6 is given in figure 9. (There is no simulation of reductions in this figure!).

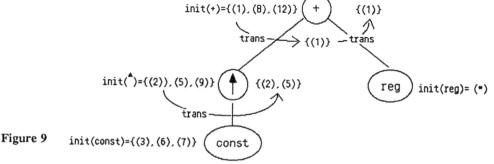

Figure 9 init(const)={(3), (6), (7)}

The automaton for this pattern set is shown in figure 10. The following convention is used:

$init[op] = z_0$ is represented as op ---> z_0

The transition from state z_{i-1} to z_i by f_i at the ith child, expressed by $trans(z_{i-1},(i,f_i)) = z_i$, is represented as

(i,f_i)
z_{i-1} -------> z_i

Final states are enclosed in bold face boxes.
Transitions which are not explicitly mentioned lead to the empty state. Every transition out of the empty state leads back to the empty state.

We will now simulate the reduction. As already mentioned in the previous chapter, the first step is to insert into every final state containing a full pattern (i) all those subpatterns which could be matched as result of the reduction by (i). In our example, all subpatterns with root label "reg" (set (*)) are added to every final state that contains a full pattern of a rule with a result pattern "reg". The result of this first step is shown in figure 11.

If such a new final state f is involved in a transition of the kind $trans(z,(i,f)) = z'$, then it may be possible that z' should contain additional subpatterns according to the definition of transitions. The simulation of the reduction may cause certain subpatterns to be no longer eliminated on the transition from z to z'. Look at the following transition in the subautomaton of ↑:

f1´

(2), (5), (9) —(1, fc)→ (2), (5) + (*)

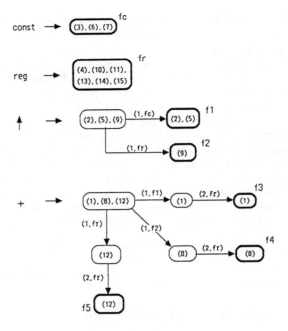

Figure 10

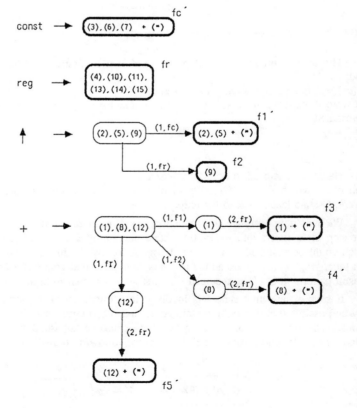

Figure 11

After the transition state *fc* has changed to *fc'*, by simulating the reduction <const> ==> <reg>, pattern (9) will be a possible match, too. Pattern (9) is no longer eliminated by the transition to f_1'.

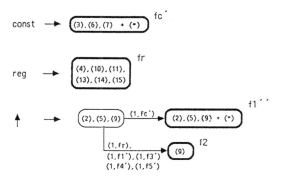

The effects produced in this way by the final states changed in the first step, yield the automaton of figure 12. Remember that some transitions to the empty state not shown in the previous figure are also changed.

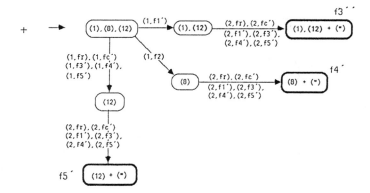

Figure 12

After each step an automaton is produced using transitions on final states of the previous automaton, that is, final states which may exist no longer in the current automaton. For example, f_1' of figure 12 has changed to f_1''. The process continues until the set of final states is no longer changed. The process terminates because during each step a state f_j (existing before the step) may only produce final states f_f, satisfying $f_j \subseteq f_j'$, and because only a finite number of combinations of subpatterns exists.

The final result for our example is shown in figure 13.

The major disadvantage of the bottom up automaton generation is the exponential worst case behaviour (see [HoDo82]). But examples using realistic patterns have shown good results. Preliminary experiments on the basis of small rule sets didn't support our fears that the

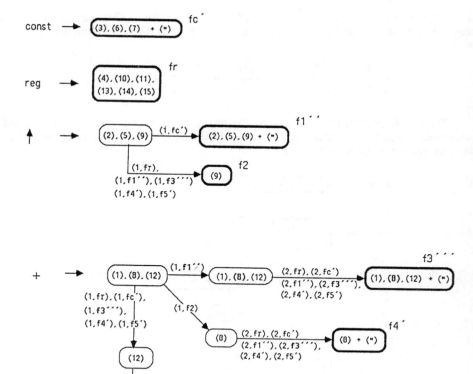

Figure 13

simulating automaton becomes significantly larger than the non-simulating one (the worst case behaviour of the two kinds of automata is naturally the same). There were even rule sets where the number of states (when identifying states containing the same subpatterns) decreased and only the number of transitions to non-empty states increased slightly . Further experiments using realistic machine descriptions will show, whether these good results will be confirmed.

Finally, we have to discuss the generation of the partial history graphs for every final state. The iteration process makes this generation obvious: In the basic (non-simulating) automaton a partial history graph is associated to each final state describing the reduction rules of its full patterns. If during an iteration step a new final state *f'* is produced on the basis of a final state *f*, then *f'* takes over the partial history graph of *f* and the reduction rules corresponding to newly added patterns are integrated. If an application of a reduction rule may induce an application of a chain of further reduction rules, then they are linked together. Possible cycles may be represented. Figure 14 shows an example.

The construction of the history graph can be prepared at generation time in the following way. There is a static number of leaves resulting from previous reductions in each (sub)pattern in a state. Therefore a static assignment of positions in a vector can be computed for all the

history graph of f3´:

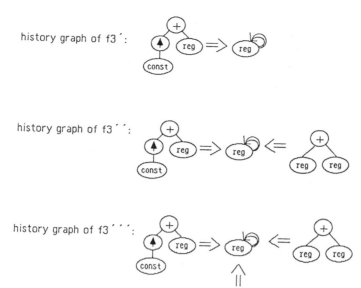

history graph of f3´´:

history graph of f3´´´:

Figure 14

leaves in all the (sub)patterns in a state. For each transition of the pattern matcher a program (or a table entry) can be generated, which uses these address assignmentsto transport the root addresses of partial history graphs to the point of next reduction. Precomputations on the basis of the rule costs will decrease the graphs for example by shortening rule chains.

4. The top down analyser

The most prominent property of the top down analysis automaton of Hoffmann/O'Donnell is its small generation cost. It takes time linear in the number of subpatterns. On the other hand the analysis time costs are significantly higher than those of the bottom up automaton: the worst-case behaviour is O(number of nodes of the subject tree * number of subpatterns).

A top down analyser tries to recognize paths from the root to the leaves of patterns within a given subject tree. The paths are represented as strings of labels and child positions. For example, pattern number (1) of figure 6 can be described by the strings

    + 1 ↑ 1 const

and + 2 reg

The task of matching tree patterns within a tree is reduced to the problem of matching all strings of tree patterns and recording successfully matched strings of patterns at nodes in the subject tree.

At generation time a finite automaton is build up on the basis of the pattern strings (see Hoffmann/O'Donnell using the principles of Aho/Corasick [AhCo75]).

A top down automaton for the patterns of figure 6 is shown in figure 15. A subject tree is analysed in preorder traversal. The transitions of the automaton are controlled by the label of the visited subject tree node and by the position of the visited child when descending the tree.

Entering a final state (represented by bold face boxes) means that a full path of a pattern matches. This fact has to be reported to the start node of the path. If a traversal stack is used at run time, we can precompute the relative distance on the stack, where we can find the start node of a path when entering a final state. If we have a match vector for every node with one counter for each full pattern (initialized by 0), then a match of a path of a full pattern (i) increases the counter (i) of the match vector at the start node of the path. A counter equal to the number of different paths of (i) indicates a match of the pattern.

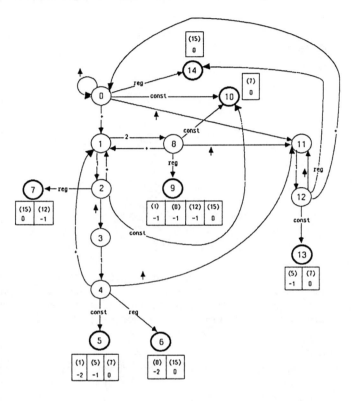

Figure 15
$$
\begin{array}{|c|}
\hline
(i) \\
\hline
-j \\
\hline
\end{array}
$$
: a path of pattern (i) has been recognized, the start point of this path can be reached j units under the top of the traversal stack

Figure 16 shows an analysis example using the automaton of figure 15. At each node we show the match vector and the transitions made by the node labels.

This top down analyser will now be modified to simulate the reduction process. A problem with the top down analyser is that the state computed for a node considers no information at all about the subtree at this node. The state is only determined by the upper context. On the other hand, a reduction process using only patterns of the sort described above is inherently bottom up. Thus, the information about the result of the transformation process is only computed when the subtree is completely traversed. Thus, we have to visit each node a second time in postorder. At this time, the match vector of the node informs us about which reduction

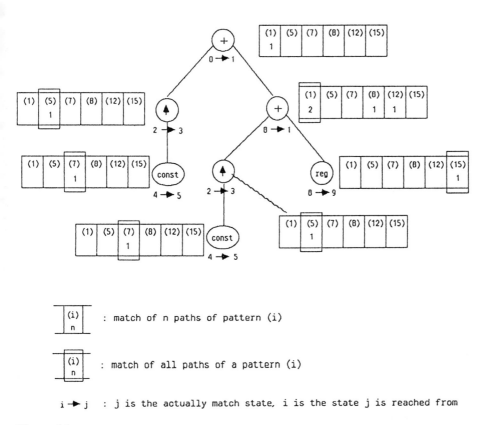

(i)					
n					

: match of n paths of pattern (i)

(i)
n

: match of all paths of a pattern (i)

i → j   : j is the actually match state, i is the state j is reached from

Figure 16

rules are applicable and which result they produce. Say, a rule having a result pattern <op> can be applied at node n. This means that a path leading to n would continue with the label op, if this rule would be applied at n. If we remember the state z entered before the node label is taken into account, the transition entered from this state z following the edge labelled op supplies a state containing all information about possible matches basing on the simulated application.

If this new transition produced additional matches at the node itself, then we have to consider the results of those rules again. The effects of such chains can be precomputed for each non-transfer rule and possible cycles may be broken.

Figure 17 shows the simulation for the example of figure 16.

For *each* label produced by the simulation of a (chain of) reduction rule(s) an additional transition has to be made. Each additional match has to be reported to an ancestor node. This means an additional cost at analysis time which is significantly higher than the run time of the simulating bottom up automaton.

The simulation process of the bottom up automaton only increases the generation costs, not the run time costs (not mentioning the possible higher access costs induced by larger tables). The top down simulation method only affects the run time behaviour. The generator of the bottom up analyzer as programmed by the first author is being integrated into the PCC-environment by Nicole Leitges with support from SIEMENS AG München.

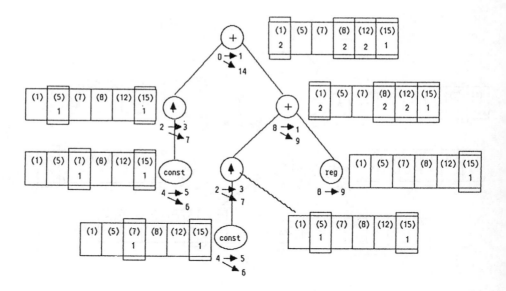

Figure 17

5. Conclusion

A bottom up and a top down pattern matcher for code selection have been presented. Both pattern matcher first compute all possible covers for an IR tree, then a cheapest cover can be selected by dynamic programming performed in parallel. The bottom up pattern matcher performs static targeting: all transfer rules are simulated in the states of a reduction simulating automaton. The top down pattern matcher performs dynamic targeting by making several additional transitions instead of a single one. But both approaches treat the problem on the pure syntactic level.

The bottom up automaton may grow exponentially with the size of the machine description. The generation cost for the top down automaton is linear. On the other hand, the analysis time performance of the bottom up automaton is much better than that of the top down automaton. Experiments will have to reveal the advantages for realistic machine descriptions.

6. References

[AhCo75]   A.V. Aho, M.J.Corasick, Efficient String Matching: An Aid to Bibliographic Search, CACM, June 1975, Vol. 18, Nr. 6

[AhJo76]   A.V. Aho, S.C. Johnson, Optimal Code Generation for Expression Trees, JACM, Vol. 23, No 3, July 1976

[AhGa84]   A.V. Aho, M. Ganapathi, Efficient Tree Pattern Matching: An Aid to Code Generation, POPL 1985

[GaFi82]   M. Ganapathi, C.N. Fischer, Description-Driven Code Generation Using Attribute Grammars, POPL 1982

[GiSc88]   R. Giegerich, K. Schmal, Code Selection Techniques: Pattern Matching, Tree Parsing, and Inversion of Derivors, Proceedings of ESOP'88, LNCS 300, Springer Verlag 1988

[Gieg88]   R. Giegerich, Code Selection by Inversion of Order-Sorted Derivors, to appear in Theoretical Computer Science, North Holland

[Glan77]   R.S. Glanville, A Machine Independent Algorithm for Code Generation and its Use in Retargetable Compilers, PhD Dissertation, University of California, Berkley, December 1977

[GlGr78]   R.S. Glanville, S.L. Graham, A New Method for Compiler Code Generation, POPL 1978

[Henr84]   R.R. Henry, Graham Glanville Code Generators, PhD Dissertation, University of California, Berkley, 1984

[HoDo82]   D.M. Hoffman, M.J. O'Donnell, Pattern Matching in Trees, JACM 29,1, 1982

[Kron75]   H. Kron, Tree Templates and Subtree Transformational Grammars, PhD Dissertation, University of California, Santa Cruz, 1975

[Lune83]   H. Lunell, Code Generator Writing Systems, Software System Research Center, Linköping, Sweden, 1983

[Moen85]   U. Möncke, Generierung von Systemen zur Transformation attributiertern Operatorbäume: Komponenten des Systems und Mechanismen der Generierung, Dissertation, Universität des Saarlandes, Saarbrücken, 1985

[MWW85]   U. Möncke, B. Weisgerber, R. Wilhelm, Generative Support for Transformational Programming, ESPRIT Technical Week, 1985

[Weis83]   B. Weisgerber, Attributierte Transformationsgrammatiken: Die Baumanalyse und Untersuchungen zu Transformationsstrategien, Diplomarbeit, Universität des Saarlandes, Saarbrücken, 1983

GENERATION OF INCREMENTAL INDIRECT THREADED CODE FOR LANGUAGE-BASED PROGRAMMING ENVIRONMENTS[1]

KHALID AZIM MUGHAL[2]

Abstract

We present an approach to generating incremental threaded code for language-based programming environments from the specification of the runtime semantics of the programming language. Language-based environments (LBEs) that support incremental code generation have usually done so using ad hoc techniques for incremental recompilation. Our aim is to provide one uniform operational model based on attribute grammars that allows the specification of the runtime semantics, and thus code generation, to be incorporated with the specification of the syntax and static semantics of the language.

The proposed semantic model of incremental code generation allows specification of compact code. It severely limits the repropagation of semantic information in the program tree due to changes in the code caused by modifications to the source program. Extended with interactive execution, this representation also facilitates the implementation of such debugging features as control-flow tracing, single-stepping and value-monitoring at the source level.

We have demonstrated the feasibility of the proposed model by implementing a program editor for Pascal. The specification is written in the Synthesizer Specification Language (SSL) and forms the input to the Cornell Synthesizer Generator (CSG).

1 Introduction

We are interested in providing code generation to support program interactive program and debugging. The main problem is mapping of the internal representation of the program maintained by the LBE to an executable form. The techniques are implemented in the incremental framework provided by CSG [Reps & Teitelbaum 1988].

---

[1] This work was partially supported by the Norwegian Research Council of Sciences and Humanities.
[2] This paper is based on excerpts from the author's dr.scient thesis [Mughal 1988].
Author's address:
UNIVERSITY OF BERGEN
DEPARTMENT OF INFORMATICS
ALLÉGT. 55, N-5007 BERGEN, NORWAY.
Phone: 47-5-212879   Telefax: 47-5-212857
Internet: khalid%eik.ii.uib.no@uunet.uu.net

We are concerned with *formal* specifications for *generating complete* LBEs. There are primarily three schools of formalisms for such specifications. The *semantic actions* approach as exemplified by the GANDALF editors [Habermann et al. 1982]. The *attribute grammar* [Knuth 1968] approach as exemplified by CSG [Reps & Teitelbaum 1988] and POEGEN [Fischer et al. 1984]. The third approach is based on *denotational semantics* [Stoy 1977] and is primarily employed in compiler generators: SIS [Mosses 1976], [Paulsen 1981]. EDS [Pal 1986] is a denotational semantics based generator for LBEs. However there are systems that employ a more hybrid approach for such formal specifications: PSG [Bahlke & Snelting 1985], PECAN [Reiss 1984a]. *Action equations* are advocated for such specifications in [Kaiser 1986]. A parallel development in this direction of tool generators can be seen in the field of compiler-compilers: GAG [Kastens et al. 1982], HLP [Räihä 1984], SIS [Mosses 1976].

2 Incremental Recompilation

In order to provide efficient execution facilities, we have to address the problem of incremental recompilation: minimize the amount of computation necessary to generate and maintain executable code in the face of source program modifications. We would like to reuse as much of the old code as possible after a program is modified. Before we look at some approaches to the incremental problem, it will be useful to distinguish between the *granularity of recompilation* and *extent of recompilation* [Reps & Teitelbaum 1988]. By granularity of recompilation we mean the *size* of program fragment which can be modified before recompilation is necessary to reflect the source program change in the generated code. The extent of recompilation refers to the amount of code that must be recompiled to reflect the change made to the program.

Hand-crafted LBEs that provide runtime facilities vary in their approach to providing incremental recompilation. In the Cornell Program Synthesizer [Teitelbaum & Reps 1981] incremental recompilation is dependent on the language construct modified. The granularity of recompilation coincides with the extent of recompilation for a control construct, an assignment or an expression. However modification of declarations requires more extensive reanalysis of the program. The extent of recompilation can thus be the entire procedure.

The DICE (Distributed Incremental Compiling Environment) system [Fritzson 1984] supports incremental recompilation at the statement level in a host-target machine configuration. DICE provides statement level granularity of recompilation and supports source-level debugging. The extent of granularity is primarily updating the code for the statement on the target machine. In the MAGPIE system [Delisle et al. 1984] [Schwartz et al. 1984], the granularity of recompilation coincides with the extent of recompilation which is the entire procedure. PSEP [Ford & Sawamiphakdi 1985] uses again a different approach to incremental recompilation where editing and code generation are concurrent processes. In the PSG system only incremental compilation is possible, not incremental recompilation. PSG performs incremental compilation during top-down derivation of the abstract syntax tree (AST) by series of refinement steps. PECAN editors [Reiss 1984b] limit the recompilation to what is called a *compilation unit* which may be a statement or a procedure depending on the context.

In CSG, its attribute evaluation mechanism can be employed for incremental recompilation. Code can be defined as instances of attributes attached to nodes of the AST. After program modification, the attribute-updating mechanism also updates the code attributes that need reevaluation. Consequently the extent of recompilation in our model is dependent on the number of code attributes that need updating. CSG provides two (limited) ways for controlling the *granularity* of recompilation for creating editors with execution facilities. One is to specify that certain program fragments can only be edited as an entire unit. The second method makes use of *demand attributes*. Such attributes are given values only when a demand is placed on them. For example when such an attribute is an argument to another attribute which needs evaluation. We present ways in which to limit the *extent* of recompilation due to changes in the value of code because of program modifications. [Reps & Teitelbaum 1988] and [Reps & Teitelbaum 1987] are the authoritative references on CSG. [Reps & Teitelbaum 1988] and [Reps 1984] describe efficient methods for incremental attribute evaluation in LBEs.

3 Incremental Indirect Threaded Code

Our code generation model is based on incremental semantic analysis. [Reps 1983] is a discussion of static semantic analysis in LBEs. We are interested in applying the power of this incremental model for implementing runtime facilities for LBEs. Any efficient implementation realizing this goal must take the following two factors into consideration: it must minimize the change propagation affecting code generation due to program modifications, and secondly, it must provide an efficient execution of the generated code. The execution paradigm is interpretation of generated code on a von Neumann machine. Thus we provide immediate program translation and interactive execution.

Since we want to make use of the incremental attribute mechanism for code generation, we can define an attribute that represents the code for a node in the AST. The code for the program is thus fragmented and attached to various nodes of the AST as attribute values.

One scheme for maintaining this fragmented code would be to *synthesize* the code for the *root* of the AST from the code fragments at the subordinate nodes in the AST. Thus the attribute value of the code at the root of the AST would represent the code generated for the program under development. This approach is used in [Milos et al. 1984] for the generation of a Pascal P-code compiler. They describe a *semantic grammar* [Paulsen 1981] which is an amalgamation of *extended attribute grammars* [Watt & Madsen 1983] and denotational concepts [Stoy 1977]. Appropriately transformed P-code is then run on the SECD machine [Mosses 1976]. This might provide for efficient execution of the code but is very inefficient for incremental updating of the generated code. In an incremental attribute evaluation scheme, any change to a code fragment of a subordinate node would mean propagation of this change to the root of the tree.

Another approach would be to coalesce or linearize this code just prior to execution time. This would introduce the overhead due to the extra step of coalescing the code every time the program was executed. It would avoid excessive change propagation but would entail additional book-keeping in mapping the code back to its respective node in the AST for debugging purposes. This extra book-keeping is also necessary for the previous approach.

We describe a scheme where the code fragments are "threaded". In order to thread the code fragments, we must know the entry point to a code fragment and this entry point must be made available to other code fragments that "exit" to it. This is modeled in our scheme by using two attributes **entry** and **completion** which explicitly define the entry to a code fragment and the entry to the next code fragment to execute on the completion of execution of the current one. **Entry** and **completion** attributes are used to thread the code fragments. Entry to and exit from code for language constructs is only possible via these two attributes respectively. Hence the term threaded code [Bell 1973] appropriately describes our code generation strategy

We will describe this approach in terms of code generation for statements found in a block-structured language like Pascal. For a *statement* node, we define a *synthesized* attribute **entry** that indicates the entry point corresponding to the code of that statement and whose value is then available to the statement's parents and siblings in the AST. These nodes can exit to the *statement* node using the **entry** attribute value. In addition, we define an *inherited* attribute **completion** whose value the *statement* node inherits from its parents or siblings and can incorporate in its own code. The value of the **completion** is effectively the entry point of the next code to be executed after the current statement is completed. These two attributes thread the fragmented code together while allowing the individual code fragments to remain attached to the nodes of the AST as attribute values.

Since we are using attribute grammars to specify generation of threaded code, we have to be careful about *circularities* in our specification. The diagram in Figure 1 shows the *flow of control* in the linked code structure for the **while** loop using **goto** instructions. This is based on the traditional semantics of a **while** loop:

a) evaluate the loop condition.

b) if condition is not true, go to d.

c) execute the loop body and go to a.

d) ...

A **while** loop is typically defined by the following production:

Statement$1 ::= **while** expr **do** Statement$2

In the AST representing the **while** loop, the code for the loop condition is generated in the subtree with root *expr*. The code for the loop body is generated in the subtree with root *Statement$2* and the code for the loop test is generated at the node (corresponding to the above production) for the nonterminal *Statement$1*. Figure 2 shows the flow of control in the **while** loop when we use the **entry** and **completion** attributes of the nonterminals *Statement$1, expr* and *Statement$2* to thread the **code** of these nonterminals. The flow of control in Figure 2 corresponds to the flow of control shown in Figure 1. However, in Figure 2, the threading of the code for the loop test, body and condition of the **while** loop via the **entry** and **completion** attributes leads to circularity in the *dependency graph* of these attributes. The dependencies are in reverse, opposite to the flow of control arcs shown in Figure 2.

The Cornell Synthesizer Generator however requires a noncircular attribute grammar as its input. In general, the circularities that cause problems in SSL are due to the circularities in the *attribute equations* of the specification. An attribute variable A on the right side of a semantic

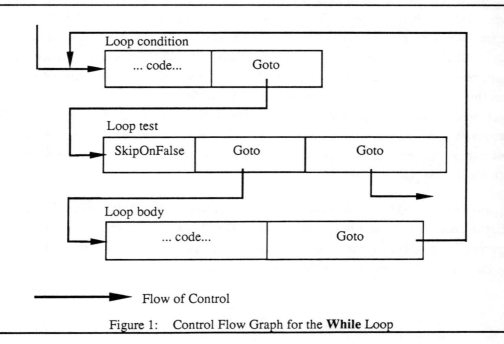

Flow of Control

Figure 1:   Control Flow Graph for the **While** Loop

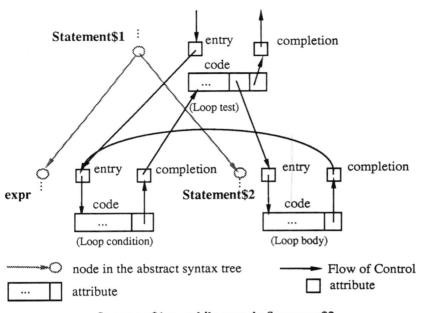

Statement$1 ::= **while** expr **do** Statement$2

Figure 2:   Threaded Code for the **While** Loop

equation for attribute variable B, introduces a dependency from A to B. We overcome the circularity problem by introducing a level of indirection in the generated code by making use of the built-in, primitive "type" ATTR of *attribute references* in SSL. If A is an attribute variable, then &&A is an ATTR-valued expression whose value is a reference to A. &&A is called an *attribute reference*. The semantics of the && operator are such that a semantic equation defining an attribute B in term of &&A does *not* introduce any dependency from A to B.

We can represent the links in the generated code by ATTR-valued expressions. When a production is applied, an attribute occurrence of the code fragment is created. **Entry and completion** are then *attribute references* to this code created by the && operator. This strategy effectively breaks the circularity mentioned above as the values of these attributes are no longer dependent on the value of the code fragments. Hence we have dispensed with the use of a fix-point operator for mutually dependant code values by the use of attribute references. In Figure 2 we can think of the flow of control arcs (or threads) as being attribute references. SSL does not provide a standard dereferencing operator for ATTR-values. During execution, a special dereferencing operation performs the indirection required to access the next code fragment, given the ATTR value from the current one. Thus we have an execution scheme based on *indirect* threaded code, analogous to that described in [Dewar 1975].

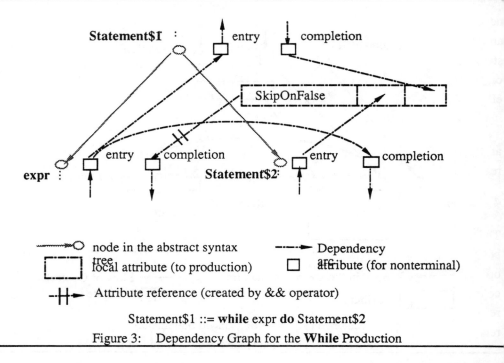

node in the abstract syntax tree ⟶○

local attribute (to production) ⌷

Attribute reference (created by && operator) ⊣⊢▶

Dependency ⟶

attribute (for nonterminal) □

Statement$1 ::= **while** expr **do** Statement$2

Figure 3:   Dependency Graph for the **While** Production

We also define the code as a *local* attribute of the *production*, rather than that of the nonterminal *Statement*. Code as an attribute of a nonterminal would require specifying attribute equations even for cases where the nonterminal does not require the specification of code. Code as a local attribute thus allows for generation of much more compact code. Another major consequence of this approach, combined with the use of attribute references for linking the code, is that change propagation due to change in the value of the code is limited to the production in which the code fragment is defined.

Figure 3 shows the dependency graph for the attributes in the **while** *production* in the AST. In this particular production there is only one local code attribute which is threaded in the overall code for the **while** construct using **entry** and **completion** attributes. The arc ⊣⊢ does not represent a true dependency and breaks the circularity cycle mentioned above. The value of *expr*.**completion** is an attribute reference created by applying the && operator to the local code. Note also that the entry point to the **while** loop is the entry point of the *expression*. This is made available to whatever statement that precedes this production in the AST via *Statement$1*.**entry**. The interpreter is thus able to transfer control directly to the expression rather than leapfrogging first to this production and then jumping to the expression. This also allows for the generation and execution of compact code.

As pointed out earlier not all nodes need to specify new code. In many cases it is only necessary to thread the existing code properly to reflect the flow of control using their **entry** and **completion** attributes. A case in point are the grammar productions for a sequence of statements were the threading information in their **entry** and **completion** attributes is passed on to the other nodes but no new code is generated. Threading code in this manner allows for efficient execution as the sequencing of instructions is indicated by the code's threads.

Another advantage of this approach is that it also facilitates the tracing of control flow in the attributed syntax tree during program execution, requiring a simple mapping from the attribute reference to its production in the tree.

4 Continuations and Completions

The incremental indirect threaded code generation scheme described in the previous section can be thought of as a *completion semantics* [Henson & Turner 1982]. A *completion* is an operational representation of a *continuation* in the denotational semantic model [Stoy 1977]. A continuation specifies what function the "remaining program" computes, and is defined in reverse - opposite to the flow of execution in the program. A completion is a concrete representation of this function.

The correspondence between the continuation structure of a program and a flow graph of a program is expounded in [Sethi 1983]. Each statement defines a continuation in terms of a supplied continuation and the denotations of its subcomponents. A special notation for *pipes* is used to specify the construction of flow graphs for the control constructs of the C programming language. A special combinator *cycle* is used for recursively defined continuations as in the case of loops. The edges of the flow graph are analogous to the threads in the generated code in our scheme.

In [Reppy & Kintala 1984], a case is made for automatically generating complete *AG-based* LBE specifications from *continuation* semantics by techniques similar to those in [Sethi 1983]. The executable representation is similar to our scheme: *code trees* containing op-codes for an abstract machine are generated and executed by an interpreter for the corresponding abstract machine. In contrast to our scheme, it however uses semantic functions with side effects to mutate the internal values of generated code trees.

5 Implementation Status

A specification for a Pascal editor with full *static semantic checking* is distributed with the CSG release [Teitelbaum et al. 1987]. This specification has been augmented with the runtime semantics of Pascal to provide runtime facilities.

SSL Pascal-I, which is described in [Mughal 1988], is an implementation of a complete program editor for a subset of Pascal where both the runtime semantics and the runtime environment are realized in SSL. The generated code is P-code [Nori et al. 1975] defined and modified in SSL to produce incremental indirect threaded code. SSL Pascal-I demonstrates the implementation of non-trivial control flow aspects of language constructs such as loops, recursive procedure call, different modes of parameter passing (including procedure parameters), handling of labels and non-local gotos, and other structured statements. SSL Pascal-I supports only primitive data types in Pascal as these can be easily represented directly by data types of SSL. The runtime management includes a tail-recursive interpreter and a runtime shallow-binding store, also implemented in SSL. The program editor incorporates such debugging facilities as control-flow tracing, single-stepping and value-monitoring at the source level.

SSL Pascal-I demonstrated the feasibility of incremental indirect threaded code, but the implementation of the *runtime facilities* was not efficient due to the limitations of the specification language SSL. Experience gained from this implementation has been valuable in the next undertaking of providing efficient runtime facilities for editors generated in the framework of CSG [Teitelbaum et al. 1988]. The interpreter is written in C and the code instructions are defined as a *primitive data type* CODE of the specification language SSL. Constructors are provided for all P-code attribute values of the primitive data type CODE. Thus the specification of code generation from SSL Pascal-I carries over to this scheme almost in its entirety. However the execution environment is stack-frame based implementing deep-binding in contrast to the shallow-binding-by-name scheme of SSL Pascal-I. The deep-binding scheme calls for the calculation of address offsets of variables during incremental threaded code generation. The code generation scheme of SSL Pascal-I is thus modified with respect to the offset calculation. The new scheme also supports structured and dynamic data types of Pascal. Debugging features include flow tracing, single-stepping, limited execution resumption after program modification and a form of COME command [Alberga et al. 1984]. For obvious reasons, the interpretation in C is far more efficient than the one in SSL Pascal-I. It is hoped that this Pascal editor will be released with the next version of CSG.

6 Summary

We have presented a viable non-ad hoc scheme for the specification of runtime semantics based on indirect threaded code in the framework provided by the CSG. It allows the implementation of non-trivial control flow aspects of many language constructs and facilitates implementation of certain runtime features. We believe this approach can be generalized to generate LBEs with runtime facilities for other block-structured languages. Ultimately one would like to provide the editor designer with a generic package for implementing runtime semantics and debugging facilities, with "hooks" into the system for tailoring and augmenting the runtime model. We believe this work to be a step in that direction.

7 Acknowledgements

I would like to thank Professors Tim Teitelbaum and Tom Reps for allowing me to work on the Cornell Synthesizer Generator Project. Support from the rest of the CSG Task Force, both past and present, is also deeply acknowledged.

8 References

[Alberga et al. 1984]
Alberga, C.N., Brown, A.L., Leeman,Jr. G.B., Mikelsons, M., and Wegman, M.N.
A Program Development Tool.
IBM J. Res. Develop., Vol. 28, No. 1, January 1984, 60-73.

[Bahlke & Snelting 1985]
Bahlke, R. and Snelting, G.
The PSG - Programming System Generator.
In Proceedings of the ACM SIGPLAN '85 Symposium on Language Issues in
Programming Environments, Seattle, WA., June 25-28, 1985, 28 - 33. (SIGPLAN Notices
20, 7, July 1985.)

[Bell 1973]
Bell, J.R.
Threaded Code.
Communications of the ACM 16, 6 (June 1973), 370 - 372.

[Delisle et al. 1984]
Delisle, N. M., Menicosy, D. E., and Schwartz, M. D.
Viewing a Programming Environment as a Single Tool.
In Proceedings of the ACM SIGSOFT/SIGPLAN Software Engineering Symposium on
Practical Software Development Environments, Pittsburgh, Penn., April 23-25, 1984, 49 -
56. (Joint issue: SIGPLAN Notices 19, 5, May 1984, and Software Engineering 9, 3, May
1984.)

[Dewar 1975]
Dewar, R.B.K.
Indirect Threaded Code.
Communications of the ACM, 18, 6 (June 1975), 330 - 331.

[Fischer et al. 1984]
Fischer, C.N., Pal, A., Stock, D.L., Johnson, G.F., and Mauney, J.
The POE Language-based Editor Project.
In Proceedings of the ACM SIGSOFT/SIGPLAN Software Engineering Symposium on
Practical Software Development Environments, Pittsburgh, Penn., April 23-25, 1984, 21 -
29. (Joint issue: SIGPLAN Notices 19, 5, May 1984, and Software Engineering 9, 3, May
1984.)

[Ford & Sawamiphakdi 1985]
Ford, R. and Sawamiphakdi, D.
A Greedy Concurrent Approach to Incremental Code Generation.
In Proceedings of the 12th Annual ACM Symposium on Principles of Programming
Languages, New Orleans, Louisiana, January 14 - 16, 1985, 165-178.

[Fritzson 1984]
Fritzson, P.
Preliminary Experience from the DICE system: a Distributed Incremental Compiling
Environment.
In Proceedings of the ACM SIGSOFT/SIGPLAN Software Engineering Symposium on
Practical Software Development Environments, Pittsburgh, Penn., April 23-25, 1984, 113 -
123. (Joint issue: SIGPLAN Notices 19, 5, May 1984, and Software Engineering 9, 3,
May 1984.)

[Habermann et al. 1982]
Habermann, A. N., Ellison, R., Medina-Mora, R., Feiler, P., Notkin, D.S., Kaiser, G.E.,
Garlan D.B., and Popvich, S.
The Second Compendium of Gandalf Documentation.
Dept. of Computer Science, Carnegie-Mellon University, 1982.

[Henson & Turner 1982]
Henson, M.C.and Turner, R.
Completion Semantics and Interpreter Generation.
In Conference Record of the 9th. ACM Symposium on Principles of Programming
Languages, Albuquerque, N.M., January 25-27, 1982, 242-254.

[Kaiser 1986]
Kaiser, G.E.
Generation of Runtime Environments.
In Proceedings of the SIGPLAN '86 SYMPOSIUM ON COMPILER CONSTRUCTION,
Palo Alto, Calif., June 25-27, 1986, 51-57. (SIGPLAN Notices 21, 7, July 1986.)

[Kastens et al. 1982]
Kastens, U., Hutt, B., and Zimmermann, E.
Lecture Notes in Computer Science, vol.141: GAG: A Practical Compiler Generator.
Springer-Verlag, New York, 1982.

[Knuth 1968]
Knuth, D.E.
Semantics of context-free languages.
Mathematical Systems Theory 2, 2 (June 1968), 127 - 145.

[Milos et al. 1984]
Milos, D., Pleban, U., and Loegel, G.
Direct Implementation of Compiler Specifications or The Pascal P-Code Compiler Revisited.
In Conference Record of the 11th. ACM Symposium on Principles of Programming
Languages, Salt Lake City, Utah, January 15-18, 1984, 196-207.

[Mosses 1976]
Mosses, P.D.
Compiler Generation Using Denotational Semantics.
Mathematical Foundations of Computer Science, Lecture Notes in Computer Science,
Springer-Verlag, New York, 1976, 536-441.

[Mughal 1988]
Generation of Runtime Facilities for Program Editors.
Dr.scient. thesis, Dept. of Informatics, University of Bergen, Norway, May 1988.

[Nori et al. 1975]
Nori, K.V., Amman, U., Jensen, K., Nageli, H.H., and Jacobi, Ch.
The Pascal <P> Compiler: Implementation Notes.
Revised Edition.Instituts fur Informatik, Eidgenossische Technishe Hochschule, Zurich,
1975.

[Pal 1986]
Pal, A.A.
Generating Execution Facilities for Integrated Programming Environments.
Ph.D. dissertation, Dept. of Computer Science, University of Wisconsin - Madison, Wisc.,
1986.

[Paulsen 1981]
Paulsen, L.
A compiler generator for semantic grammars.
Ph.D. dissertation, Dept. of Computer Science, Stanford University, Calif., 1981.

[Reiss 1984a]
Reiss, S. P.
Graphical Program Development with the PECAN Program Development Systems.
In Proceedings of the ACM SIGSOFT/SIGPLAN Software Engineering Symposium on
Practical Software Development Environments, Pittsburgh, Penn., April 23-25, 1984, 30 -
41. (Joint issue: SIGPLAN Notices 19, 5, May 1984, and Software Engineering 9, 3, May
1984.)

[Reiss 1984b]
Reiss, S. P.
An Approach to Incremental Compilation.
In Proceedings of the SIGPLAN '84 SYMPOSIUM ON COMPILER CONSTRUCTION,
Montreal, Canada, June 17-22, 1984, 144-156. (SIGPLAN Notices 19, 6, June 1984).

[Reppy & Kintala 1984]
Reppy, J.H.and Kintala, C.M.R.
Generating Execution Facilities for Integrated Programming Environments.
Technical Memorandum, AT&T Bell Laboratories, Murray Hill, 1984.

[Reps 1983]
Reps, T.
Static-semantic analysis in language-based editors.
In Digest of Papers of the IEEE Spring CompCon 83, San Francisco, Calif., Mar. 1983.,
411 -414.

[Reps 1984]
Reps, T.
Generating Language-Based Environments.
M.I.T. Press, Cambridge, Mass., 1984.

[Reps & Teitelbaum 1987]
Reps, T. and Teitelbaum, T.
The Synthesizer Generator Reference Manual.
2nd Ed., Dept. of Computer Science, Cornell University, Ithaca, N.Y., July 1987.

[Reps & Teitelbaum 1988]
  Reps, T. and Teitelbaum, T.
  The Synthesizer Generator.
  Springer-Verlag. To be published in fall 1988.

[Räihä 1984]
  Räihä, K.J.
  Attribute Grammar Design Using the Compiler Writing System HLP.
  Methods and Tools for Compiler Construction, B. Lorho (ed.), Cambridge University
  Press, 1984.

[Schwartz et al. 1984]
  Schwartz, M. D., Delisle, N. M., and Begwani, V. S.
  Incremental Compilation in Magpie.
  In Proceedings of the SIGPLAN '84 SYMPOSIUM ON COMPILER CONSTRUCTION,
  Montreal, Canada, June 17-22, 1984, 122-131. (SIGPLAN Notices 19, 6, June 1984).

[Sethi 1983]
  Sethi, R.
  Control Flow Aspects of Semantic Directed Compiling.
  ACM TOPLAS 5, 4 (October 1983), 554-595.

[Stoy 1977]
  Stoy, J.E.
  Denotational Semantics.
  MIT Press, Cambridge, Mass., 1977.

[Teitelbaum & Reps 1981]
  Teitelbaum, T. and Reps, T.
  The Cornell Program Synthesizer: a syntax-directed programming environment.
  Communications of ACM 24, 9 (September, 1981) 563-573.

[Teitelbaum et al. 1987]
  Teitelbaum, T., Mughal, K., and Ball, T.
  A Pascal editor with full static-semantic checking.
  Included with the Cornell Synthesizer Generator, Release 2.0.
  Dept. of Computer Science, Cornell University, Ithaca, N.Y., July 1987.

[Teitelbaum et al. 1988]
  Teitelbaum, T., Mughal, K., and Ball, T.,Belmonte, M. and Schoaff, P.
  A Pascal editor with execution and debugging facilities.
  To be included with the Cornell Synthesizer Generator release.
  Dept. of Computer Science, Cornell University, Ithaca, N.Y., fall 1988.

[Watt & Madsen 1983]
  Watt, D.A., and Madsen, O.L.
  Extended Attribute Grammars
  The Computer Journal, Vol. 26, No. 2, 1983, 142 - 153.

This series reports new developments in computer science research and teaching – quickly, informally and at a high level. The type of material considered for publication includes preliminary drafts of original papers and monographs, technical reports of high quality and broad interest, advanced level lectures, reports of meetings, provided they are of exceptional interest and focused on a single topic. The timeliness of a manuscript is more important than its form which may be unfinished or tentative. If possible, a subject index should be included. Publication of Lecture Notes is intended as a service to the international computer science community, in that a commercial publisher, Springer-Verlag, can offer a wide distribution of documents which would otherwise have a restricted readership. Once published and copyrighted, they can be documented in the scientific literature.

Manuscripts

Manuscripts should be no less than 100 and preferably no more than 500 pages in length.
They are reproduced by a photographic process and therefore must be typed with extreme care. Symbols not on the typewriter should be inserted by hand in indelible black ink. Corrections to the typescript should be made by pasting in the new text or painting out errors with white correction fluid. Authors receive 75 free copies and are free to use the material in other publications. The typescript is reduced slightly in size during reproduction; best results will not be obtained unless the text on any one page is kept within the overall limit of 18 x 26.5 cm (7 x 10½ inches). On request, the publisher will supply special paper with the typing area outlined.
Manuscripts should be sent to Prof. G. Goos, GMD Forschungsstelle an der Universität Karlsruhe, Haid- und Neu-Str. 7, 7500 Karlsruhe 1, Germany, Prof. J. Hartmanis, Cornell University, Dept. of Computer Science, Ithaca, NY/USA 14850, or directly to Springer-Verlag Heidelberg.

Springer-Verlag, Heidelberger Platz 3, D-1000 Berlin 33
Springer-Verlag, Tiergartenstraße 17, D-6900 Heidelberg 1
Springer-Verlag, 175 Fifth Avenue, New York, NY 10010/USA
Springer-Verlag, 37-3, Hongo 3-chome, Bunkyo-ku, Tokyo 113, Japan

ISBN 3-540-51364-7
ISBN 0-387-51364-7